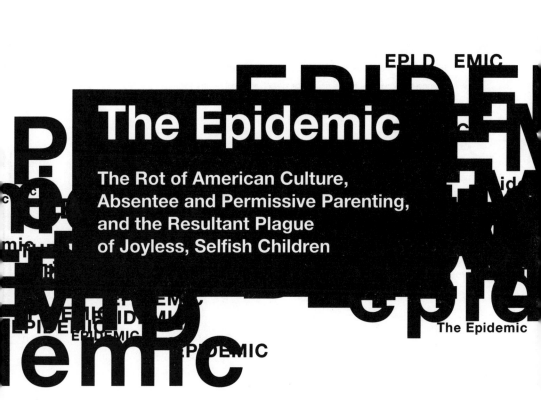

The Epidemic

The Rot of American Culture, Absentee and Permissive Parenting, and the Resultant Plague of Joyless, Selfish Children

The Epidemic

Robert Shaw, M.D.

With Stephanie Wood

 ReganBooks

An Imprint of HarperCollins*Publishers*

The names and identifying characteristics of parents and children featured throughout this book have been changed to protect their privacy. Any resemblance to actual persons, living or dead, is purely coincidence.

FIRST EDITION

Designed by Nancy Singer Olaguera/Richard Ljoenes

Printed on acid-free paper

Library of Congress Cataloging-in-Publication Data

Shaw, Robert, 1927 Feb. 19-
    The epidemic : the rot of American culture, absentee and permissive parenting, and the resultant plague of joyless, selfish children / Robert Shaw with Stephanie Wood.—1st ed.
        p. cm.
    Includes bibliographical references.
    ISBN 0-06-001183-1 (acid-free paper)
    1. Conduct disorders in children—United States. 2. Behavior disorders in children—United States. 3. Children with social disabilities—United States. 4. Social skills in children—United States. 5. Parents of children with disabilities—United States. 6. Parenting—United States—Psychological aspects. 7. Child rearing—United States—Psychological aspects. I. Wood, Stephanie, 1961- II. Title.

RJ506.C65S33 2003
618.92'89—dc22

                                                            2003057834

03 04 05 06 07 ❖/RRD 10 9 8 7 6 5 4 3 2 1

For our now and future children

"Finally! A book that critically examines the great disservice permissive parenting has done to our attitudes toward children's development. Dr. Robert Shaw guides us through the conflicts of our modern age: whether and when to condone, punish, ignore, or agree to the demands children place on us. With a wise and knowledgeable tone, Dr. Shaw conveys his belief in our ability to do a good enough job while he helps us see our blind spots and weaknesses. This book will stay with you from your child's conception to adulthood and then be passed on to your children's children."

—Carol J. Eagle, Ph.D., professor emerita, Department of Psychiatry, Albert Einstein College of Medicine, and author of *All That She Can Be*

Contents

Waking Up!

The true test of civilization is, not the census, nor the size of cities, nor the crops—no, but the kind of man the country turns out.

—Ralph Waldo Emerson, *Civilization* (1870)

WHEN THE NEWS reports began to break in the spring of 1999 about the catastrophe at Columbine High School in Littleton, Colorado, where two teenage boys had mercilessly slaughtered twelve fellow students and a teacher and injured twenty-three others, my first thought, like that of many of you, was, "What makes a young person capable of planning such an atrocity for months—and then carrying it out?"

To commit this cold-blooded crime, these boys had to be extremely detached and alienated from everyone around them— their parents, families, teachers, peers, and community. They had to have been living such an abstracted, "virtual" existence that they could not feel the impact of what they were doing strongly enough to stop their behavior, which was much like the meaningless killing in a video game. They must have been completely cut off, totally lacking in the understanding that there were people they could talk with about their feelings of loneliness, emptiness, despair, resentment, and rage.

No one seems to have foreseen such an outcome, but the disintegration of their personalities can't have happened overnight. Why didn't their families and others in the community notice and get involved? On May 4, 1999, columnist Thomas Friedman raised this issue in the *New York Times:*

> The events of Littleton knocked the stuffing out of the country. . . . They [the American people] are sincerely troubled by Columbine, and what it might say about their own schools, their own communities, and their own kids. . . . The shootings in Littleton were not by deprived inner city youths who could be written off as psycho. Rather, they happened in a *Leave It to Beaver* neighborhood. . . . Until we hear from parents in this story, until we unearth the psychological smoking gun that explains how a young man of privilege could go to the prom on the weekend and then shoot up his schoolmates the next week, it is going to gnaw at the country.

As sad as the events of Columbine were, they did not surprise me. These children were not an aberration. They were the natural outcome of the way we have been raising children from comfortable and even affluent families today. They were developmentally crippled by the child-rearing attitudes and practices that have spread like a virus from home to home in this country.

Over the past ten or fifteen years I've become more and more aware of this epidemic, but now it has reached the point that calls for us to intervene. Wherever I go—in stores, on the street, in restaurants, in people's homes—I see repetitious scenes of whining, and tantrums, and—even more upsetting—an increasing number of kids who look sullen, unrelated, and unhappy. These kids are in the early stages of what I believe is a serious epidemic of disturbed children; those who become school shooters are simply at the far end of the spectrum.

The behavior of these discontented, joyless children is so

common these days that many people no longer consider it abnormal. We rationalize it, normalize it, call it a "phase" or a "stage" at each point along the way.

I want to shock you into opening your eyes and truly confronting what is happening in the lives of our children. What are the signs of this epidemic?

- Far too many children today are sullen, unfriendly, distant, preoccupied, and even unpleasant. They whine, nag, throw tantrums, and demand constant attention from their parents, who are spread too thin to spend enough time with them. Feeling guilty and anxious, the parents in turn soothe their kids with unhealthy snacks, faddish clothing, toys, and media. Many kids, even very young ones, treat their parents with contempt, rolling their eyes and speaking rudely.
- Teachers describe today's children as much less educable and complain that managing their behavior takes up more and more time, leaving less time for education. Many schools have become like prisons, with metal detectors and security guards.
- A host of new "clinical diagnoses" have been invented to explain why children seem totally spoiled, untrained, and unsocialized, and an incredibly large number of children have been diagnosed with attention deficit hyperactivity disorder (ADHD) and bombarded with psychoactive drugs.
- Newspapers carry daily stories of school shootings, sadistic bullying and hazing, and robbery sprees.
- Blaring, rapid-paced television shortens our children's attention span, teaches passivity, draws them into the consumerist spiral, and bombards them with sadistic, sexist images.

What do these things have in common? *They are signs that our society has become toxic to children.*

• • •

I know what conditions create kids like this, and I can tell you how to avoid these problems for your children or how to remove them from the grip of the epidemic if it has taken hold. My clinical experience has been very broad. Over many years I have interacted with thousands of children and families with a broad range of behavior disorders: anxiety, school and learning problems, family problems, psychosomatic illnesses, eating disorders, and the spectrum of autistic syndromes. I've taught professionals and directed psychiatric programs in New York City at Mount Sinai Hospital, the Coney Island Mental Health Center, and the Albert Einstein School of Medicine, where I ran the Child and Family Mental Health Program for the entire South Bronx. I have also run the child and family psychiatric services for the city of Berkeley, California. With my wife, Judith Shaw, a psychotherapist who works primarily with families, I founded the Family Institute of Berkeley, which is devoted to the treatment of families and the training of clinicians in our approaches to family and couple's therapy.

I have worked in settings that serve comfortable and even wealthy families. I have spent many years working in inner-city ghettos. I have seen it all, and over the years it has become clear that we as parents have gradually adopted attitudes and practices that constitute a prescription for disaster.

We used to be clearer about the importance of parenting, but somehow we've forgotten what children actually require in order to grow into happy, responsible adults. We've lost our sense of what matters most in our children's lives—and when we do know, we're not spending the time and energy to make it happen. Then there's a great conspiracy of silence. It's not politically correct to say that some of our lifestyle choices are not in the best interests of our children, despite our loving intentions, and that they compromise their opportunity for the connections and rituals and nurturing that are so necessary to children's healthy development. We have abandoned the notions of decency and morality that once led parents to "know" what to do with their children. And we have trivialized the notion of what it takes to support the sacred passing of humanity from one generation to the next that occurs in the incredible love affair of mother and child.

This book is about your children, your grandchildren, and their future. It is about what you can see around you, not about some mysterious disease or some horrific teenage crime committed far away from your comfortable home. You will notice as you read that I do not very often select examples of the epidemic from my practice, as is usual in books by psychiatrists. Rather, I select my examples from the life I see outside of my office, in the world around me—around the neighborhood, in restaurants and stores and at friends' houses. This epidemic is best illustrated by the behaviors and attitudes that I know are right in front of you too. These stricken children and parents are not tucked away on therapists' couches—they are everywhere, right out in full view.

This book is not a "how-to" book but a "what-is-necessary" book. It is a blueprint to combat the toxic elements of our culture: the pressures it puts on parents, the absence of relaxed family time, the outright abandonment of the traditional values of honesty and effort, the devastating impact of media saturation, and the consumerism that pushes constantly to undermine contentment and increase our urge to acquire. In no way can possessions substitute for the greater rewards produced in life by hard work, by accomplishment through performance, by good deeds, by affection given and returned. The human soul prospers by sharing, caring, relating, understanding, fulfilling. Despite the good intentions of their parents, many children today are inadvertently being raised to take and never give back, to accumulate but never share, to own but never value. And sadly, we live in a culture that is increasingly controlled by people who are victims of the epidemic themselves and thus unable to pass the values of empathy and moral training on to their own children.

I believe that child-rearing should be our greatest opportunity for fulfillment, pleasure, and joy. Some of you may be experiencing that. But as I look around today, I see that becoming less and less true for many families. I have committed my career to helping parents of all backgrounds raise well-adjusted, expressive, likable children. And even more important, my own children and my marriage have remained the major (and extraordinarily rewarding) focus of my life. My ultimate goal is to show parents how to find true happiness in raising their families and how to guide their children in ways that nurture their souls. At the same time we must work together to defuse the violent and explosive time bomb that is ticking away in the hearts of the millions of children who have been shortchanged.

Our society has become crippled. We can no longer count on the traditional supports—such as extended families, religious institutions, community programs, and reliable public schools—that once helped nurture and educate our children. It is terribly sad to me that parents need to be told how to find a niche of safety for their children in a society that is no longer protective of them.

Yet there is hope, since this epidemic is not a disease of children themselves—it's a problem of how they are being raised. All parents need to do is change their behavior, and the children will get better. The pages that follow define the problem, dissect the well-meaning but dangerous parenting methods that contribute to it, and provide clear-cut directions on how you can prevent your child from being sucked into this epidemic. The need is urgent; the time is now. A look at the nightly news—or even a walk down your block or into your neighborhood stores—will show you why.

1

Stricken Children, Stricken Families

You are the bows from which your children as living arrows are sent forth.

—Kahlil Gibran, *The Prophet* (1923)

WE ARE IN CRISIS. Large numbers of children, even including those who could be considered privileged, are no longer developing the empathy, moral commitment, and ability to love necessary to maintain our society at the level that has always been our dream. The emotional, psychological, and moral well-being of the current generation of children has reached a frighteningly low point, and it's going to require a powerful shift in thinking to save them. A few short years ago we were in serious denial that there was such a problem, but recent catastrophic events in our society are forcing us to face the inevitable: our culture no longer offers what children need to truly thrive. Look around you. While happy families were once the norm, more and more often we see parents and children today rushing frenetically from one task to another—children whining, bickering, tantruming, pouting, parents nagging, complaining, and trying to ignore their unruly, surly offspring. Can you go to any store, restaurant, or library without seeing these joyless children screaming, throwing food, or pulling packages and books off shelves? Are you comfortable seeing such scenarios—or tempted to look the other way?

For some strange reason, our way of dealing with this has been not to look, not to notice, not to care. But we can no longer turn a blind eye: there is a mountain of evidence now telling us what's truly good—and really bad—for kids, and in this book I want to help you find the strength to do what has to be done so that you can raise happy, productive, and pleasurable children. I want to help you take a close hard look at your lifestyle, your values, your goals, and what your precious children could become. I want to help you create the kind of family environment necessary for their future—and nothing less than the future of civilization.

Our awareness that something bad was happening in our society became clearer on April 20, 1999, when, with serpentine coldness, Eric Harris and Dylan Klebold slaughtered twelve fellow students and a teacher and injured twenty-three others in the once quiet halls of Columbine High School in Littleton, Colorado. Then came the horror of September 11, 2001: there isn't a person alive then who will forget the day religious radicals hijacked four passenger-filled planes and crashed them into the twin towers of the World Trade Center and the Pentagon, killing thousands of innocent people and leaving a grieving nation of widows, orphans, relatives, friends, citizens.

Two separate horrors, conceived at opposite ends of the world: the idyllic, well-to-do suburbs of Colorado and the barren, sand-beaten deserts and caves of Afghanistan. What could these perpetrators and pivotal events possibly have in common? Both showed the extreme to which children can be led to develop. Both showed the merciless cruelty that can come from people who are alienated from themselves and lacking in empathy. Both sets of perpetrators were terrorists, many from privileged families: one group comprised Islamic fundamentalists hell-bent on holding the world hostage to their ideology; the others were younger but equally confused domestic terrorists, if you will, filled with hate and despair, also hell-bent on control and totally lacking in empathy. The religious radicals indifferently slaughtered strangers for an ideal; the alienated, angry, grandiose teenage shooters terrorized those they knew: friends, teachers, people who should have mattered to them. These were relationships that should have had value in their lives, yet they didn't. We can identify somewhat with crimes of rage; on some level we can imagine people becoming greedy or desperate enough to rob a bank or embezzle from their companies. But we cannot connect with senseless slaughter; the mind of the high school shooter is beyond our comprehension.

When you hold a baby in your arms and see her sweet face looking up at you, you hope and expect that she will naturally grow up to be a well-developed, compassionate person. However, it doesn't happen naturally—children can be trained to a variety of outcomes, including these two tragic situations I just described. As a culture, we need to start noticing that the path to severe dysfunction is often subtle. I will help you identify what is causing this epidemic and encourage you to take a close, hard look at what you do yourself and how it affects your children. Like termites, the epidemic of problem behavior can silently burrow into your life and do great damage before it's discovered. If we as parents don't "train" our children in constructive, safe, and expressive ways of operating in our society, their natural drive to connect with someone or some idea may well lead them toward some of the most destructive behavioral manifestations. They'll be "trained" all right, but perhaps by wayward peers, gangs, the media, or radical religious cults.

Teachers and grandparents have been complaining for years that today's children are out of control, and Columbine made those concerns an overriding reality. The events of September 11 revealed how tragically wrong things can go when humans grow up devoid of empathy. We looked the other way—until the behavior became so horrific that it could no longer be ignored. This book is meant to be such a wake-up call. The day of reckoning has arrived: we simply can't afford to raise our children this way.

WE DETERMINE OUR CHILDREN'S FUTURE

Children are extremely malleable and plastic, and how we rear them is the major determinant of their outcome. I believe that the parenting trends that have evolved over the last thirty years promote the development of unattached, uncommunicative, learning-impaired, and uncontrollable children. We are experiencing an epidemic of school problems, both learning and behavioral. Teachers everywhere report that children are arriving ill equipped to engage in school because they lack focus, purpose, connection, an ability to fit into a rules system, and a desire to learn. At the extreme, our culture may well be breeding a generation of unattached, predatory children who are cognitively smart but lack the capacity to appreciate the feelings and positions of other people.

This epidemic seeps like a fog into all of our culture. Parents find themselves enslaved by a materialistic, overachieving society that leads them to spend so many hours at work and so much money that they can't make the time to do the things necessary to bond with their children. They are worried that they might crush their children, stifle their self-esteem, or kill their creativity, to the extent that they lose all sense of proportion about the role of a young child in a family. They rarely put limits on their children or permit them to experience frustration, and they overlook their children's moral and spiritual development. As a result, essential values like empathy, effort, duty, and honor do not develop. And on top of that, they abandon their children to the influence of the media—children waste so much time on such mind-numbing electronic entertainment as television and video games that their literacy, social development, and creativity are all inhibited. These unbonded, untrained children agitate in ever-widening circles of problem behavior until they finally bump up against real limits—which all too often have to be supplied by institutions such as schools or, eventually, the law.

What are the chances that this will happen to your child? The answer lies within the lifestyle choices you make. Each and every decision that moves your family away from what we know is good for children—secure attachment to a primary caregiver; a safe, structured, and ordered environment; lots of free time to exercise creativity and imagination—increases the level of risk to your child's development. The choices are tough ones, and with each decision you set the odds one way or the other.

FACING UP TO THE EVIDENCE

Proof of the epidemic is in the news every day. Children appear to be functioning at an acceptable cognitive and social level, but clearly they haven't developed a solid center of moral and emotional control if so many turn around and attack their peers, their parents, and the authority figures in their lives. In the years since Columbine countless attempts have been made to dissect the whys and hows of this tragedy. At first there were rumblings of how normal the boys seemed—playing sports, working in a pizza parlor, attending the prom. Then the news media reported on the teasing and ostracizing they had experienced in the student community and the cliques of "jocks" and "nerds." Harris and Klebold belonged to a socially outcast Goth-like group known as the Trench Coat Mafia, for the black trench coats they wore to school. It certainly seems as if that attire should have raised a few eyebrows. Members of the Trench Coat Mafia were allegedly teased mercilessly by the more fashionable jocks. Ultimately the public found out about the poisonous thoughts that Eric Harris posted on his personal website, the violent tales he penned for a creative writing class, and the ammunition he amassed in his bedroom and his family garage. We learned that the two boys videotaped their plans in Harris's home while his parents slept soundly upstairs, and that Eric Harris had been on the antidepressant medications Zoloft and Luvox. Both boys had criminal records—they had been arrested for stealing electronics from a van—and Harris had told his probation officer that he had homicidal and suicidal thoughts. Indeed, the juvenile justice officials involved have claimed that Harris and Klebold "conned" them into believing the anger management program that was part of their sentence had worked—proof of the boys' intellectual and cognitive ability to move within an acceptable social framework.

There were ample clues to Harris's potential for violence. His parents had consulted professionals and clearly knew things were not going well, so why did they continue to grant him a level of privacy that allowed him to keep weapons in his bedroom? And why did the police allow him to slip away? Is it that they saw so much disturbance in today's youth that nothing was shocking anymore? Sadly, as far as I am aware, both families have chosen to remain silent about what went on in their homes and with their children and apparently are unwilling to help other parents with similar difficulties by telling their story.

So far our society has chosen to deal with the true-life horror of Columbine and other school shootings as unrelated, isolated events. But let's review them as a group, and you'll see just how neatly the pieces fall together. You'll see how common these emotionally abandoned, morally stunted children are. No one is communicating with them, even when they themselves seem to be crying out for help through their words or behavior. Then, when the behavior explodes, those who might have seen and helped express their surprise that this child could have perpetrated such a crime. Here are a few recent examples:

- On March 5, 2001, a fifteen-year-old outcast at Santana High School in the idyllic burb of Santee, California, opened fire on his classmates, killing two and injuring thirteen. The perpetrator, Charles Andrew "Andy" Williams, lived alone with his father, a seldom visible presence in his son's life. Andy reportedly spent after-school hours hanging out at a skateboard park, drinking beer, and getting stoned. His mother lived across the country on the East Coast. News reports indicated that she had last spoken to her son "just after the Christmas holidays," some two months before the crime, and had denied his request to come back east and live with her. After the shooting spree she declared Andy "lost." High school friends and even one adult—the live-in boyfriend of Williams's best friend—later revealed that the boy had spoken of his plans for the shooting, but no one took him seriously enough to alert authorities. Indeed, Williams later told ABC news reporter Diane Sawyer during an exclusive interview from his jail cell that he had hoped the dozen students he told about his plans would stop him, but instead they egged him on.

- A fourteen-year-old girl at a parochial school in Pennsylvania shot a classmate in the arm in the school cafeteria, just days after the Santana High School incident. The perpetrator, who claimed the classmate was talking about her behind her back, had recently transferred to the small Catholic school after having trouble fitting in at her local public school. She had apparently been giving off warning signs for years, in the form of depression, self-mutilation, and paranoid behavior.

- One January 27, 2001, two boys, sixteen and seventeen years old, from Chelsea, Vermont, lied their way into the home of two Dartmouth College professors, then murdered them in an effort to get their ATM cards and PIN numbers so that they could steal enough money to relocate to Australia. The boys, who had attempted four other such robbery-murders before succeeding on the fifth try, were described as "likable" and "bright" by shocked residents of the quiet New England town. The older of the two, high school senior Robert Tulloch, was on the debate team and served as president of the student council. The other, James Parker, was known as the class comedian. Still, some students described the pair as "cocky" and said they treated other classmates as if they were stupid. These were admittedly very cognitively bright young men, but they were emotionally stunted.

Reports of thwarted school massacres—by both individuals and groups of friends—continue to pop up on the news wires: in New Bedford, Massachusetts; Cupertino, California; Royal, Kansas; Elmira, New York. Just as I was finishing this book, a fourteen-year-old Pennsylvania boy with no history of discipline problems walked into his middle school and killed his principal, then turned the gun on himself. The only possible motive at press time, according to one of the local authorities, was that "something was building up inside him that he couldn't control."

Almost always the setting is a middle- to upper-middle-class community, and the perpetrators are described as being from "good families." These are apple-pie schools with green-as-Granny-Smith playing fields and graffiti-free walls punctuated with rainbow artwork. There are no metal detectors at the entrances or police officers patrolling these hallways. Too often they get installed only after violence occurs.

These privileged teenage killers are demonstrating the ravages of the epidemic at its most dramatic end stage—as does the climbing adolescent suicide rate, destructive assaults by young computer hackers, the neat disposal of unwanted babies in Dumpsters by high school and college students, and the prevalence of hate crimes and neo-Nazi ideals among people not yet old enough to vote.

Consider, too, the so-called American Taliban, John Walker Lindh. How could a boy become so influenced by a militant fundamentalist religious cult that he allegedly took up a gun and fought against his own country? This matter was thoroughly discussed in a major article in *Time* magazine. According to that report, Lindh's parents were the quintessential easygoing, laid-back, let-it-all-hang-out Marin County, California, couple. The father stated that his marriage had essentially ended six years earlier than the couple's formal divorce, and their seeming lack of standards was such that their sixteen-year-old child could walk around town in Muslim garb without what I consider to be effectively getting their attention. Joining a religious group that is foreign to your family is a very significant event and should be thoroughly examined. It implies a rejection of and distancing from one's family values. John Walker Lindh was a seeker of spiritual perfection—a quest common to children who have never found a firm moral connection at home. He was grabbed by the certainty that fundamentalist religious cults offer, in addition to an outlet for hostility, as he trained to destroy "sinful" creatures.

On another level I can see that his parents were victims too—victims of a society that has fallen into the habit of not giving kids the kind of supervision that allows parents to model for their children what they think and feel about life. Many people are proud of their permissiveness ("hey, everything has value") and their ability to be flexible. Without supervision, however, there is no family interaction, so children don't get to see parents demonstrating their own moral stance. Children need a firm moral center, the kind of anchoring that helps them pick appropriate friends, make the right decisions, and view others empathetically. Without it, they're easy prey for a gang or cult leader.

There are many signs of unsupervised children in our world, kids who are floating and drifting in the epidemic: reports of high school students in upscale school districts who create websites detailing the names and acts of sexual promiscuity of female peers; the New Jersey high school student who was indicted by the Securities and Exchange Commission for manipulating stock trades on the Internet; an affluent group of Greenwich, Connecticut, high school students going on a robbery spree at neighborhood liquor, deli, and convenience stores; a group of upper-middle-class girls from a suburban Chicago high school conducting a senior initiation "hazing" that turned into an orgy of violence; and skyrocketing statistics indicating that teenage girls suffer physical and emotional abuse from their dates at a rate equivalent to that of domestic violence by adult partners. It's not just about kid-on-kid violence: these children are demonstrating unethical, immoral, even criminal behavior right under their own roofs, on their home computers. In the case of the Chicago high school girls, their rampage was said by the authorities to have been fueled by the large amounts of alcohol that were supplied by some of the parents.

Our first reaction is to normalize these events. Parents, friends, and teachers all jump up and insist that the perpetrator is "a good boy," "bright," "well behaved," "popular," and certainly not capable of such an act. When publicity makes us confront the problem despite our denial, instead of turning to communication and healing, we try to legislate aberrant behavior with metal detectors, guards, limitations, and regulation of well-adjusted students as well as the problem children. We can no longer be sure that childhood taunts like "I'm going to get you for that" aren't literal. Students needn't carry a gun or knife to school to get into trouble: nail clippers or scissors tucked in your backpack can get you suspended in some districts just as easily. Consider the immediate suspension of a Florida high school valedictorian because a kitchen knife was discovered on the floor of her car. Never mind that both she and her mother tried to explain that the day before they were moving her belongings to an apartment on the college campus to which she'd been given a scholarship. This sort of knee-jerk reaction is but another symptom of the lengths we've been driven to by our fear of our own children. Our comfort and safety have been shattered, and we're trying to point the finger everywhere but at home. We are frightened of our children.

THE ROOTS OF THE EPIDEMIC

Where does it all begin? The epidemic of which I'm writing cannot be imagined as a function of poverty, of the inner city, or of a minority race. It is occurring in the homes of comfortable, educated parents. Its symptoms can be observed in every classroom, every playground, every supermarket and restaurant, and in more and more households across America. The evidence begins early and can be observed anywhere, in both parental and childhood behavior:

- The parents of an eighteen-month-old leave her with a baby-sitter while they work all day. The sitter, in turn, plops her in a high chair to watch an endless parade of Barney videos. The child's response: she enters meltdown mode the minute Mommy arrives to take her home. Naturally Mommy can't wait to escape back to the office the next morning.
- The two-career parents of a three-year-old, too tired to cook, drag him out to yet another restaurant at the end of his own long day. The child tosses his food on the floor, whines incessantly that he wants to leave, and then climbs off his seat, under the tables, and around the chairs of other patrons, ruining their meals as well. The parents pretend not to notice so they can finish their conversation.
- A father goes to pick up his four-year-old from a play date. The child spits in his face, then screams all the way out the door. The father, clearly not used to being in control of his son, begs and cajoles ("we'll stop for ice cream on the way home") in a desperate effort to end the embarrassing scene.
- Parents on the way to a child's birthday party make a stop at the toy store with their own five-year-old in tow. They explain that they are here for a present for Suzy, not her.

The child throws a fit in the toy store until her parents give in and leave with two purchases. One can only imagine the scene at the party when the other child opens her presents.

- A ten-year-old refuses to do his homework and is failing several subjects. When his mother tries to help him, he gets up and walks away. She wants to take him off the basketball team until his grades improve, but her husband refuses, insisting that sports are all he's got going for him. The child's behavior continues, unmanaged, as the mother gives up and the father hides at the office.

- The parents of a twelve-year-old are hosting a small party. The boy has already eaten dinner, but just as the hors d'oeuvres are being put out, he skulks silently into the room wearing a cold, deadened expression and begins to help himself. His mother quietly approaches the boy and asks him to leave the food for the guests. The boy gives his mother a defiant glance, proceeds to eat some more, then grabs another helping as he heads for the door. When she then asks if he would give a message to the baby-sitter, he snaps back, "No!" A few months later the boy is expelled from his school for breaking in at night and seriously vandalizing school offices, and his defensive parents, backed by advisers and lawyers, protest his punishment. Then, at the age of fourteen, he and a friend are arrested for burglarizing a store.

As parents, our lives are filled with these *critical moments* on issues both large and small. They may seem insignificant at the time, when you just need to get through that restaurant dinner or trip to the toy store, but how they're handled sends a vitally important message to your children about the nature of their relationship with you. From that sleep-deprived decision in the wee hours that it's easier to let a toddler come into bed with you than not, to that evening when you're too tired or lazy or even afraid to stand up to a rebellious teen, by not acting you *are* acting—and potentially in a harmful way. The younger children in the previous examples whose parents tolerate their public meltdowns now will likely be the same ones who are underachieving, disrespectful, vandalizing teens later. Throughout this book I will point out such critical moments in parenting as they occur in the anecdotes and case studies you will read about, to help you see and understand the mixed messages that your actions—or lack thereof—are conveying to your children.

Today's parents seem to have absorbed the notion that a child's life should be totally serene, totally self-expressive, and totally free from frustration. But creating an atmosphere that feels satisfactory to the child all the time does her a disservice. Interestingly enough, it was Anna Freud, the daughter of Sigmund Freud and herself a prominent child psychoanalytic theorist, who recognized the dangers of this development. According to Robert Coles, M.D., in his brilliant study *The Secular Mind*, Anna Freud worried that the obsessive attempt to avoid having children feel unnecessary guilt or disappointment was leading to an increase in what we call today "narcissistic personalities." She felt that people striving to provide the best childhood for their offspring were more likely to constantly say "yes" and that their children would learn too little about "no."

When you look at it this way, it's easy to see how the breeding ground of the epidemic goes all the way back to infancy. Of course a newborn still adapting to her overwhelming new world needs and deserves immediate and constant attention. But by six months of age or so, a baby should have developed the capacity to doze off on her own and sleep through the night, or entertain herself with a toy for brief periods while a parent goes about the everyday tasks of life, such as cooking or making a phone call. Yet more and more often we see high-demand older babies who react intensely the minute they are put down and who continue to awaken their now zombielike parents hour after hour throughout the night demanding complicated soothing routines. These infants grow into temperamental toddlers who refuse to accept routines and resist toilet training well past the age when they are capable of it. (The manufacturing of a totally new product—large-size disposable diapers for preschoolers—is but one example of this trend.) As four- and five-year-olds who should be evolving into happy, eager-to-please little people, they continue to react with tantrums when limits are set and suffer emotional collapse in the face of frustration.

It is totally human and expected that children are going to test their parents and other authority figures—not to do so would be abnormal. Rather than seeing all limit-testing as a bad thing, however, we must recognize its merits in helping the child safely determine what is expected of him in the world. The trouble is that indulging and distancing parents have allowed limit-testing to go beyond an acceptable level. When parents don't teach their children acceptable behavior, defiance becomes the norm. Of course a one-year-old tries to pull hair or bite; he needs to be taught not to, or he will continue to do it. Of course a two-year-old will throw a tantrum; he must learn that such behavior is not permitted and will not get him his way, or he will continue to do it. Of course a two- or three-year-old will feel reluctant to share her toys; she must be taught that it's a nice thing to do, or she will continue to refuse to. Of course a three- or four-year-old may try to run into a dangerous street; he must learn that he can't. Not enforcing appropriate limits is neglecting the teachable moments that ultimately civilize and protect your child.

Many of today's children have gotten the message that their frightened, guilt-ridden parents will give in if they put up enough of a fight. So rather than trying to please their parents, they oppose, resist, and irritate; their parents, in turn, cringe and cower and cave in. Control has come to replace attachment and love, skewing development in an abnormal direction that has become accepted. Palatable labels ranging from "high-energy" to "hyperactive" to "temperamental" to "oppositional" are bandied about like personality traits that must be tolerated.

Parents are lulled into believing these behaviors are the norm by the parenting gurus who preach child-centric theories: "Never let your baby cry," "He'll use the potty when he's ready," "Discipline is disrespectful," "The child's feelings should come first" (well before yours, of course).

The media are part of this problem as well. In one recent issue of a popular child-rearing magazine I saw the following query from a reader: "My three-year-old is a delight in most ways, but if I ask her to do something, she'll say no, throw herself on the floor, and tell me I'm not her mommy anymore. I've raised her to express her feelings, but have I gone too far?" The answer from a noted pediatrician: "Her behavior is perfectly normal for a three-year-old."

It is extremely sad to me to think of the children whose parents are being influenced by statements like this. If this were normal, why would anyone want to have a child? Children are being injured in their emotional development every day by being allowed to behave in totally inappropriate ways. That a pediatrician is alleged to have accepted this as normal indicates to me how far this epidemic has penetrated into the fabric of child-rearing. Yes, a child might do something like this on a rare occasion, with provocation and under stressful circumstances. But one time should be enough. It is possible for a parent to make it clear that he or she will not bargain under duress. Children are very bright and learn the rules rapidly. The problem is that we are teaching them the wrong rules.

Those children who progress down this distorted developmental track are much more likely to become angry and alienated and to assume a cold or contemptuous attitude toward others, especially authority figures. At home they are secretive, sullen, broody presences. In school, behaviors such as distractibility, indifference, overdiagnosed attention deficit hyperactivity disorder (ADHD), disdain for adults, whining, and nagging detract from their ability to learn. Well-intentioned parents then take them to psychiatrists, who prescribe the latest medications to calm them down, help them focus in school, and become more manageable. Indeed, the number of children and adolescents who take psychiatric drugs such as Ritalin (for ADHD) and Prozac (for depression) more than doubled between 1987 and 1996, according to a study of 900,000 children and adolescents published in the *Archives of Pediatric and Adolescent Medicine* in January 2003. Just over 6 percent of those children took at least one psychiatric drug in 1996, compared with 2.5 percent in 1987. Yet a very small number of these children have actual distortions of ability—slightly more than 4 percent, according to the National Institute of Mental Health (NIMH). The vast majority test normally and show little improvement on medication. In effect, ADHD has become a rationalization for kids who aren't in productive relationships. They are being subjected to chemical warfare just because their parents have been misled by cultural attitudes that breed intolerable behaviors. Indeed, psychiatrist Peter Breggin, M.D., author of *The Ritalin Fact Book*, refers to the scientifically approved list of ADHD symptoms as "a list of behaviors that annoy adults" in a 2002 *New York Times Magazine* article titled "Preschool Meds." He estimates that nearly six million kids are now taking Ritalin. Even more alarming, that many of these medications are being prescribed to preschoolers "off label," Breggin and other experts suspect, meaning that they have never been FDA-approved to treat children under age six and the long-term effects are unknown. As a result, NIMH has launched a controversial new study on the safety and effectiveness of generic Ritalin for children ages three to five, the results of which are expected in 2004.

To the parents of these out-of-control children, the daily indignities are frustrating but easy to rationalize: "She'll grow out of it," "I'm too tired to deal," "He's a high-spirited kid," "It's probably just puberty." But the saddest fact is undeniable: family life for many has become too much work and too little fun. Sheer lack of time and performance pressure on both adults and children have diminished the importance of seemingly less productive pursuits like playing peek-a-boo with a gurgling baby, sitting down to a family board game, or chasing twinkling lightning bugs under the summer stars. Instead, we find ourselves slaving after children who laugh in the face of our weak attempts at discipline, demand to be amused all day, and stay up late because we're too exhausted to put up the struggle it takes to get them to bed. These kids are fully in charge. No wonder they have piles of untouched toys—the real live playthings that are their parents are far more entertaining.

Meanwhile, modern moms and dads are encouraged by a culture in overdrive to push and prod and force their children onto an endless track of achievement, to desperately keep squeezing one more enriching activity into their already too-tight schedules. The not-so-subliminal message: if Johnny doesn't do it all, he'll never keep up with the multitalented majority, he'll go the state university route instead of Ivy League, and he may never discover his true calling and reach his potential. Driven by such superficial goals and constant consumerism, parents abdicate their children's day-to-day routines to others so they can work longer; meanwhile, the beautiful home sits forlornly, the dining room table goes unused, and the long family weekend away gets postponed when work calls. They feel regret, but they can't mobilize themselves to stop and relax and enjoy their family life.

As they grow older, our stricken children spend much of their time pursuing entertainment rather than accomplishment: TV, video games, mall roaming, computer hacking, substance abuse, promiscuous sex. Prematurely on their own, they put their asocial, disaffected peers before their parents far too soon. Taking a page out of our own playbooks, they derive their self-worth from possessions, demanding special sneakers or the latest high-tech toy. It is as though they live on a bed of quicksand that will swallow them if they are not cool or fashionably correct.

When these children get into trouble academically, we are also seeing a cultural tendency to literally dumb down standards. Like many states trying to improve education standards, California enacted a law requiring all students to pass an exit exam or be denied a diploma beginning in 2004. Now the Board of Education is considering delaying the denial of diplomas at least a year, and possibly dropping the test standards, because the first round of students taking the exam are failing in astounding numbers: as of January 2003, 38 percent of high school juniors had not yet passed the math portion, which is set at a tenth-grade level, with a low passing grade of 55. This is the class that will be required to pass the exam for a diploma in 2004, unless the plan is delayed. Reasons cited for the failures include, of course, poor schooling in the earlier grades and low-quality remedial classes, but also kids who skip too many classes and parents who fail to support their children's education.

California is not alone: Texas, Michigan, and Colorado are all reportedly in the process of redefining their state education standards to "reduce"—at least on paper—the number of student failures. This situation has all the hallmarks of the epidemic: helpless educators dropping the standards to make it look as though kids are learning more than they really are, outraged parents who fear their children may not get into college, and students who are categorically unable to meet the requirements of school. Furthermore, since the test results demonstrate that the economically disadvantaged kids are doing almost as well as wealthier kids, we have to conclude that the supposed educational advantage of the privileged child is waning. I believe this is because the parenting practices of middle- and upper-middle-class families are growing more similar to the practices I was only too familiar with during my years working in inner-city ghettos. Once kids from privileged families experience the same type of parenting failures found in the ghetto, the educational results are going to start to become similar as well.

Before the days of dumbing down and propping up, we held high standards for children at home as well as in school. As they grew, kids contributed more and more to the family: doing chores like washing the dishes, mowing the lawn, watching over younger siblings. Now they retreat to their rooms to instant-message cyber-buddies on the Internet or overdose on the violent, sadistic, sexist messages of much contemporary music. Certainly the argument can be made that teenagers hardly need the supervision that toddlers require, that it's downright impossible to know what they're doing when they're supposed to be at school or working in the pizza parlor or tooling around with a driver's license in their back pocket. A teenager wouldn't be normal if he didn't demand some level of privacy, nor would he grow into a fully functioning adult if his parents didn't provide it. Yet there is a difference between giving a child some space and never communicating, between getting into some mischief and committing a truly immoral act, between being embarrassed about being caught and simply hiding your behavior because you don't want to be stopped.

Never before has the degree of dysfunction I have described afflicted privileged families in the numbers we're seeing today, nor has it begun so early. The American Academy of Child and Adolescent Psychiatry estimates that 5 percent of children and adolescents suffer from depression, and suicide has risen to become the third-leading cause of death among teens.

These stricken children are proving ill equipped to cope in the more demanding world beyond their homes. A recent study of more than thirteen thousand college students seeking psychological counseling revealed that their emotional difficulties were far more complex and more severe than those of students in the past. Researchers at the counseling center at Kansas State University found that the percentage of students treated for depression or suicidal tendencies doubled in the twelve years from 1989 to 2001. More than twice as many students were taking some type of psychiatric medication. Problems related to stress, anxiety, learning disabilities such as ADHD, family issues, grief, and sexual assault also rose.

I find it painful but no surprise that these constantly placated children are growing into adults who are unable to take the rough-and-tumble of life. Because they were never given the chance to develop the inner resources to deal with the stresses of responsibility and accountability, they are landing in college counseling offices, leaving schools responsible for their mental health.

THE BIGGEST MODERN PARENTING MISTAKES

Sigmund Freud thought that a son whose mother adores him totally will have a better chance of success. The more totally enraptured she is of him, the more believing in his ability to accomplish anything, the more capable he will then become, empowered by her love and the security and confidence and capability it provides. On the other hand, if you don't expect much of your child, he is less likely to achieve as much. You'll have handed it all to him—all, that is, but his future. I believe that the practices parents choose for the quick fix—placating a tantrummer, providing mindless entertainment, satisfying end-less consumer addictions—whittle away at a child's character development in the long run. And what little ethical foundation we manage to provide is devoured by our toxic culture.

Yet I see in my practice how easy it is to turn the tide when I am able to help parents become clear about what must happen in order for their children to develop fully. In this book I call for nothing less than a return to the basics that our children really need—a secure bonding experience; structure and order in their day-to-day lives; and the supervision and moral training that lead to the ability to resist negative societal influences.

I believe that the following practices put children at increased risk for emotionally skewed development:

- Failing to establish a strong emotional bond with your child by not giving him the necessary time and attention.

- Not reading to, talking to, or playing with young children to provide the experiences we know help them acquire literacy.
- Accepting the idea that excessive nonparental care will be an adequate substitute for your relationship with your child.
- Not having firm rules and routines that you administer calmly, fairly, assertively, and without guilt or hesitation.
- Not conveying to your child—through both actions and words—the moral, ethical, and spiritual values you believe in (or not having moral, ethical, and spiritual values in the first place).
- Allowing your child inappropriate control over his life. A certain amount of control, doled out as a child is ready to handle it, is wonderful; too much control when your child is ill prepared for it is disastrous.
- Yelling at and threatening your children. You can be firm and reliable in reinforcing rules without resorting to these tactics. When you lose your temper, it says that you have delayed handling an issue until your frustration and impotence have become overwhelming. You can act firmly right away; you don't have to wait until you get angry.
- Overidentifying with your child, to the extent that you assume he wants what you want, will fulfill your own aspirations, or will perform in a way that enhances your self-image. In short, expecting your child to build your ego and solve your doubts.
- Expecting too much while demanding too little. For instance, letting him loll around playing video games all day, then expecting him to win honors at school.
- Not allowing your child to experience the rewards of earning and achieving on his own.
- Overexposure to media.
- Not giving your child the type of activities and experiences that promote his ability to sit quietly, concentrate, and lis-

ten, then expecting schools to "fix" him. Not even the very best private schools or most stellar public education systems can accomplish the same goals with underdeveloped children as they do with those who are well adjusted and ready to learn.

- Failing to talk things through. Direct, honest, complete communication should be the constant characteristic of your relationship with your child.

When parents commit these all-too-common mistakes in an effort to suit their own needs and concerns or through ignorance or lack of energy, they thwart their child's natural course of development. When you put off toilet training because you're too busy to deal with it, or allow your six-year-old to keep crawling into your bed at night because you're too tired to put up a fight, or dole out money on demand instead of insisting on an allowance, or let curfews slide, you will cripple your child in the long run. These developmental tasks can feel endless at times, but it's naive to think that children will turn out fine if you just leave them alone. Values are not instinctual; they are passed on to your children day after day, in your every interaction with them. That is why, with effort, even very deviant children can be helped to gain the values they need.

WHERE DO WE GO FROM HERE?

From the moment of conception to baby's first birthday, parents are given charts and graphs galore outlining in tremendous detail all the milestones they have to look forward to: how big the mother's belly will grow each week, when she'll feel that first abdominal twitch that soon becomes a karate kick to the ribs, the unmistakable cramps of early labor, what to pack for the hospital. After Mom is mercifully done watching her own weight gain, the obsession becomes graphing how many pounds and inches baby gains, how long he nurses, how often he poops, when his first tooth erupts, he rolls over, he sits up, he climbs down, he crawls around, and ultimately when he toddles away from you. Then suddenly, Mom and Dad are on their own. There are fewer guidelines to fall back on, no true barometers to tell them how their child is doing. They've survived that initial proving ground of keeping him alive and growing, so it's time to take a breather, right? All that's left is his socialization. How ironic that the hardest work to be done is yet to be done.

What do parents really need? Visible, concrete evidence that their child is indeed developing appropriately. They need to know what to expect and when: moral milestones (when a child feels empathy toward others, demonstrates loyalty to a friend, or knows that telling a lie is wrong), behavioral barometers (when she understands the word "no," stops grabbing toys in the sandbox, or accepts delayed gratification), and social standards (when she says "please" and "thank you," doesn't interrupt, or uses tact in dealing with peers). In fact, I think you will be surprised as you read on at just how early kids are capable of meeting these expectations. Without this understanding, the insidious epidemic festers, little by little, stage by stage, and we become confused about what is normal and what is not. We run the risk of accepting our confusion and frustration and living with abnormal children as though it is right and good—and our problem if we're unhappy.

The following chapters provide an antidote to our child-toxic society: a progressive map from infancy onward to help you see your way through the fog of frustration, the toxic messages, the cultural clamor that gets in the way of the family life both parents and children deserve. This map will take you from the earliest elements of bonding, dealing with fear, disappointment, and frustration, developing empathy and moral understanding, and literacy attainment, to the ways in which parents can begin to

2
Teaching Your Child to Love

They do not know love that do not show their love.

—William Shakespeare, *Two Gentlemen of Verona* (1594)

THE CHILD SUCKLES, snuggled against her mother's warm skin, smelling, listening to her mother's heartbeat, her eyes locked on her mother's eyes. What is it that passes silently between them? Much more than milk. This is the earliest stage of the connecting process, a relationship that begins for humans during the close contact that occurs while tenderly feeding. What's really going on during that loving, snuggling, nuzzling, nurturing act is the passing down of the essential ingredients for being human. Here, against the mother's heart, in her arms, embraced by her sounds, her warmth, her love, her totally entranced attention, is where babies, feeding from the breast or a bottle, receive the capacity for intimacy and empathy, where they learn what love feels like, where they receive the seeds of successful moral/ethical development, where they begin to absorb the sounds of their native language that evolve into future literacy.

Babies are not as simple to nurture as other living things. Unlike the mighty oak, whose seeds contain all the information needed for it to become a complete tree in the normal range of environmental circumstances, human offspring transcend mere biology. Our humanity is formed not just by food and water and shelter but also by dialogue—particularly by dialogue with the mother. She alone has that unique instinctual drive that prepares her to engage in a developmental dance with her newborn. She is the only one flooded with hormones that open her to a transforming ability to love and connect as nothing else in human experience does. The newborn, too, is programmed to respond to her overtures—locking his eyes on hers, gurgling, suckling—in a way that makes her want to connect even more. Their behaviors reinforce each other, she stimulating or soothing him, he drinking it in or turning away when he wants some respite from the stimulation. In this way, the mother essentially regulates the tension and joy in her child's life and teaches her child to be an addict of what we in the psychiatric profession call the state of "attachment": an intense feeling of affection, devotion, and intimacy that forever binds one person to another—in this case, mother and child. The more the child feels attached to the mother, the more secure he is in his acceptance of himself and the rest of the world. The more love he gets, the more he is capable of giving. Attachment breeds self-control, self-esteem, empathy, and affection, all of which lead to an increasing ability to develop literacy. We don't know why, but it seems to be true. Attachment is as central to the developing child as eating and breathing.

Evolution has worked to refine the complexity of this emotional exchange between mother and child. The urges to nuzzle, sniff, and feed are all present in other mammals, but they don't need the very long socialization process necessary for development in our species. They push their young out into the world much sooner. The human mother is attuned in a way that supports not just physical growth but speech, literacy, even the ability to handle the stress of a complicated world. Consider the infant brain as in some ways analogous to a computer. It has a seemingly infinite number of connectors just waiting to be plugged in, an architecture that allows for the development of incredibly complex behavior. But without a program that helps direct its thoughts and actions—the software, so to speak—it amounts to little. As you will see, the baby's interaction with the mother provides the software and significant, crucial parts of the hardware. Depending on the skill of the programmer, the outcome can be a disappointment or an incredibly powerful machine.

The hardware that is present even at birth is incomplete. It has cosmic potential, but on its own only limited actual capability. Through the research of neurobiologists over the past twenty years, we've arrived at the realization that the mother's interaction with her child shapes the human hardware that is the brain. She is the programmer who, during the critical first two years of life, provides a social and emotional give-and-take that determines which brain connections (synapses) and nerve tracts will develop to their full potential, as well as those that will wither. In an optimal situation, the number of synapses reaches its peak between one and a half and two years of age, and then they are pruned for efficiency. This is why, for example, a very young child can easily become bilingual early in life but that capacity diminishes as he grows; for most children, new language acquisition becomes more difficult the older they get.

Just like learning to dribble a basketball or turn a perfect cartwheel, these early stepping-stones to literacy evolve from practice, practice, practice. The mother coos in response to the baby's murmurs, looking into his eyes as he follows her lilting singsong of what's become known as "motherese": "First we're going to get our diaper changed, then we're going to go for a ride in the stroller," or "There's the red ball—let's play with it," or "What a big boy! Mommy wants a kiss!" For children who don't experience this dance of sounds and language and affection, learning to read requires more effort, and their acquisition of literacy is similar to learning a second language rather than an instinctual and enjoyable accomplishment. These kids will ultimately be less likely to read for pleasure.

Mothers who are emotionally in tune with their babies offer such conversation without even thinking about it. One mother told me she never even realized she did it until she saw herself on videotape with her firstborn a few years later and heard herself babbling every minute to the then-speechless child, in a gentle voice she barely recognized as her own.

I say all this knowing that fathers can be extremely maternal and a total substitute for a child past early infancy. But I feel nature has conspired to flood a woman with hormones that fine-tune her responses and open her to a special kind of harmony with her newborn that makes her extremely difficult to replace. When the fledgling family of mother, father, and newborn arrives home from the hospital, the bond begins first between mother and child as she feeds and cuddles her offspring, and the father becomes a full partner by aiding the mother in her efforts: delivering the baby from his crib for nighttime feedings, changing the diaper afterward, giving his wife a massage. As the baby grows and moves to cup- and spoon-feeding, he can enter into this nurturing process as well.

As more children enter the household, additional bonds evolve—sibling with sibling as well as mother with toddler, father with infant, parent with parent—so that avenues of affection and support increase exponentially. In this way the family is a living organism that grows and matures and nurtures itself. When children begin to outnumber their parents and parental time must be divided more efficiently, older siblings are as likely as parents to pass on the family devotion to care, concern, and nurturance, as well as the code of behavior and morals, to their younger brothers and sisters. While the mother helps an older child with homework, for example, another sibling may respond to the baby's whimpers with a hug, song, or game of peek-a-boo to entertain him, ensuring that there is a sufficient amount of bonding going on at all times.

instinctual and enjoyable accomplishment. These kids will ultimately be less likely to read for pleasure.

Mothers who are emotionally in tune with their babies offer such conversation without even thinking about it. One mother told me she never even realized she did it until she saw herself on videotape with her firstborn a few years later and heard herself babbling every minute to the then-speechless child, in a gentle voice she barely recognized as her own.

I say all this knowing that fathers can be extremely maternal and a total substitute for a child past early infancy. But I feel nature has conspired to flood a woman with hormones that fine-tune her responses and open her to a special kind of harmony with her newborn that makes her extremely difficult to replace. When the fledgling family of mother, father, and newborn arrives home from the hospital, the bond begins first between mother and child as she feeds and cuddles her offspring, and the father becomes a full partner by aiding the mother in her efforts: delivering the baby from his crib for nighttime feedings, changing the diaper afterward, giving his wife a massage. As the baby grows and moves to cup- and spoon-feeding, he can enter into this nurturing process as well.

As more children enter the household, additional bonds evolve—sibling with sibling as well as mother with toddler, father with infant, parent with parent—so that avenues of affection and support increase exponentially. In this way the family is a living organism that grows and matures and nurtures itself. When children begin to outnumber their parents and parental time must be divided more efficiently, older siblings are as likely as parents to pass on the family devotion to care, concern, and nurturance, as well as the code of behavior and morals, to their younger brothers and sisters. While the mother helps an older child with homework, for example, another sibling may respond to the baby's whimpers with a hug, song, or game of peek-a-boo to entertain him, ensuring that there is a sufficient amount of bonding going on at all times.

seemingly infinite number of connectors just waiting to be plugged in, an architecture that allows for the development of incredibly complex behavior. But without a program that helps direct its thoughts and actions—the software, so to speak—it amounts to little. As you will see, the baby's interaction with the mother provides the software and significant, crucial parts of the hardware. Depending on the skill of the programmer, the outcome can be a disappointment or an incredibly powerful machine.

The hardware that is present even at birth is incomplete. It has cosmic potential, but on its own only limited actual capability. Through the research of neurobiologists over the past twenty years, we've arrived at the realization that the mother's interaction with her child shapes the human hardware that is the brain. She is the programmer who, during the critical first two years of life, provides a social and emotional give-and-take that determines which brain connections (synapses) and nerve tracts will develop to their full potential, as well as those that will wither. In an optimal situation, the number of synapses reaches its peak between one and a half and two years of age, and then they are pruned for efficiency. This is why, for example, a very young child can easily become bilingual early in life but that capacity diminishes as he grows; for most children, new language acquisition becomes more difficult the older they get.

Just like learning to dribble a basketball or turn a perfect cartwheel, these early stepping-stones to literacy evolve from practice, practice, practice. The mother coos in response to the baby's murmurs, looking into his eyes as he follows her lilting singsong of what's become known as "motherese": "First we're going to get our diaper changed, then we're going to go for a ride in the stroller," or "There's the red ball—let's play with it," or "What a big boy! Mommy wants a kiss!" For children who don't experience this dance of sounds and language and affection, learning to read requires more effort, and their acquisition of literacy is similar to learning a second language rather than an

These first emotional experiences are no less than the crux of our socialization. When handled appropriately, the nurturing of these early months is where the child learns that joy comes from union, from pleasing and getting along with that first significant person and then with all the people yet to come in his life. We all thrive in close relationships, from that initial bond with our mothers to the friends we make in school, the teachers who educate us, the bosses we work with, and the spouses we marry. Then the cycle repeats itself as we produce our own children and bond with them. The bond perpetuates itself.

That is precisely why taking care of your marriage is integral to also taking care of your child. Divorce is nothing less than a failure of the child-rearing pact you made with your partner. I'm not willing to accept the notion that children aren't damaged by divorce. They may not be ruined for life, but the breakup of a marriage makes it infinitely more difficult for you and your child to do your jobs well. There will be much more wear and tear on their psyches and yours than in a comfortable, happy, two-parent home. For this reason I urge you to pick your partner carefully and provide the most stable family setting you can for your child.

FROM FRAGILE BOND TO FEELING BABY

Just like the inherent, life-sustaining reflexes to root for food and suck when a nipple is discovered, all babies are born with the capacity to attach, which includes the ability to identify sources of warmth, comfort, and food; to make the appropriate expressions, sounds, body postures, and tensions to promote mothering behavior; and to "dance" with the mother in give-and-take interactions that make the child feel good and that soothe him when he doesn't. But the capacity to attach requires the reciprocation of a sensitive, constant primary caretaker to become true attachment. Without that critical feedback, the ability atrophies, and the probability of attachment and emotional wholeness diminishes. For example, research shows that clinically depressed mothers are less likely to speak in the captivating tone of motherese, which may cause their infants to miss out on the nonverbal learning of sensations and cues connected with feelings of being cared for and loved. Indeed, as these children progress through the preschool years, they are less cooperative and have more problem behaviors. They also tend to score lower on tests of school readiness, expressive language, and verbal comprehension. In contrast, children in the same studies whose mothers were never depressed, and thus were able to be more emotionally available and sensitive, did better on cognitive and language tests, were more helpful and cooperative, and exhibited fewer problem behaviors. The latest child development research suggests strongly that the emotional state of the mother determines the emotional state of the newborn much more than do genes.

Children who miss out on sufficient early connecting may look normal, but they are likely to be neurologically and physiologically different. The part of their brains that mediates emotional reactions is thought to develop less functionally than in children who've had adequate nurturance. How could this occur? As I said before, the newborn brain has yet to be fully programmed. All the equipment is there, but the only part that is fully functional is the most primitive, the lower brain stem, which controls the bodily functions needed for survival. That means newborns have enough instinctual social skills to get us to respond to their needs, but not enough to form full-fledged relationships. As mothers interact with their babies, however, fostering those essential synapses, brain maturity extends up into the higher centers, enabling them to better control the primitive reactions. The midbrain limbic structures—including an area called the amygdala, about which important research is now going on—evolve to the extent that a baby can consciously feel emotions, and then use his upper brain (cortex) to manage those feelings. For instance, he may initially resist and become upset when tucked into his crib at night, but he will eventually calm down and settle himself to sleep.

During the first year of life the development of the prefrontal cortex, and especially the right orbital higher centers, enables the baby to fully receive sensory input from outside, as well as from memories, fantasy, or dream life, and it helps him learn to evaluate the appropriate meaning of the input he receives. As the in-tune, nurturing mother interacts with her baby, his brain develops enabling circuits, and an increasing degree of attachment takes place. In this process the knowledge of how to be with people gets built into the child without ever being discussed. Loving relationships are learned like bike riding. You can't transmit how to do it with a lecture. It has to be lived. That is the challenging secret of emotional intelligence.

Recent findings by Richard Davidson, Ph.D., director of the Laboratory for Affective Neuroscience at the University of Wisconsin at Madison, correlate a tendency to be either upbeat or depressive to the balance of certain components of the prefrontal cortex/amygdala circuits. As the mother croons to and bonds with her newborn, she is setting the balance of this system in a way that promotes the development of a happy and positive child, much like the calmness that is induced by meditation.

The nervous system also reacts to what is sensed in the environment, producing either anxiety-arousing sympathetic hormones or calming and soothing parasympathetic hormones. Mother-child interactions determine how much of these hormones the child produces, which in turn regulates his emotions.

As the brain further matures each month, new possibilities arise for empathy and connection, which leads to the secretion of endorphins and other messengers that promote warm, wonderful, and joyful feelings. If a new figure is perceived as an object of interest, the child's arousal and endorphins will be just right for curiosity to develop. But if the child feels overwhelmed, he'll have an alarm reaction and resist the new person's overtures. Sometimes it's not even an unfamiliar person who causes this negative response—it's simply not the person with whom the baby feels most secure. Given the same neuroanatomy, the securely attached baby, the one who has had the best early interactions, will have more complex brain circuits on which to draw and will make more socially appropriate reactions. The less secure infant will have a more limited repertoire of responses in such a situation.

The earlier this process of attachment occurs, the better. But even damaged relationships can be turned in a better direction. When I was chief of the Child Psychiatry Inpatient Service at Mount Sinai Hospital in New York, I developed a "Mother Bank" as an intervention into the treatment of infants who were pulling out their hair, banging their heads against the bars of their cribs, scratching themselves raw, or rejecting food or comfort. Since I attributed these problems to an inability to bond, we engaged a troop of grandmotherly volunteers to hold and feed and coo to these aberrant infants. The volunteers also supported the emotionally challenged mothers, who felt like failures because they were unable to soothe their children. When the mothers came to visit their babies, the volunteer grandmothers who had been spending several hours each day with the babies would talk to the mothers and encourage them in their roles, calming a baby and then putting her into her mother's arms. This way, the mother would get to experience the baby in a pleasurable state and feel more confident in her own skills.

Within weeks to a few months, these very disturbed infants began to respond to affection and to abandon their self-destructive behavior. And the mothers themselves were empowered in taking over the nurturing process. This tells us that even extremely deprived youngsters can improve and that detached mothers can be helped to build new bonds with their children. Cuddling and loving is the elixir; connection is the result.

Many of the neglected Romanian orphans who were adopted by American families are another case in point. Most of them had spent their early months lying alone in their cribs day after day, with nothing to look at or hear or touch. They experienced minimal human interaction beyond the meeting of their most basic needs for survival. Research shows that even the ones who have been placed in loving homes for several years often continue to exhibit serious developmental, social, and behavioral problems. Four-year-olds typically behave like two-year-olds, and playing with peers is one of the biggest problems because of their underdeveloped social skills. Almost all of them tend to be indiscriminately friendly with strangers because they remain desperate for any form of attention, but they are unable to attract it in socially acceptable ways. This is not necessarily surprising: the more a child has had to cope on his or her own, the greater the tendency to become manipulative.

When I occasionally see couples who are able to make profound alterations in the way these kids grow, I find support for the notion that children can be reached at almost any age and circumstance and restored to an amazing state of functioning. One family I know adopted a little boy from the Ukraine who had spent the better part of his first year of life in a hospital and then an orphanage. His new parents were not permitted to see the orphanage when they adopted him, so they are uncertain of the actual conditions he was living in, but the mother told me, "When I looked him in the eyes for the first time, I knew there was a wonderful kid in there." It's exactly that attitude, that conviction that you can do something for a child, that helps him respond to your attention and affection. I also suspect that in this case some of the workers in that orphanage were as loving and caring as the women in our Mother Bank at Mount Sinai. Remember, too, that children have a tremendous plasticity that allows parents to mold and shape them in more positive ways, no matter how hopeless the situation seems. This Ukrainian boy is a perfect example; today at age three, he is one of the most charming and well-adjusted children you could ever meet.

THE ELEMENTS OF RISK

This incredible relationship between mother and child is absolutely unique, the single most sacred thing in our culture. There is no more a substitute for this interaction than there is for food. No vitamin or supplement carries all the virtues of real food, and the attuned mother providing comfort and security is the perfect vehicle for giving a child the greatest chance for fulfilling his or her potential. It is a maternal responsibility that may well be the major portion of the parental package. Assuming a healthy set of genes, what passes from mother to child determines that child's future more than any inherited chromosomes, and secure attachment is more important than any innate temperament.

Popular culture has moved us away from this most fundamental aspect of maternity and its rewards, and the risk is that children will be less than they could have been. I don't mean to say that a child won't grow into a great, wonderful, talented individual if his mother works and spends less time with him, but such conditions do, in fact, provide less support for that to happen. Now, at what level does reduced support become critical? We have no way of knowing for sure, so the risks for each lifestyle decision cannot be precisely measured.

This critical issue of combining a career and creating sufficient bonding time will be discussed more fully in chapter 4. Here I cannot emphasize strongly enough that the decisions that reduce those optimal conditions should not be taken lightly, yet our culture has led us to do just that. In fact, the mother-child relationship is under direct attack. There has been a pervasive lack of appreciation for the role that mothers play, going back to the 1950s. The full-time housewives of that era were often isolated within their nuclear family, with little opportunity for adult diversions or even conversation. At the same time they were expected to be everything to everyone. It's not just that these women were left unfulfilled by their lack of opportunities; they were also treated as marginal by society. Naturally they wanted to get out of the house and work, and the expanding economy on the eve of the technological revolution helped bring what was once a possibility to reality. Today women are pressured to have a career, which may be entirely right for some and a reluctant decision for others. Their having a career may work for their children if handled well, or it may become a real threat to their development if stress or time constraints or inadequate child care interferes. We are led to believe that women can and should have it all, but this is simply not an easy situation to manage for every woman, or an acceptable way to grow up for every child.

Careers themselves are hardly what they used to be. The nine-to-five, Monday to Friday ideal has morphed into a sixty-hour workweek. Suburban sprawl requires lengthy commutes so that families can purchase housing within their financial grasp, and the technology that was supposed to make life more convenient has actually kept us on call full-time.

Where does this leave the woman who wants to have a longer maternity leave or to clock out at five so she can maintain her bond with her child? Maternity leave itself has become an oxymoron: the woman who can afford to go without pay longer is too important at the office to make a complete exit, so she remains tethered to her responsibilities by fax machine, cell phone, and laptop, all the while trying to establish the critical mother-baby bond. This newborn's substitute for motherese may well be the beep-beep-beep of the fax tone, the pinging e-mail alert on the computer, or the stern, business-as-usual tone his mother takes on when talking to colleagues. At the other end of the spectrum are those women whose jobs are such that they could take leave but can't afford to give up the paycheck. These mothers must rush back to the office before their bodies have had a chance to recover, let alone their hearts and souls.

Then there is the issue of financial independence. Stories abound of women who gave it all up to raise the children, only to see their husband skip out the door, leaving them with little or no financial support. These issues simply won't be resolved until we find a way to provide a social structure that makes it safe to be a mother. Meanwhile, this lack of social support compels each woman to exercise tremendous creativity to make things work out for her children.

Happily, there is an increasing number of options for more flexible situations today: for instance, telecommuting, consulting, or running a home-based business can free up time for parents to be with their children. Or they can choose to alternate work schedules so that one of them is home with the children while the other is out, and vice versa. Other possibilities: moving closer to a grandparent who can help out; sharing a nanny with another family so that each can have higher-quality at-home care rather than group care; even single mothers or fathers sharing a residence so that they can back each other up while the other works. We don't discard the option of creativity when our boss wants to improve a client proposal or we're trying to finance a house—what, then, would possess us to do so when it comes to our child's well-being?

Yet many of us either don't see the options or are afraid to consider them, even temporarily, while our children are young and vulnerable. For many women, work has become the main element of their identity, particularly those with demanding careers that have required a significant time investment. Let's take a look at one woman who came to me for advice because she had delayed marriage and family and now was at an urgent crossroad, uncertain of the best path for her:

Andrea is thirty-eight and single. She has been involved with Mike for two years, and both would like to make the leap to marriage. The trouble is that Mike wants to have a family, and Andrea, a high-powered attorney, is ambivalent about the idea. She enjoys her job and the nice lifestyle that comes with her income. She's not naive enough to think her life won't change with a child, and she's unwilling to switch to soccer mom status. Still, if Andrea tells Mike she wants to take a pass on the kids, he may well take a pass on her. She's not getting any younger and dreads the thought of winding up alone. For the same reason, of course, the baby carriage is going to have to follow right behind the marriage, as the nursery rhyme goes.

So what does Andrea decide? "I'll have the baby and hire a nanny," she ultimately convinces herself. "Other women work kids into their lives, so why can't I?"

CRITICAL MOMENT: Andrea is deciding whether a baby can fit into her demanding lifestyle. She has done none of the planning necessary to ensure an optimal environment for raising a child. The sheer act of assuming a baby will conform to her needs is a mistake: clearly Andrea doesn't know the significance of what she is deciding, or the impact it will have on both her own and her child's happiness and well-being. We are best off if we have children because we want them, not because they are the latest accessory or a bonus that will help cement a relationship.

Of course, Andrea was looking to society to provide her with the answers, and the one she got was, "Why shouldn't I be able to pull it off?" She had the income to hire the best in child care and maintain that hard-won career. But Andrea would still have to come home and find the energy to nurture this baby she had brought into the world. Even though she herself was comforted by material trappings, a child wouldn't find security in a luxury stroller, a designer nursery, French immersion videotapes, or a spot on the waiting list at the most exclusive preschool in town. Attachment isn't something that can be scheduled into a Palm Pilot full of appointments. Yet our culture is leading many parents into attempting to do so.

Andrea's story reminds me of a family I observed on the beach recently. The baby sat alone in his stroller, directly facing the hot sun without any sort of hat to shield his eyes, while the mother and father were off to the side smooching. It was clear that they weren't finding enough time for themselves and needed this interlude, but that left their little child totally alone and in relationship with no one while his parents were having what they considered a family outing. Now, all couples have moments when they'd rather be alone together, their desires free to unfold without the interruption of children. But I had the sense that this couple—and probably many more just like them—feel this way *a great deal of the time.* Many people today have grown up believing that they are entitled to a good time, that that's what life is all about. They put their pleasures ahead of their children, then feel guilty and become placating slaves to the children to make up for it. Consequently, no one has a good time in these households. Young men and women like Andrea are at serious risk for this sort of life if they become parents for the wrong reasons.

If you're a working mother, you have no doubt experienced the very normal gamut of emotions about your choices. It's so hard to know what's right, to not be affected by the many pressures. While it is extremely difficult and requires tremendous planning to do it all, it is possible for attachment to occur even if a mother works. The two are not mutually exclusive, though working full-time outside of the home does present an additional set of challenges (hardly a surprise to the families living that life). Sheer time together is critical to the process, but it's also important that the time be mutually pleasurable. Naturally there are women who don't feel they can be happy at home with a child all day, and if such a woman has the courage to stand up for her feelings, her children may well be better served if she is able to go to work on some sort of basis. When you try to act from what you don't really feel inside, it becomes harder to become effective at it. The best thing for a baby is when her mother thrives on what's happening between them. The question is not really so much about working or staying home as it is about whether bonding is paramount in your life—it's about finding that mother-child attunement for yourself. Going to work is fine if you return home hungry for your baby, as eager to reattach yourself as the child is for you. But you must know going into it that doing both of these jobs well—the job of nurturing a child and the job of earning a paycheck—takes tremendous stamina and devotion.

The woman who comes home exhausted needs to find ways to enjoy her precious moments with her child. It's natural to crave some downtime, but why not work your baby into it: put her in the bathtub with you, or invest in a jogging stroller and go for a run together. Work it out with your partner that one of you goes straight home from work on alternate nights, while the other gets an hour or so to go to the gym or for a massage—whatever lessens your stress but also provides some one-on-one interaction for your child in the process. That is the essence of not just parenting but parenting *well*. Anything less introduces that first element of risk and diminishes the child's chances at emotional wholeness. Anything less is the first step into the abyss of the epidemic.

HEEDING THE WARNING SIGNS

Lisa and Ed have been married ten years. They desperately want a child and have done everything in their power to make that happen. They've tried every fertility drug, artificial insemination, and two in vitro fertilization procedures. Their money and motivation are wearing thin. Not to mention that both of them are about to turn forty. Imagine their elation when on their third and—they had decided—final attempt at in vitro, the procedure works. Lisa is pregnant! She cuts back on her office hours, quits the workouts she's normally religious about, swears off anything and everything rumored to complicate or threaten pregnancy: caffeine, artificial sweetener, even the supposedly safe acetaminophen that's the only option for those nagging hormonal pregnancy headaches. And they wait.

When baby Alexander is born, they dote on him like any nervous new parents—and then some. Throughout her three-month maternity leave Lisa nurses and rocks and sings and coos, complete in her joy, reveling in this much-anticipated prize. No matter the sleepless nights, the colicky crying spells, the fact that their once-prolific social life has dwindled to an odd conversation with the neighbors as they take their evening stroll, Alex tucked in his modern-day pram with all the bells and whistles.

Fast-forward to the six-month anniversary of Alex's birth. Lisa is back at work full-time, with a schedule she has dreamed up to keep her close at hand and child-care expenses to a minimum. On Monday Alex's grandmother keeps him. On Tuesday a neighbor with three children baby-sits him in her home. On Wednesday Lisa telecommutes, working from home with an electronic setup that helps her do pretty much everything but make lunch. It's a little frantic trying to squeeze in phone conversations and e-mail only when the baby is quiet, but it's better than another day away. And she can always finish her work at night after Ed gets home. On Thursdays she bundles Alex off to her sister's for the day. Friday it's back to Grandma's.

All seems to be working well, except for the fact that Alex is getting more and more demanding. Lisa assumes he's just getting bigger and wants more stimulation, so she invests in an array of products—baby videotapes, exercisers that let him bounce and twirl and spin, electronic busy boxes that are as sophisticated as computers, and even an interactive Barney stuffed with a high-tech computer chip—to keep him happy. But he's not—unless he's being held. When her neighbor, who's getting pretty exasperated trying to pacify Alex all day while tending to her own kids, suggests that maybe Alex is feeling a little insecure, Lisa immediately gets defensive. "Insecure? I've turned my life inside out for him!" she snaps.

CRITICAL MOMENT: Alex is at risk for what we child psychiatrists call an "insecure" or "anxious" attachment. A different caretaker every day—no matter how loving each one is—just doesn't suffice. Infants need a sense of stability in order to feel loved. If a baby doesn't know who will be there when he awakens from his nap, who will offer his next bottle or spoon his pabulum, whose voice will croon the next lullaby, his world is upside down in a way difficult to imagine. His mother needs to approach her child-care situation from the perspective of what will help Alex feel secure, not what suits her work schedule or budget.

Lisa had the right intentions. She loved her child, loved being a mother, yet she'd gotten mixed messages about how to go about it. She could have found a cheap day-care center where he'd just be another diaper to change, but she'd been told that the next best thing to herself was a doting relative, so she'd taken advantage of her mother's and sister's availability. She has truly struggled to arrange more intimate care that also works for her lifestyle. The trouble is that it doesn't work for Alex. He would probably do better in the home care situation across the street, since small groups are better than big ones.

Many parents at this stage are too busy and preoccupied trying to keep it all together to heed the warnings. If you have an infant who is increasingly upset, anxious, and inconsolable, you will have to consider intervening. It may require a lifestyle change—cutting back on your work hours, rethinking your child care. Once you make the commitment to create a better caregiving relationship for your child, you'll see possibilities you may not have noticed before; indeed, the opportunities will become obvious. Lisa, though frustrated at first, was nevertheless sensitive enough to pick up on Alex's signals and her neighbor's concerns. She gave up her erratic arrangement and hired a live-in caregiver to provide some stability. Turning off the cell phone, fax machine, and computer when the workday is done can also help you feel emotionally present for your child.

It can feel like a lot to ask of an adult who up until now has had complete control of her schedule. I encourage you to consider that family life will ultimately feel more fulfilling. Your child will be much more satisfied and less demanding in the long run if you provide him with what he needs. As one East Coast mom said of life with her infant: "You just have to allow yourself to feel frustrated, then figure out where you're going to take that. It's hard to go from an office, where your productivity is measured by the hour, but maybe this is one of the lessons my child is here to teach me. Yes, she's clingy, but she's very bright-eyed and cheerful and seems well adjusted to me. I know I'm going to miss this incredible intimacy when she grows up and doesn't want to be held anymore."

As this mother is discovering, when the attachment process works, it's fulfilling for both participants. And a beautiful scene to the observers as well:

A mother, a grandfather, and four children ranging from infancy to school age are having lunch on a restaurant patio. The kids sit at the table for a very long time behaving cooperatively and even productively. Two of them color, the oldest reads a small paperback book, and the baby sits comfortably in his high chair interacting with his mother and the sister sitting on the other side of him. The grandfather is at the other end of the table, playing jovially with each of the children.

After a while the mother leaves the table to go to the restroom, and the grandfather moves over to her seat to be with the baby. He is as upbeat and actively engaged with the infant as with the older children, and the little boy responds with interest and joy. Still, as time goes on and the excitement continues, the baby appears to be a little overstimulated—making louder noises, straining harder and harder to hold his grandfather's finger, and finally starting to fuss. By that point his mother returns, takes him into her arms, and begins her soothing, comforting dance of motherese. Within minutes he quiets down and dozes off in her lap.

What's so right about this picture? Often, observing today's families is a painful scene: the miscues, the estrangement, the embarrassed parents, the children spinning out of control. But this group clearly stood out as representative of the loving quality of life every family deserves to have. The older children were secure and independent enough to amuse themselves, and well schooled in appropriate restaurant behavior. Not just the mother but the grandfather, too, clearly had a warm and affectionate relationship with each of them. And the baby, although he eventually became out of sorts, did very well in a situation that required him to adapt to unfamiliarity, outside stimulation, exhaustion, and his mother's absence. Many infants go through separation anxiety, a state of discomfort that develops when the child is cognitively mature enough to recognize his primary caregiver, then becomes distressed when she leaves his sight. This baby, at a critical moment, had the inner resources to remain patient, secure in the fact that Mom would return and the family members he knew and loved were nearby to maintain his sense of order. The grandfather did his best and did it well, but was simply not as attuned to the child's needs as the mother. In this powerful example, only when the baby began to tire emotionally did he start to exhibit anxiety, yearning for his mother to return and restore his equilibrium, as she so beautifully did.

MISUNDERSTANDING SEPARATION ANXIETY

The term "separation anxiety" is one of the most widely misunderstood concepts in parenting. The original term was used by child development theorists to describe the alarm reaction of an infant placed in the hands of someone other than the primary caretaker. But over time popular child-rearing gurus began to normalize it by referring to it as a phase and promoting the idea that parents should expect it, often in significant amounts. Yes, researchers can show that infants act with some apprehension when their mother leaves and is replaced by a stranger. That should be simple common sense. I am sure it is true of older children and adults as well under certain circumstances. But some of the measures I advocate will surprise you in their ability to ease or prevent separation anxiety altogether.

The well-being of the infant is so bound up with the connection to her mother that the child actually loses something precious when her mother disappears. However, the child can very gradually learn to maintain a mental image of her mother so that she becomes less bereft at her absence. Other people can acquire the mantle of importance merely by being around the mother and child, pitching in, talking to both of them, all while the mother exhibits comfort in the other person's presence. Thus, the child rapidly learns to be at ease with another person if the mother can accept the separation without excessive guilt or sadness. That said, some mothers do not want to feel that someone can replace them even for a brief interlude. It is such feelings of overinvolvement that can aggravate the situation for the child. Likewise, the child who is unable to put himself to sleep or entertain himself without help from his parents is going to have fewer reserves to draw on when thrust into an unfamiliar situation.

I consider a child who is exhibiting excessive anxiety about separation from the mother in a regular way as manifesting insecure attachment. What do I mean by excessive? If an infant or toddler becomes very upset and cries when his mother hands him to a familiar caretaker, something is awry. The child has not internalized a stable image of his mother to assure him that she will come back. Most child-rearing books will tell you it is the child's problem, not the parents', so parents insist, for instance, "We can't go out to dinner because Jimmy won't accept a sitter, and we don't have the heart to force him." No, we don't want to traumatize Jimmy, but there are plenty of ways to make him feel comfortable:

- First and foremost, make sure you are spending enough intimate bonding time with your child—talking, reading, playing.
- Start early on in your child's life to have other familiar adults—Grandma or an aunt or a close friend—help with caretaking tasks such as feeding and diapering. If you're breast-feeding, express some milk so Dad can give a bottle once a day too.
- Provide your child with the opportunity to practice small separations at home: when he is playing contentedly, for instance, move into the next room and talk to him from there so he knows you're available even when he can't see you. Pop back in periodically so he can have some "emotional refueling."
- Have a new sitter come over when you are home so she and your child can become acquainted gradually.
- The next time the sitter is over, go for a short walk or errand, but don't stay away too long.
- When you leave your child, even your newborn, always say good-bye and explain where you are going and how long you'll be. Never sneak out.
- Provide your preschool child with a tangible sign that you'll return: tell her, "When the little hand on the clock gets to four and the big hand gets to twelve, I'll be home." Or give the sitter three storybooks, tell your child she can have a story each hour, and when the last story is done, you'll be returning.
- Leave your child with a token of you, a picture she can kiss or a tape of you reading a bedtime story in case she becomes anxious while you're out.

Young babies, oddly enough, are often soothed easily by a competent stranger. They are still so totally in their bodies and not yet in their minds that they can respond to the firm support of the holding, the warmth, and the food even though the giver is not familiar. As the child develops, she becomes aware of personal attributes and begins to derive emotional support from the reliable presence of a specific person. At that point separation fears can become more apparent. If parents don't become frightened or guilty, this can be handled like everything else—with reassurance, comforting, gradual introduction of the person, and so forth. If the parents cannot manage this, they should seek help from a counselor just as they would if they had trouble breast-feeding or getting their child to sleep.

In short, exaggerated separation anxiety is a symptom that something has gone wrong. We want to free children of their limitations, not design life to accommodate unnecessary fears and phobias. Our society, unfortunately, has been doing just the opposite: working hard to make life free of unpleasantness, to the extent that we cook different dinners for everyone in the house and leave caregivers with extensive instructions about what our children will and won't tolerate. In every pre-epidemic society, children ate what was served. Children's broad acceptance of foods can be seen within different ethnic groups. Foods we may think are difficult are normal in other cultures. The fact that we don't have this flexibility even at mealtimes testifies to the reach of the epidemic.

We have to face the fact that when we have young children we can't put to bed, when we can't go out for a romantic dinner or a date with friends, when we can't sit in a restaurant with a young child behaving well and participating in the conversation, when we can't put our child down in a safe place with toys and go take a shower, we have created a situation or environment that isn't working. Something needs to be done to correct it. We think that making life easier for our children will make them happy. It won't.

HOW IS MY CHILD DOING?

During the first year of life, a securely attached baby will evolve from needy newborn to an interactive, busy, and engaging little personality who is a pleasure to be around the vast majority of the time. Even the youngest infants should have periods when they sleep or lie contentedly, and you should be able to go about your life in an organized fashion. If you're instead feeling overwhelmed, you need help. Use this checklist to determine how that process is going.

- Your baby should enjoy social interaction so much that she attempts to initiate it on her own—for instance, making gurgling noises to get your attention or peeking from behind a corner or a blanket.
- Your baby should be capable of occupying herself for brief periods of time.
- Your baby should be generally content even when not being held.
- He should show a healthy curiosity for exploration and make physical attempts to get where he wants to go by scooting, crawling, cruising, or even walking.
- She should sleep through the night and nap relatively predictably during the day.
- You should feel confident and comfortable with your ability to care for and soothe your baby.
- You should be able to accomplish what's on your day-to-day to-do lists without having to constantly placate your baby.
- You should generally enjoy your baby's company.
- You should be able to devote time to your marriage, having an enjoyable dinner alone some evenings or going out with your partner.

3

Starting Down the Right Path

Everybody gets so much information all day long that they lose their common sense.

—Gertrude Stein

WATCH A LITTLE GIRL WITH A DOLL: she coos and sings to it, changes a pretend diaper, gently rubs its back as she rocks it, then delicately tucks it into a miniature crib. For most women, the attachment to their babies began in their own childhood, when they imitated their grown mothers in the nurturing process. By the time you begin to plan your own pregnancy, the dreams and aspirations of what your child will be like and how you will raise him or her are well formed. But on the day that little blue line travels across the home pregnancy test window, cultural forces start to bear down on you, shattering the confidence of that wise little girl who once knew exactly what her baby needed. Everyone—from your obstetrician or midwife to your girlfriends, your mother-in-law, your water-cooler colleagues—offers up opinions on what to eat, what to wear, what to avoid, and what to sing to your growing belly. Formula or breast milk, cloth or disposable diapers, crib or bed, work or home, nanny or day-care center, pacifier or thumb, permissive or firm when it comes to early power struggles such as tantrums and toilet learning—these are but a few of the many polarizing issues that pit parent against parent, family against family. The truth is that what really fits for you, what you know is right, is going to work. What is forced upon you because it is fashionable is very likely not to.

This chapter is designed to free you from the clutter of all the advice givers and restore your common sense, which is going to be your best tool. There is no reason to believe that any adviser knows for sure about the best child-rearing practice or has more common sense than you innately have yourself. I include in that statement the advice of pediatricians, psychologists, lactation consultants, nannies, early childhood educators, self-anointed or media-appointed gurus, family, and friends—and even what I say in this book. There are so many contradictory theories and prescriptions that clearly no one has proven either side of any of the issues. When we are clear about scientific fact, there will no longer be any argument. Meanwhile, the effect of the contradictory advice of all these people is to create doubt and ignorance. It is fine to listen to their suggestions, but if the advice does not really resonate inside you ("Now, that could work! I feel that that would do it!"), you should not attempt it.

Of course, no parent intentionally chooses to follow a path that will hurt his or her child, so it's natural to feel nervous about such decisions. But every human being has the ability to feel his or her way as a parent. Too much advice alienates us from our instincts and common sense. You have a live-in parenting expert who shows you every day the effects of what you are doing: your child. Anything that is not going well with your child is a sign that your parenting practices are not working.

Why are there so many new parenting practices when we should know how to raise kids by now? The pendulum seems to swing every thirty or forty years in child-rearing. It's understandable that parents raised in the 1960s and 1970s, when liberation was the unifying theme, wanted to pass these freedoms on to their children. They had a dream of personal liberation, freedom from constraints and moral imperatives, and they fulfilled that dream by offering it to their children. But as I will demonstrate throughout the book, unregulated freedom is harmful to kids.

Every generation also tends to want to do better, to make up for the insufficiencies of their own childhood. Just as an ambitious employee always feels he could do his boss's job better if given the chance, an ambitious parent wants a better life for his child than he had. Having your own child is the perfect opportunity to make up for discipline you felt was unjust ("I'm not letting that happen to my kid") or for that used bike that paled in comparison to your buddy's spanking new ten-speed. Of course, our society has also made tremendous advances in medicine, education, technology, and opportunities for women, and it's only natural that we want our children to benefit from this new knowledge and have access to state-of-the-art everything. And that includes the latest psychological and developmental advice. Doing things the way our parents did feels like a throwback—it's out-of-date. We know better now.

Or do we? Why are we constantly seeking to discover some perfect practice that will make everything all right? Evidence is in fact mounting that modern practices may be detrimental. Today's parents fully believe they are doing the right thing by raising their children according to philosophies currently accepted as the norm. The real irony here is that many astonishingly popular practices, which I will discuss in more detail shortly, are in fact counterproductive, having evolved from well-meaning but mistaken ideas about the nature of the relationship between child and parent. Because the most radical viewpoints are frequently the ones demanding to be heard, our children have become the guinea pigs of an endless parade of child-rearing "experts" who spout untested theories and write mass prescriptions without knowing individual parents and children, then leave struggling families to prove them. But the problem with untested theories is that they have led us to get worked up over the wrong issues instead of following our instincts and intuition about what our children really need. For example, we have passionate camps devoting themselves to preaching the horrors of formula, when it may be that what hampers our children is not the form of nourishment they receive but too little bonding time and a lack of structure and discipline. We let our concern about ruining self-esteem get in the way of handling day-to-day issues such as going to bed on time and behaving well in public places.

The zealous onslaught of pressure to adhere to some rigidly applied, politically correct view rather than one's own inner prompting begins early, when parents are uncertain about the new, significant responsibilities of child-rearing and little decisions seem to take on monumental importance. Let's go through a number of parenting trends and examine how the instinctual process becomes conflicted and then thwarted. First, a case study about the decision to breast- or bottle-feed.

THE FOOD OF LOVE

When Melanie walks into my office with her four-week-old son, it is apparent from the tentative way she holds him that she has never been intimate with her baby. She has not made the transition to a loving, cuddly mother; she is not quite sure about what she is carrying in her arms. Timothy is a somewhat frightening package, held by his mother, yet unknown to her.

Melanie's pediatrician has informed me that mother and child are having feeding problems, that Timothy is always hungry but never interested in her breast. He is discontented after a nursing attempt; his mother is unsatisfied after supplying a bottle of formula. Melanie finally admits that she has come to hate feeding the baby, bottle or breast. "I feel I'm a failure because breast-feeding revolts me and the bottle embarrasses me," she says. Melanie is caught in the notion that there is a right way: breast-feeding. But for whatever reason, she doesn't want to breast-feed, and the alternative makes her feel terrible because she isn't living up to what she thinks is the preferred standard.

The situation is becoming alarming: instead of gaining weight, Timothy has actually lost a pound and a half. Her pediatrician and a lactation consultant with the La Leche League, a prominent breast-feeding support group, have both insisted that Melanie try harder and express breast milk for the supplemental feeding. The lactation consultant came to Melanie's house to teach her how to express her milk, but Melanie is producing less and less because Timothy is not nursing and she is not pumping to stimulate her milk production.

If Melanie isn't helped to change her attitude, this downward spiral is going to become a disaster. When she tells me she feels that "normal women" breast-feed, I say, "Are all these women who bottle-feed really abnormal?" I also note that statistics show that a significant number of women bottle-feed, especially after the newborn period, and most go on to raise perfectly happy, healthy children. In view of this fact, shouldn't she change her thinking? "Why breast-feed when neither of you are doing well?" I ask her. I sense that when she examines this question, her certainty about breast-feeding starts to fade.

The first thing Melanie needed to understand was that she had a choice between two workable and legitimate methods: breast- or bottle-feeding. Why breast-feed when she hated it and neither the baby nor their relationship was thriving? Next, she needed some assistance with bottle-feeding so that the baby could get enough food until she felt comfortable doing it herself. Finally, she needed a rest from some of the baby caretaking responsibilities until her anxiety eased a bit. Unfortunately, her husband was required to travel on business a great deal and she was frequently alone.

The solution: I suggest that Melanie ask her mother, who lives about two hours away, to move in temporarily and help her out, especially with the feeding responsibilities. The new grandmother is delighted to oblige, and within a matter of days the three return to my office. Melanie is proudly holding her baby and smiling. Timothy is content, not fidgeting or fussy. Grandma has been successfully bottle-feeding him, and everyone is feeling better.

I say to Melanie, "It is a wonderful thing that you can know deep inside what you really like and what you don't. As you know, there are many moms out there who don't like breast-feeding either. They are managing to push through it, and I'm not sure that that's really good for their babies. Things often do work out when you respect your own feelings."

Melanie ponders these possibilities for a few days and watches how Timothy gazes contentedly at his grandmother when he is finished feeding. She decides she wants to elicit that herself. She tries the bottle, first at home. It works. Then at a friend's house. Then the park. She finds herself telling the other women in the park that she is relieved to feel comfortable feeding her baby. In about five weeks Melanie and Timothy are successfully launched in the feeding, bonding, and attachment process, and Grandma goes home. Melanie is now back in touch with her own common sense and respect for her inclinations.

CRITICAL MOMENT: Breast-feeding, inherently a great act of attachment, was actually interfering with the bonding process, because Melanie felt she had to join the right nutritional political party rather than listen to her own head and heart about what she preferred. The point is that you need to be confident in the decision you make. Feeding is going to be the first and most significant bonding experience for you and your baby, and it must be pleasurable for both of you, no matter what form it takes. I hope that you know that your own feelings will tell you what works for you, and what works for you will work for your child.

Melanie was not alone in her confusion. Another mother I counseled was pressured to continue breast-feeding exclusively by advocates who insisted that her child would develop "nipple confusion" if she introduced a supplemental bottle. Just listen to her comments:

> I keep on getting conflicting advice from all kinds of "experts," and I'm ready to go insane. My lactation consultant says one thing, La Leche League says another, the pediatrician says something diametrically opposed to the former two, and the books say yet another. Who is right? I don't actually think my daughter, Jenna, has nipple confusion. Most "experts" say to wait until breast-feeding is firmly established before introducing the bottle (a different nipple). Well, what the heck does that mean? A couple of weeks? Six weeks? So we've given up the idea that she'll be confused, and I think our instincts are right. She takes the bottle and the breast with equal gusto. No furrowed brows or looks of general bewilderment. I think we're okay.

This mother hadn't missed one feeding for over a month and was exhausted. Now she is experiencing relief. I am beginning to think the whole concept of nipple confusion has been invented to enable people to be more in control of mothers—to explain difficulties caused by all the pressure put on them. Here's another story:

Krista has just given birth to her second son, and having breastfed the first one exclusively, with no relief for the first couple of months, she announces to one of the nurses in the postpartum ward that this time around she plans to give herself a break now and then by letting her husband bottle-feed with her breast milk so that she can sleep more.

The nurse gives Krista a horrified look and hastens from the room, returning shortly with three other nurses and a new-mother counselor from the hospital. They are there, they inform Krista, to alert her to the dangers of "nipple confusion." Not only will the baby get confused and maybe not go back to the breast, but a baby who is not completely breastfed the first few months (time not specified) might be less intelligent than one who is exclusively breastfed. "Studies prove it," they insist.

Krista, who luckily has a mind of her own, retorts that she was bottle-fed, her husband was breastfed, and she knows for sure that she is much smarter than her husband! She says this just to get them "off their high horse," she tells me later. And it works—they all start laughing. Krista goes home from the hospital and breast-feeds most of the time but gives herself bottle breaks when necessary, and she is thoroughly enjoying her newly expanded family.

This issue of nipple confusion illustrates perfectly how these gurus seize people's souls and reduce them to frightened, conforming slaves. All things being equal, there are a lot of good reasons to breast-feed: infants who are breastfed have lower rates of many garden-variety illnesses, from diarrhea to ear infections, allergies to diabetes, and some research even indicates that breast-feeding may enhance cognitive development. Mothers themselves have reduced risk of breast and ovarian cancer, experience more rapid postpartum healing, and are able to lose pregnancy pounds faster owing to the increased metabolism necessary for milk production.

Many women who are open to breast-feeding have an easy time of it. Others find it challenging but have the support of a good friend, grandparent, or experienced lactation consultant to help them over the humps. Still others know they have no interest in nursing and no qualms about the bottle-feeding choice. Why do some women choose not to breast-feed when the sheer act promotes attachment? Many lifestyle factors conspire to defeat the process. While almost 70 percent of new mothers leave the hospital nursing their newborns, by six months that number falls to just above 32 percent. Some of that decrease can be blamed on the return to work: inadequately short maternity leaves and a lack of flexibility and understanding on the part of employers are but two of the culprits. Even mothers who choose to stay home may have a tough time of it. Some don't have the emotional support or educational resources to make breast-feeding work. Many are too overwhelmed with the demands of other children or an overcrammed lifestyle to carve out the necessary time.

There are ways to re-create the physical intimacy of breast-feeding. You can find the same bonding experience by holding the baby against your chest, making that extraordinary eye-to-eye contact, or establishing that profound psychic connection you both get from being skin on skin, heart to heart, many times a day for minutes and hours at a time. Avoid as much as possible the temptation to leave your baby alone in an infant seat or stroller with a bottle propped between his lips.

Remember, too, that formula is fine; it's been good enough for several generations, and improvements are continuing in the effort to make it more comparable to breast milk. So you see, your baby will be fine either way. The first thing you need to do is make the decision about whether breast or bottle is the best fit for you. If you opt to breast-feed, cultivate an optimistic attitude and create an environment that will help it work: line up an experienced friend or lactation consultant you can call on for help; create some physical space that's comfortable for you (a rocking chair, stool, nursing pillow, soft lights); and introduce a supplemental bottle as soon as you feel your milk is established enough so that your partner can help out with middle-of-the-night feedings. Don't be afraid to experiment—try a glass of wine or a beer if you're having trouble with letdown, eliminate offending foods from your diet if your baby is gassy, and use a pump to build up your milk supply or remove excess when you're uncomfortable. And always remember: it's the nurturing act, rather than the nutritional choice, that makes the real difference.

THE POLITICS OF EATING AND SLEEPING

It's sad to say that eating and sleeping have become political issues in the child development field, but they have. Our culture is so organized around creating an endlessly contented child that the current recommendation, both medically and psychologically, of feeding infants "on demand"—that is, whenever they indicate they're hungry—has become a political football. Historically, demand feeding refers to a quick and consistent response to your baby's request for food, rather than trying to feed him on a preset schedule. But the original meaning of the concept has become perverted. On a psychological level, demand feeding lets your baby know that you are always there to meet his needs, a major milestone in the attachment process. And certainly newborns need frequent feedings to grow and thrive. But eight-month-olds don't require a meal every two hours, or in the middle of the night, and to continue to slavishly feed an older infant every time he whimpers is a mistake. If you do not train your child to suckle constantly, he will naturally space out his own feedings as his body is able to hold more food per meal and stay full longer. Conversely, if a bottle or nipple is placed in his mouth every time he manifests some form of discomfort, he becomes habituated to that form of soothing. Your baby will have been trained to be suckle-dependent and may gain excess weight in the process; you may end up resenting his twenty-four-hour-a-day demands. Excessive feeding will also slow down the shift your child should make during the course of the first year from passive suckler to active explorer. Yet, utter the word "schedule" and people will look at you like you're considering child abuse. It simply isn't so.

A generation or two ago, it was common practice to feed babies at consistent intervals and put them down to sleep at the same time each day. The sooner you got them on a schedule, the theory went, the more secure they'd feel and the more sane family life would be. Well, there's certainly a germ of truth to that. Babies do thrive on predictability. You will feel better physically and emotionally once life regains some semblance of normalcy, and you will therefore be better able to nurture your child. The difference between then and now is that we now understand the importance of flexibility in the early months. But there also comes a time when we need to begin to institute a routine, and neglecting to do that is as harmful to development as it is to ignore your baby's hungry cries. There is a middle ground here, one that some gurus and their camps can't seem to recognize. Life is not the sharp black and white that ideologues demand. There are all kinds of grays that work fine.

Teaching self-soothing is not emotional neglect. Attempts at routine do not put the parents' convenience before the baby's needs, thwarting emotional security and the attachment process. Babies crave and thrive on a consistent, predictable routine. There is absolutely no reason not to facilitate this process, and if parents follow their natural nurturing instincts, there is relatively little risk in helping it along. You learn as early as the first two or three months whether your baby is crying out of hunger or from some other frustration. If he's just nursed, been changed, has been awake for a few hours, and continues to fuss, it's likely that he's simply overstimulated and needs to rest. Offering yet another feeding or continuing to rock him probably won't do any good. Put him in his crib and let him fuss it out a few minutes on his own. It's very likely that he'll quickly doze off and take a nap. Then watch for the same cues and repeat the process at about the same time the next day. This is not the same as refusing to feed him until the clock strikes a certain hour. This is not rigid, calculated scheduling. It's following your baby's signals and helping him learn how to soothe himself and what to expect out of life. He's trying to tell you something, and you are satisfying his request. Call it a schedule, call it a routine, call it a happy accident—it's trusting your gut, and it works.

In fact, developing a routine promotes attachment. Your baby will grow to recognize the sound of your voice, the scent of your body, the sight of your breast, and know that when any or all are near, she's going to start to feel better. If she's going to evolve into what's typically known as an "easy" baby—one who is adaptable and sociable and regular in bodily habits—you'll see within two to three months that you are all she needs to begin to fall gently into an easy, predictable pattern: feeding at fairly regular intervals, falling asleep on her own and resting for longer periods at night, and behaving contentedly when awake. Then, sometime between four and six months, a traditional and effective routine has been established: sleeping through the night, feeding every three to four hours during the day, and taking two fairly predictable naps, one midmorning and one mid to late afternoon. Now life is good.

Most experts would call this process of settling into a routine a developmental accomplishment. I would also make the leap and call it a sign of secure attachment. A baby who is secure in his world and his relationships is more content, able to occupy himself when left unstimulated for a short time, and able to quickly soothe himself to sleep. You may even see your baby develop the ability to wait patiently for a few minutes as he observes you warming his bottle or preparing his cereal, secure in the notion that you understand what he's asked for and are about to provide it. This period of predictability ushers in what many parents refer to as the honeymoon period—a stage that starts at about three or four months and continues until near the end of the first year. This time is blissfully easy and downright delightful compared with the stressful newborn months and the high-maintenance toddler phase when baby becomes mobile and adventuresome. If you're not experiencing this honeymoon period, get the help you need.

What happens when you neglect to establish a routine? Your child gets to six or eight or ten months of age and remains as demanding as a newborn. Many experts would have you believe that you have a "difficult baby" and there's nothing to do but suffer through your plight. I'm here to tell you that it simply isn't so. If you resolve the problem by deciding your child is "difficult," you are less likely to examine what goes on between you and your so-called difficult child. You are less likely to seek help and less likely to learn to do things in a way that's better for both of you. Don't accept the notion that you have any form of a problem child. It is you who needs the help.

Remember: no normal, healthy infant requires a nighttime feeding beyond six months of age. Nor should he be hanging off your breast, sucking on a bottle, or tethered to your hip all day long. Babies this age no longer need to suck for emotional gratification, nor should they need to be amused by you 24/7. They should be playing with toys, exploring their world, moving on to physical milestones. And you shouldn't be slaving away, frustrated, exhausted, and resentful. Certainly, the baby who is clingy or prone to crying jags will take longer to reach a contented, predictable pattern, but these are the infants who most need that structure in their lives and who are looking to you to provide it. It's the calmness and predictability of routine that helps them regulate their out-of-control emotions.

THE CRYING GAME

These so-called difficult babies are an early testing ground for the epidemic, as it's all too easy to allow them to take control and never let go. Any reasonable parent would respond to such a baby's constant need for soothing, but some unwittingly continue to pacify every whimper and demand—even as their baby leaves the colicky newborn period. That's why it's not uncommon for formerly colicky infants to also have sleep problems. They've never learned to soothe themselves, and their parents feel helpless and often guilty that they cannot relieve the pain. Then they fall into the habit of substituting placation for the frustration that children need to help them grow their personality structure. Doing that is physically exhausting, emotionally draining, and no fun. Take a look at what happened with this couple:

> Rick and Julie's first child, Megan, starts to cry somewhere around the end of her second week, and it doesn't take long for them to realize that their baby is colicky. No matter how many times they are told that it isn't their fault, there's no known cause of colic, and it will end by the three-month mark, the couple feels devastated, embarrassed, and disappointed in themselves.
>
> Julie forces herself to keep breast-feeding, since mother's milk is typically gentler on the newborn system, but nursing sessions are frequently chaotic, with Megan spitting out her nipple and resisting any attempts at affection. Julie modifies her diet as directed by her pediatrician, in case something she is eating is causing her baby discomfort, tries supplementing the nursings with predigested, hypoallergenic infant formulas to combat any allergies, and keeps a battery of pacifiers on hand. Fans, dishwashers, and other sources of white noise are employed as often as possible. "If anyone looked in the window and saw us trying to watch TV with the vacuum cleaner running by itself in the corner, they'd think we were nuts, but sometimes that's the only way to get through the evening," Julie says, laughing, but with an edge to her voice.

The three-month mark ticks by, then the fourth, and there is still no relief from baby Megan's incessant wails. Finally, sometime between five and six months, the couple realizes that the crying jags are truly becoming less frequent. Still, life is far from calm. Megan rarely naps long enough or predictably enough for her mother to accomplish anything, and nights are, well, a nightmare. Megan seldom falls asleep before eleven or twelve o'clock, and that is far from the last Julie hears of her daughter. Even though Megan is no longer being fed in the wee hours, every time the pacifier falls from her mouth, she wakes up and goes ballistic.

Rick, who rises for a long commute to work at 5:00 A.M., crawls into bed well before his wife and daughter, and Julie can hardly expect him to make the middle-of-the-night runs to the crib while she is home. Julie worries about how she is going to cope when Megan turns nine months old and she herself has to go back to the office full-time. It is hard for Julie not to wonder what she did to deserve a baby like this.

CRITICAL MOMENT: Rick and Julie have had to spend months just trying to help their child reach a minimum level of contentedness, and now they need to do an about-face and let her cry a little to learn to settle herself. That makes them vulnerable to the "cry-it-out" controversy—yet another overreaction to a more structured child-rearing style. The parents and experts who think allowing a baby to fuss a little before falling asleep is emotionally neglectful tend to be the same ones who most fear the concepts of bottle-feeding and developing routines. But just as with feeding, there are differences in today's more enlightened approach that are equally in tune with both a child's emotional development and need to learn to self-soothe.

Parents like Rick and Julie must be empowered to take control, not be made to feel guilty. They need to close their ears to the idea that anything that is easier on parents has to be bad for the baby. It is not about putting your own comfort first. It is about creating a harmonious family environment that is pleasurable not painful, affectionate not adversarial. It is the first step in helping baby fit into society—the society of your home, from which he will venture forth into the world. None of this can be accomplished if you're all severely sleep-deprived.

I do not advocate letting an infant scream at all costs, for hours, to teach him a lesson. Indeed, in those three to four newborn months the parents of some babies may need to stand on their heads—and they should—to keep those babies soothed. But there is a point when all children need some structure to their routine, and a baby like Megan may need help recognizing that. Resistance to adding this structure, to training your baby to sleep well and predictably, is another element of the practices leading to the epidemic, one that gives the child too much control and parents too much guilt.

You may be reeling at just the thought of a plan that involves letting your child cry. It sounds cruel, unfeeling, stern. But children need to learn to bear frustration, anger, and disappointment, and there is a very good, gentle, tested method of accomplishing this that won't harm your baby. Using this method will improve the whole family's day-to-day existence—and in the long run, your child's character. You may simply need to set up a predictable bedtime routine: bath, feeding, lullaby in a dimly lit bedroom, tucking her into her crib while still drowsy, then leaving her alone to settle herself. Return at periodic intervals to soothe your baby if she continues to fuss—every five minutes or so at first—but don't take her out of the crib. As her crying begins to peter out, stop going to her and she'll drift off. The first night or two may produce some hysterics, but most babies quickly catch on that it's bedtime and they must go to sleep.

You are not abandoning or damaging your child. Your child

knows you are there. He may get a little mad at the change in behavior, but it's not as if he's being totally neglected. And later he's going to get mad about a lot of things: not being allowed to put his finger in an electrical socket, or not getting an ice-cream cone instead of dinner, or not being allowed to stay up late on school nights. Are you going to give in then? One would hope not. Look at it this way: you will not only have reclaimed your own nights—a critical step in finding the energy and motivation to be a good parent during the day—but you will have given your baby an important gift. Good sleep habits are critical to a child's well-being—you can't learn in school if you're too tired to focus. When you rush too quickly to meet your baby's every need all night long, you miss out on an opportunity to let him learn an important skill that will serve him well into adulthood.

How does it work in real life? Getting back to Julie's plight with restless Megan, she eventually confided her distress to a few seasoned friends at a parenting group, who were quick to offer up some very helpful advice. Start that bedtime routine. Get the rocking chair out of the family room, they said, and put it in Megan's room, so she can have her last feeding and lullaby in a dark, quiet place, without the TV blaring. Then tuck her in while she's still drowsy and follow the response routine described here. Julie tried it: sure, the first day was rough, but the second was better, and soon Megan was going to bed without a peep. Because Megan had learned the art of self-soothing, she also quit demanding her pacifier at all hours. Next Julie employed the method during afternoon naptime. When the day finally came for Julie to go back to work, both mother and child were well rested and ready.

THE FAMILY THAT SLEEPS TOGETHER

Right in line with the practice of letting babies call the shots throughout the wee hours is the philosophy known as the "family bed." Proponents believe that babies will feel more secure sleeping next to their parents, and mothers will have less of a problem with nighttime nursings if they don't have to do anything more than roll over and accommodate their child. This is a very intense controversy—the only other topic that evokes such passionate feelings among parents is breast-feeding, or the lack of it. Yet there are a number of things that seem questionable to me about sharing a bed with your child. Children develop resources sleeping alone that are essential for adaptation in our complicated culture. Sure, they're going to be happy about being equal participants in what is essentially the core of the marital relationship. But in allowing them to maintain that delusion, we only postpone the day when they learn that they are not the center of the universe, and not on a par with their parents in power and presence. They are children, and they cannot inhabit an identical world to ours. Also, learning to be alone leads to increased ability to self-soothe, to tolerate frustration, and to recover from disappointment. Sharing a bed with your child clearly thwarts or delays this process.

The practical rationalizations for the family bed also don't make sense. Even if you want your child close by to breast-feed, you can accomplish this task safely with a bassinet or crib in your room. And again, nighttime feedings are no longer necessary past the first six months (even that's being generous). By that point you should be weaning your baby off of them.

I have never been clear about how having a child in your bed can be good for your marriage. What kind of intimacy can parents attempt if they have no privacy? Such an arrangement literally gives the child control over your relationship, often fostering resentment in one or both neglected partners. And finally, once a child is in your bed, it becomes very difficult to get him out. That may not seem like such a big deal with a ten-pound baby, but wait until he's a forty- or fifty-pound preschooler taking up more than his share of room. Family bed advocates insist that all kids eventually move out on their own, but your child's time frame for doing so may be well past what seems right to you. And when the next sibling comes along, where will she fit in?

This is not to say that you should never allow your child in your bed. There are times when your child really needs you nearby at night, and you should be sympathetic to those situations. When your child is sick, for instance, it can be much easier to keep an eye on spiking temperatures or vomiting episodes if he is next to you in your bed. If he has a nightmare, it's worth the few minutes of lying next to him in his room to get him peacefully back to sleep. And certainly many a brood spends Saturday mornings reading the funny papers and downing pancakes from breakfast trays in the master bed—that's the stuff that happy family life is made of.

A FIRM FOUNDATION

Setting routines about sleeping and eating leads comfortably to the next step of life with your child: toddlerhood. This is a potentially delightful stage when your child grows into a truly independent being—sometimes a bit too independent, in fact. As he becomes ever more mobile, curious, verbal, and opinionated, the two of you will butt heads over many issues as you try to keep him safe and he tries to conquer his world. Without a firm, loving foundation, these times will be trying. Once we allow our children to develop the delusion that they are in control, we have great difficulty trying to impose necessary routines, and tantrums result. These difficulties become much more than simple power struggles. The child gets upset because control has become his security measure and losing control makes him feel vulnerable and unloved. When he is thwarted in his attempts to control the world, his security crumbles.

Parents suffer, too, as the demands of their child snuff out that romantic connection that created him in the first place. Indeed, a healthy parental marriage is more critical to the mental health of the growing child than many of the other issues we now worry about. Consider the following situation in which a couple became victims of their own permissiveness.

Jack and Abbie are the parents of Zoe, who is charming and easy to manage as a small baby. As Zoe reaches eighteen months, however, she begins to refuse to do what she is asked or delays excessively. She resists bedtime and going into or coming out of the bathtub and generally defies her parents whenever she is told no. Abbie is confused. She tells me that she knows she should be doing something about her daughter's behavior, but can't bring herself to take action. She feels as if her sweet daughter is changing, and she says she doesn't know how to function with this very different child under her roof.

As time goes on, Abbie continues to ignore and avoid the situation. Zoe's demands become more insistent, and she begins to shriek and tantrum, not just at home but in her nursery school, in stores, and on the street. The child's behavior is actually beginning to threaten the couple's marriage. Jack, who is unwilling to accept his share of responsibility, says he is getting fed up with Abbie's lack of ability to parent their daughter and beginning to feel he cannot continue to live in that atmosphere and function. It is this threat to their marriage that brings them to the consultation. They both describe their marriage as otherwise very happy and working well. The couple is up against an impasse that illustrates the underlying issues in the problems with children today.

When I ask Abbie what she feels when her child refuses to do what she wants and looks at her defiantly, she replies: "I feel paralyzed. I can't move. I love her so much, I can't take the risk of doing something wrong. I hope that this is just a stage and that soon it will change.

Hoping for better, I choose not to do anything. It feels like I won't crush her spirit if I just try to talk her down."

CRITICAL MOMENT: Testing limits and probing boundaries is, of course, very normal behavior for a toddler. The problem here was that it was not being managed. If Abbie did not establish her authority, she would set Zoe on a track of isolation and endless exploration of boundaries, leaving her with a sense of power and entitlement that are a distortion of the reality of a child's life. Abbie's response should always be: "I know you would like to stay longer, darling, but time is up. We are going to get dressed now (go to bed now, leave the playground now, and so on)." There should be no question that the child will do as told.

Abbie reminded me of another mother I knew who was actually fueling her child's tantrums by putting the child in her room and then hovering nearby. When the child quieted a bit and called for "Mommy," she would go in and give the child a soothing, calming lecture on why she shouldn't be having tantrums, since "Mommy loves you and wants to make you happy." Both this mother and Abbie are charming and gracious, with heartwarming smiles. I can see how rewarding it is to a child to have her mother totally within her power, pleading with her and trying to figure out how to get back in the child's good graces. I suggest that you not talk children down. Let them have zero payoff for this behavior, and it will be extinguished.

The solution with Abbie was to help her establish a new distinction. She mistakenly thought that anything she might do in response to the tantrums "could be dangerous" to her child. She did not realize that by not doing anything, she was electing to do something. For example, the surgeon who does not operate on an acute appendix causes subsequent severe damage or even death to the patient. He cannot defend himself by saying, "I did nothing." Not operating is as significant in the patient's life as operating. Not handling your child's tantrums is also an extremely significant act with severe consequences. When I put it to Abbie in this way, she couldn't escape her ultimate responsibility.

We discussed Abbie's childhood and the fact that her mother was a strict disciplinarian who would spank all her children when they misbehaved. Abbie described the fear and anxiety she experienced when her mother got angry and she herself wasn't even sure what she had done wrong. I asked her if she was afraid she would be like her mother, adding that she didn't seem to me to be that kind of person. I suggested that her reaction to her mother was one of the issues controlling her behavior with her child, and that perhaps it was time to stop letting her mother run her life. (Doing the opposite of one's parents is being controlled by them as surely as imitating them.)

I told Abbie, "I know you love Zoe very much, and I hope that your love will overcome your fear once you know what is at stake." I also emphasized that her child's behavior was not simply a stage and would keep intensifying if she didn't do something to change the practices that were leading to Zoe's disturbed behavior. It might seem hard now, but it would be much more difficult if Zoe were four or five years old and still going to great lengths of screaming to try to get her mother to give in. I gave Abbie two strategies.

First, I told her to try to identify the first moment when Zoe started the process that led to tantrum. "If you just sit by and wait, hoping she will stop before the tantrum goes too far, that leaves the power in Zoe's hands, not in yours. But your child is not able to be her own parent." I told Abbie to watch carefully for the typical posture, facial expression, and vocal tone that preceded a tantrum. Every child very clearly shows signs beforehand. In fact, skillful mothers never see the full-blown tantrum; they head it off almost before it can get started.

Second, I told Abbie to pick the child up, telling her: "You

cannot do this anymore. Mommy doesn't like it." If Zoe continued the tantrum, no matter what the situation, Abbie needed to
take her home (if they were out) or put her in a safe but confined
place—a crib, play yard, or her bedroom. Tell her she is not permitted to come out until she stops, I said, and do not discuss the
situation further. If Zoe wouldn't remain in the room, Abbie
could use a pressure-mounted safety gate so that she couldn't
escape. Once Zoe had calmed down and diverted her attention
to a more appropriate activity, she could leave the room, and
Abbie could resume treating her normally.

The issue is this: you and your child are about to determine
just who is in charge. It is ruinous to leave your child in charge.
A parent can be both loving and firm. These are not opposite
qualities. In fact, a child cannot use her normal, two-year-old
boundary-probing to help her grow if her parent doesn't meet it
with loving control.

Whenever a child develops the tendency to tantrum, typically
between the ages of twelve and eighteen months, parents must
behave consistently and refuse to give in to the child's wishes or
fuel the tantrum with conversation. More educated parents tend
to fall back on this strategy of talking and rationalizing to make
their point. But look at it this way: if you are issued a ticket for
speeding, the police officer is attempting to correct your behavior simply by giving you the consequence; he does not spend his
time giving you a lecture on speeding or discussing how you feel
about the ticket. The same applies to a temper tantrum. Your
child comes to the realization that she is wrong through your
firm, confident response. Nor should you rationalize that your
baby doesn't "understand" her behavior. She certainly knows
what she wants and is attempting to get it; you must teach her
that this is not the way to achieve her goals, and that her goal at
that moment might be impractical.

There is a fine line between meeting your young child's needs
and totally giving over your life. As I said before, it's utterly
essential in the early weeks and months to find this balance as

your baby adapts to the overwhelming world of life outside the womb, yet there also comes a critical period midway through the first year when it's emotionally important for him to develop a degree of independence. Surprisingly soon, parents need to begin that delicate dance of letting go a little at a time, yet being there when baby needs them. This is a natural process that builds a socially and emotionally mature child. This is the child who will develop a healthy sense of autonomy for venturing out into the bigger worlds of the sandbox, preschool, and beyond.

TOILET TRAINING: THE NEXT CRITICAL STEP

Another of the current practices that thwart this natural evolution to independence is delayed toilet training. It has been an established medical fact that most children gain bladder and bowel control—that is, they are aware of the sensation that they need to use the bathroom and can wait a few minutes to do so—around the age of two or two and a half. You can observe this yourself when your toddler goes behind a table or chair, or to some secret spot, and has a bowel movement in his diaper. This wanting to hide is a key signal that your child is ready for toilet training. Yet we see many children over the age of three who are still in diapers, which manufacturers now produce in larger and larger sizes. Some noted pediatricians have even come out and encouraged parents to wait until the child decides himself that he is ready. The idea that a child will spontaneously decide to use the toilet on his own is an iffy proposition. It reminds me of the now-laughable approach that progressive schools used to take in teaching reading. Teachers would sit back until the child expressed an interest, and what do you suppose happened? Many seven- and eight-year-olds in their classes couldn't recognize a word.

The fact is that you need to condition your child to use the toilet, and while most kids are not ready to start this process before age two, waiting until age three or beyond is a disservice to both of you. If you've established a firm foundation in other areas, your child is likely to be cooperative, eager to please, and excited about growing up. Simple steps like letting her watch you and older siblings use the bathroom, buying big girl or boy underwear, and setting up a potty seat in the bathroom to practice on will make the process enjoyable and fun for your child. Then, once you've laid the groundwork, take the diapers off and put on the underwear. Disposable training pants—another clever marketing gimmick that manufacturers have invented—are nothing but pull-up diapers that allow your child the freedom to continue to urinate when and where he wants. Let him feel the sensation of itchy wet legs a few times, and he'll quickly figure out the potty is preferable.

Again, it all comes right back to common sense. When you feel anxious, uncertain, and unclear about the right away to proceed with your child, you are in the grip of the confusion produced by the sea of advice washing over you. The advisers are really saying, "You need me, you don't know, you are ignorant. I am smart, I know." It is torture to feel uncertain when your baby is crying and refusing the nipple or your toddler is throwing a tantrum in a public place. You need to know that this uncertainty is normal; it is okay that you feel that way. What is not is that you think you must find out what you "really" need to do. That fright or insecurity is just part of what we all go through when we are faced with an unfamiliar challenge.

Take a deep breath, remind yourself that the knowledge is built in and available if you just relax, wait a moment, and then see what you have an urge to do. If you summon up your confidence, in a minute or two you will get an urge to do something. Trust that urge and carry it out. I believe that most of the time, what you want to do will work and be good not just for you or your baby but also for both you and your partner. Remember, women thousands of years ago knew nothing of science, nutrition, or child-rearing gurus. They just did it, and we continue to evolve. Mothering knowledge is built into you, and the gurus are trying to talk you out of it. Maybe you will recognize that your fear comes from their injury to your natural confidence, the kind you had when you put your dolly to bed as a child, by filling your head with arbitrary rules.

The advisers are not mean. They are filled with fear themselves that you won't do it right. They worry that if they say, "Do what comes naturally," you will do something crazy or extreme or neglectful. That is the way men have historically regarded women, and the way doctors have questioned mothers' abilities, even in childbirth, which the medical community has made into a disease. It is up to you to struggle against this attitude with the same strength you have fought for every freedom you have ever won. Every child growing up has to reach a point where when a parent proffers advice she can say, "Thanks, Mom, thanks Dad, for your advice I will think about it," and then do whatever she decides is best for her unique being. When you give the same response to child-rearing gurus, you will get back your common sense.

HOW IS MY CHILD DOING?

The important thing to remember is that if your baby or toddler is content, secure, and well behaved by most standards and you are enjoying life with him, then you're on the right track. If your child is endlessly demanding and more prone to expressing dissatisfaction than pleasure, you are at your wit's end, and nothing seems to be going right, the bond is weak and unhealthy and fragile. Watch for the following clues that you may need to rethink your parenting practices; at times, an objective family therapy professional who can observe you and your child in action may be helpful. Your pediatrician or another medical professional you know and trust can refer you to a credible therapist.

- Your baby is taking far longer to settle into a predictable routine than other infants you know. (This should happen naturally or with a little prodding from you between about three and six months.)
- You can't remember getting a good night's sleep since your child was born. (The vast majority of infants are capable of sleeping all night by six months.)
- Your older baby or toddler would rather suck on a bottle or pacifier than explore. (A baby should switch from passive suckler to active explorer between six and nine months old.)
- Your child melts down if his needs are not immediately met. (He should be able to display some tolerance for delayed gratification—waiting calmly in the high chair as he sees you preparing his food, for instance—as he heads into his second year of life.)
- You find yourself frequently confused about how to handle your child's behavior and resentful of his unceasing demands.
- You have very little time or energy for your spouse, and your marriage is showing signs of strain.

4

The Truth and Consequences of Child Care

If there is anything that we wish to change in the child, we should first examine it and see whether it is not something that could better be changed in ourselves.

—Carl Jung, *The Integration of the Personality* (1939)

THE ISSUE OF CHILD CARE is an extremely contentious one. The research that's been conducted over the last decade has presented evidence that nonparental care tends to pose hazards for young children. And many working parents are caught in a conflict between their need to develop their career and their wish to nurture their baby in the best possible way. But the truth is that no one can tell you with any certainty exactly what to do about it. The evidence accumulated so far is not sufficient to tell you how much time your child can safely spend in nonparental care. But it does strongly suggest that nonparental care poses a definite risk to your child's development.

Thus, every parent has to ask and answer a very difficult question: Am I personally capable of both working and parenting well? There is no question that some people can do both. At a recent dinner party I was seated next to a woman, a family practice physician, who described how she entered her medical residency shortly after her first child was born. It was clear that she was a person capable of organizing her life so that she could do both. She arranged to breast-feed her child; she found the time to be both at school and in a program that facilitated a close connection with her child. She did not have to leave her professional life for her mothering life. They were all one for her—she was always a mother and always a doctor. I am trying to get at something subtle here that is different from just doing both. The inner resolve to do it all as one actually requires that you make creative choices. This physician chose a school that would help her work out her situation, picked a specialty that lent itself to mothering, and worked in such a way that her child could be nearby. It was clear to me that this very specially gifted person could in fact do it all. Not everyone can. Most of us know whether we are qualified to apply for a job, play in a sports league, or run for political office. We know something about our real capabilities.

And we know how much we want a baby. We can tell the degree of our yearning and also sense how we really want to spend our time. I suspect that people often do not push themselves to be sure that they really want what they are about to create and can handle all the burdens, commitments, and responsibilities that a child entails. I hope you will do all the work and thought necessary for your decision to be crystal-clear to you. For there is no more critical moment in parenting than when you make the decision to work or stay home and figure out how to execute that decision on a daily basis. It may truly be the turning point in your relationship with your child. In this chapter, you will have the opportunity to consider the options, weigh the risks, and determine a course from which both you and your child can benefit.

NEW MILLENNIUM, SAME OLD PRESSURES

The pill. Who knew back in the embryonic stage of the feminist movement what that incredible ability to control one's fertility would do for women? It held the promise of a lifetime of freedom, happiness, fulfillment, adventure, and accomplishment. Yet freedom increases the complexity of life, giving rise to more choices in a world that hasn't necessarily changed to reflect these possibilities. This freedom has confronted women with choices of how to combine work with child-rearing that aids the bonding process. What careers are best suited to motherhood? When is the best time to start a family in the course of that career? How much time can a woman realistically take off, what's the best way to negotiate it, and—most important—who will take care of the child when work is resumed?

Are women really free, or are they merely subject to yet another set of expectations? Society likes to talk as if women now have a "choice," but in reality it may well be that we've just added another layer of responsibility to the role. Even if you choose to work, you often continue in all the same roles as mother, wife, homemaker, PTA member, and so on. The support from our society is grossly inadequate. We're one of only two developed countries that do not provide paid maternity leave. Increasingly, salaried workers are expected to be on call to their employers around the clock, meaning that cell phones and pagers frequently interrupt those precious few family hours. Hourly workers are often forced to work overtime or lose their jobs. Cutting back to part-time work often entails a loss of health benefits too critical to give up. And child care, left entirely to the private marketplace, is underregulated, understaffed by often underqualified workers, and overall, inadequate for meeting children's needs.

Many women today are just accepting what is dictated by society and struggling to make it work, perhaps at the expense of their child. Staying home with a baby is a choice many of them can't envision. Even if they do, it's not politically expedient to speak of it on the job. Announce during pregnancy that you're not coming back to the office after your delivery, and you may forfeit income that would have been available during maternity leave, critical benefits such as health and life and disability insurance, and often any real authority you have in your job. Since it's a rare woman who can afford to give up those financial benefits or accept lame duck status after years of climbing the corporate ladder, most just continue to act as if they will remain equally devoted to their career for the duration of their pregnancy. Others talk themselves into the idea of "coming back," figuring they might as well give it a shot and see how it goes. And many more never even consider being stay-at-home mothers.

We know that the majority of mothers with children under age six—about 62 percent—work outside the home, according to the Bureau of Labor Statistics. And 79 percent of those with children ages six to seventeen are in the workforce. There does seem to be some evidence that mothers of babies younger than one year are choosing to stay home more often than they have done in the recent past. The year 2000 brought a slight decline in the number of working women with infants for the first time in twenty-five years, from a high of 59 percent to 54 percent. It's still too early to tell if this is a significant lifestyle direction or a product of economic trends.

Yet there's much that these numbers don't tell us: how many mothers really *want to work,* how many *have to work* for financial reasons, or how many *could afford to quit* if they were willing to rethink their lifestyle. What *is* certain, however, is that high-stress, time-pressed, two-career families are far from the optimum environment for raising children. We've had three decades of the working-mother experience, and that has given us plenty of information about how it functions. For many women, it's been wonderful. The same goes for their offspring, when their care is well handled. But there's also increasing evidence that many children and parents are suffering from the choices they have made and the rationalizations they've accepted.

I take it to be only natural that women want to express themselves in the world of work. In addition to being a devoted mother, my wife, Judith B. Shaw, has enjoyed a very successful career as a therapist, teacher of family therapy, and author of *Raising Low-Fat Kids in a High-Fat World.* In fact, both my mother and Judith's mother ran the businesses that supported our families when we were young. My coauthor, Stephanie Wood, is a successful journalist, author, and editor of parenting magazines who carried and delivered her third child during the course of writing this book. I have trained and mentored many women in the field of psychiatry and family therapy who have been mothers. The major difference for women who are successful at doing both is that motherhood remains the priority. These women are first and foremost mothers, even when they're presiding over a company board meeting, examining patients, or teaching a classroom full of other people's children. They have a wide-angle point of view that allows them to see everything that happens in their lives from multiple perspectives: their child's, their own, their spouse's, their boss's.

This type of woman doesn't have one view of her life at home and another of her life at work; she has one identity that embraces the entirety of her life. Some women manage to combine both roles easily; others are swimming in conflict. It's critical that you carefully plan a course you know you can handle, bearing in mind that the more hours you spend away from home in your child's earliest years, the more difficult it becomes to maintain that priority. Quite simply, if you or your spouse is not going to be home, it can be very difficult to find an adequate substitute to rear your child well and lovingly.

Many fathers are now accepting this role. More and more men are choosing to stay home and care for the children. Others are working alternate shifts and sharing the child-care responsibilities so that an outside baby-sitter doesn't have to be hired. Support organizations like the At-Home Dad Network and websites such as slowlane.com and MrMomZ.com are cropping up so that these men can connect with each other and share their experiences, much as women have always done on the playground or in "mommy groups." Still, while a positive development, these full-time fathers remain a minority.

Another small group of families—about 5 percent—can afford

the up to $50,000 a year it costs in major cities to hire an in-home nanny, the next best substitute for very young children. A few have healthy, active grandparents nearby who are willing to step in. But the vast majority of two-career families feel they have little choice but to turn to group child care that is often mediocre at best, and typically far from adequate. In his excellent 2001 book discussing in great detail the needs of children and the risks of child care, *The Four-Thirds Solution: Solving the Child-Care Crisis in America Today,* psychiatrist Stanley Greenspan, M.D., calls out-of-home child care "a social experiment that isn't going well." Sadly, he notes, "most of our children are being cared for in arrangements that have significant limitations."

This isn't the way it was supposed to be; it isn't the dream women envisioned in the early days of the feminist movement. Yet, it's the way we've been lulled into doing things. Hearing what comes next won't be easy, but it's time to face facts. There are certain rules to life—we don't make them and when we run into them, it can hurt. But they're undeniable rules, and we will have to live with the consequences of breaking them. The right way to raise young children falls into this category. I spend much of my professional time treating anguished parents and their children, and I can tell you this much is true: at least one of the parents has to make raising the children the top priority. If you do not, you and your child will live with the consequences the rest of your lives.

WORKING AND BONDING: CAN YOU DO BOTH?

In chapter 2, I discussed the state of attachment—an intense feeling of affection, devotion, and intimacy that forever binds parent and child and creates a deeply embedded relationship from which all other life relationships stem. Indeed, for the better part of the last century researchers studying the process of attachment have consistently found that when women return to work full-time in the first year of their child's life, that child is at risk for a diminished level of attachment. How diminished is still a big question mark. Certainly if Dad stays home in place of Mom, he can make that same essential connection. If the mother can delay her return to the workforce for the first year, the bond is likely to be stronger. Returning to part-time instead of full-time work can also protect that bond. Finding a fabulous in-home caregiver is key for those who do go back to work at this stage. (Turn to page 97 for more advice on finding quality child care.)

At the more problematic end of the spectrum is group care during infancy. Most attachment researchers feel that group care at this age is substantially riskier, even if it's high-quality—but most group child care is mediocre at best. This is tough news for pretty much everyone to accept: women who want both to be a mother and to work; fathers who want to support their wives and provide the best for their families; and legislators, policymakers, and family advocates who want to do more for working families. It's hard to be objective, because at a certain level everyone experiences the painful conflict between the needs of their child and their need or desire to work.

Addressing the heart of this conflict is the recent ongoing study financed by the National Institute of Child Health and Human Development (NICHD), a branch of the National Institutes of Health; begun in 1991, the study will continue until the year 2005 and involves more than 1,364 children in ten university research centers nationwide. Called the NICHD Study of Early Child Care, it defines child care as care by anyone other than the child's mother that is routinely scheduled for at least ten hours a week. Subjects are being followed from birth through the sixth grade, and multiple methods (interviews, observation, testing) are being used to assess their social, emotional, intellectual, and language development, as well as behavior and physical health.

There is a battle for public opinion on this point, even at the NICHD itself. Early headlines suggested that development is not significantly changed by nonparental care; that child care in and of itself neither adversely affects nor promotes the security of infants' attachment; and that characteristics of the family, particularly the sensitivity of the mother (defined for the study as being attentive, responsive, and positively affectionate toward the child), were stronger predictors of children's behavior than their child-care experience. In essence, they were shifting blame for any negative outcomes from the child care itself to the family.

Yet there were also specific and alarming findings that suggested some degree of risk: "The more hours spent in child care, the less harmonious the mother-child interaction, the higher the probability of insecure attachment if the mothers also were less sensitive [to their child's needs]," and the greater the likelihood of behavior problems when the infants grow into toddlers. The most recent reports revealed that children in group care still have more behavior problems when they reach kindergarten. The critics came out in full force on this finding, insisting that the 17 percent with increased behavioral problems is not a huge number. But when you consider that the group of children being raised primarily by their mothers have only a 6 percent chance of such difficulties, that's nearly three times as many kids. If we said that three times as many adults were suddenly likely to get breast or prostate cancer, you can bet that there would be a great demand for answers and solutions. Now consider that your child may be one of those statistics. That's why I consider child care a risk factor.

Other critics of the findings suggested that it isn't the child care itself but the fact that most child care is of mediocre quality, or that working parents are too tired and stressed, or that care providers are not trained to give emotional support.

This issue is so politicized, and the professionals so divided, that there was a backlash against some of the researchers, especially Jay Belsky, Ph.D., a former professor at Pennsylvania State University and now at the University of London in Ontario. After supporting group child care in the 1970s, Dr. Belsky, bothered by the mounting evidence, reversed his position and became vocal about his concerns. Even back then—in the mid to late 1980s—the media and many of his colleagues responded by crucifying him. He was called a misogynist who wanted to keep women at home, and his publisher allegedly removed his name from a book he coauthored because they believed it wouldn't sell. Most recently, when the NICHD released findings from the ongoing study indicating that preschool children in day care are more likely to have behavior problems, Belsky was the spokesperson and an easy target. Some of the other researchers in the study dismissed his claims, saying he had overreacted to the results.

This conflict has some of the qualities of a religious or political war. It's important to many people that researchers who say anything critical about child care be countered or discredited. An entire growth industry is at stake—as well as the parental guilt and anxiety occasioned by reports that question the merits of child care.

When researchers at Columbia University recently conducted another analysis of the NICHD findings, they found a link between mothers returning to full-time work before their children were nine months old and those children achieving lower school readiness scores. Naturally this link was met with more skepticism by the media: How could the same study produce such conflicting results? How much did those numbers really matter if *most* kids did okay? But look at it this way: many adults today grew up safely before car seats and seatbelts were available. Does that mean it's okay not to put your child in a car seat or seatbelt today? No. Increased unnecessary risk is simply unacceptable.

The children in the NICHD study who attended quality programs did demonstrate good language and school readiness skills. Of course, cognitive development sounds impressive—everyone wants a smart kid. And it makes sense that group child care would promote such precociousness: these children have to fend for themselves, so they learn coping skills sooner. What concerns me most is that their empathy may be impaired—their emotional intelligence stunted—as a result of that missing bond, that one-on-one attachment. It's quite common to be smart cognitively but crippled socially and emotionally.

It's confusing for researchers as well as parents struggling to find their way, but there's an overriding factor that can't be ignored: risks that aren't always necessary, such as those cited here, are being introduced into these kids' lives. And the political interest is around everything but the well-being of the child. All this finger-pointing from the child-care establishment and the media is just another example of how we choose to tune out any possibility that we may be doing something that doesn't work. Such defensiveness only makes it easier to ignore the risks and give up time with our children in exchange for money and power and possessions. Then we rationalize our halfhearted parenting efforts to cover our guilt and exhaustion and lack of focus because we are working so much to achieve those things.

In reality, even the most positive findings of these studies come with some strict caveats: the best outcomes for children depend on high-quality child care, which is not always available and often prohibitively expensive. In fact, the research team found that *most* child-care centers do not meet all the recommended guidelines for small group sizes (which range from eight to twenty children, depending on age), high ratios of adults to children (which range from one-to-four to one-to-ten, depending on age), and teachers and assistants having some background in early childhood education. (For more specific guidelines on what the NICHD study considers the regulable aspects of child care, you can consult the National Association for the Education of Young Children's website for accreditation criteria: www.naeyc.org/accreditation.) The findings were also contingent upon a functional, responsive, sensitive two-parent household, which can be hard to find in our overworked, overstressed age.

The work treadmill keeps speeding up as we run faster and faster—the more work we do, the more we get—and technological goodies make it harder and harder to resist employers' demands. Recent statistics from the United Nations' International Labor Organization found that since 1990 Americans have added a full workweek to their year. We now work 137 hours more a year—about three and a half weeks—than our closest rival, those stereotypical workaholics the Japanese. Work hours in every other country surveyed actually declined at the same time as ours rose.

Neither the NICHD study nor any other like it will ever finally prove that child care is good or bad—there are just too many variables that are difficult to measure, and too many individual circumstances enter into the picture. But such studies can point to risk. They are showing us what parents have always known in their hearts: we are best for our children, no matter how wonderful our child-care arrangements. And I want to suggest that every effort be made to allow new mothers and their babies freedom from time constraints so that they can bond.

We can conclude from the NICHD research that sometimes a good enough mother can compensate for the time she spends away from her child by means of her loving attunement and by finding the highest-quality care. But sometimes she can't, and to deny or avoid or fail to recognize when child care is not working for your child is a terrible tragedy for both of you. Child care in and of itself, as the researchers like to refer to it, is nothing but a tool, pure and simple, not a substitute for your relationship with your child. Don't allow the cultural forces whispering in your ear—"*Your child will be okay no matter what*"—to sway you. No one can definitively tell you what's best for your child. It depends as much on her and you as it does on statistics, and the sensitive, involved, attuned mother won't be overwhelmed by them. Yes, it's entirely possible for a child with a less sensitive, less responsive mother to actually be better off in day care where there is a caring person to meet his needs, but I don't think that's you. You're here with me now reading this book.

When you decided to become a parent, you made a commitment to put your child's needs first. You know that being a mother or father is arguably the greatest experience in life, and that it's a privilege to have that opportunity. Taking good care of your child is the same as taking good care of yourself. Parents who use child care well never forget this. We don't need exhaustive and extensive research to tell us what's common sense: if you do decide to work, you must not allow it to take too much time or energy or affection from your child.

A LOOK AT THE OPTIONS

So let's say you've weighed the pros and cons, and you and your spouse have decided you both should continue to work. How can you structure your work lives in the best interest of your child, maintain financial stability, and avoid having one parent feeling forced to give up a fulfilling job? In *The Four-Thirds Solution*, Stanley Greenspan calls for both parents to work two-thirds of the time—hence the four-thirds equation. That might mean that you work a full-time nursing job at night and your husband does part-time contracting work or sells real estate on the days you're off. Or you each have a nine-to-five office job three days a week, one of you doing Monday-Tuesday-Wednesday, the other Thursday-Friday-Saturday. Still another possibility is that one of you works full-time outside the home and the other runs a part-time, home-based business. There are many options, and I'm sure you can think up many more. The point is that, with creative solutions, mothers don't get shortchanged, because they are still able to maintain careers, fathers get to share in the child-rearing process and improve their relationships with their children, and the children, of course, benefit from receiving primary care by a parent most of the time. The need for nonparental care is kept to a minimum.

I applaud Greenspan for this sort of creative thinking and his willingness to speak out on the dangers of too much nonparental care. For too long we have listened to child-rearing experts couch their criticisms so as not to offend parents, especially working mothers. The real goal here is not to take away from parents the opportunity to work but to give back to children the kind of upbringing they need to thrive and reach their full potential. For some families, that reckoning is going to involve what looks like a big lifestyle sacrifice. But many, many others will be all too happy to make such changes when they realize at last that their child's well-being is at stake, as well as the overall happiness of the family. They simply need the complete picture.

The two main issues are the number of hours your child will be away from his parents and the type of care you choose for those hours. Every option before you brings a certain element of risk, and it's up to you to decide if that risk is too high. Clearly, the longer you or your spouse can be with your infant the better. At least a year of at-home care by a parent is a big step in the right direction; going back to work after only three months constitutes a real risk to your child and requires nothing short of excellent care and heroically good parenting. I strongly urge you to avoid this situation and be creative when it comes to your child's well-being: work at a company that offers flextime and on-site child care so that you can visit and feed your baby during the day; cut back to part-time work or telecommute to minimize those other-care hours; work alternate shifts so that one parent can be at home at all times. This last option can present a challenge to a marriage, of course, but if both partners see it as a workable solution for a finite period of time—say, until the child starts school—it becomes less of a burden.

Above all, don't think of child care as dictating your life. You have the right and the ability to create the kind of child-care situation you want—you don't have to settle for what's out there. That's what Jane, the New England mother of a four-year-old, does, and it works for her.

My child-care strategy is not what facility I put my son in, but rather something larger and more encompassing—a way of caring for him that somehow strikes a balance between having a mommy who's around and a mommy who works. The smartest thing I did was to drop out of the corporate world before I had my son. This gave me time to establish my home business. My husband and I also bought a reasonably priced house so that one of us wouldn't feel completely pressured to work full-time. I think where people really get screwed up is when they build a life where they have to work like dogs, to the detriment of their kids, to keep it up.

When my son was an infant, I had a woman come to my house to watch him, and since I was there, too, I could still breast-feed him and check on him throughout the day. When he turned two and needed some socialization, I took him to the sitter's house instead for the same number of hours. Now he's four and in a group preschool/day-care facility from 9:00 A.M. to 4:00 P.M. My son greets me every morning with soft, relaxed eyes, and we actually have time for breakfast together. I cut out of the office at four, we go get a Popsicle and squeeze in a bike ride or walk the dogs, and then his dad comes home. I have the flexibility to meet any situation, and needless to say, this has been good for our marriage and the family as a whole.

What makes Jane an especially useful role model was her willingness to structure a life that would be optimal for her child and for herself before she even had him. It's okay to strive for a situation that's good for you too—raising children shouldn't be a sacrifice. Jane approached parenting as a critical priority. At forty-one, she was a borderline baby boomer who was lucky enough to benefit from some of the frustrating "trying-to-have-it-all" struggles of those women a decade or more older. Jane had two younger sisters who decided to buck the trend and not even attempt working and mothering at the same time in the early years. One left her position as an investment banker for a while, then eventually went back part-time. The other stayed at home for seven years, then got her real estate license so that she could work flexible hours around her children's schedules.

Jane herself is happy with her life and would like to see more women be flexible in how they work and parent. "We hear a lot of people telling us to quit our jobs completely, or other experts who say kids are perfectly well adjusted being raised in day-care centers and as latchkey kids," she notes. As Jane has discovered, there is indeed a happy medium that all parents and children should be able to enjoy and thrive within—if they simply take the time and creative initiative to discover it.

Another child-care innovator is Liz, a full-time executive for a major hotel chain. It has never been economically possible for her to stay at home, but she has taken great pains to arrange child care at each stage of her son's life that filled his needs.

My heart breaks for those mothers who have no choice but to put their six-week-old infants into day care. I visited every center in my area but felt there were just too many kids and too few adults to give my son, Luke, the care he needed. I was able to stay home for three months with Luke, and then my retired father took care of him until he was eighteen months old. My dad had worked six days a week when I was growing up, and he truly enjoyed this opportunity. Even now, at five, Luke and his grandparents are inseparable. On weekends or days that we don't see my parents, they will always find some sort of excuse to stop by or call to talk to Luke.

When Luke became a toddler and I recognized his need to be around other kids, I still couldn't find a center I liked—they all seemed to have a production-line feel and a pungent cleaning-fluid smell—so I chose an energetic young woman who watched three boys in her home. She had a great piece of land in a semirural setting with lots of toys and a play set. She also gave me a five-page contract outlining her rules of service, suitable clothing, toys, meals served, and a list of referrals. I was impressed that she was so thorough. Some days I was even asked to provide an extra set of play clothes so that the kids could get dirty, which I thought was great. It was important to me that Luke had some serious fun, and he did.

Now five, Luke attends a Montessori school from 8:30 to 3:30 daily, and he is thriving. I chose it because of the homey feel and the fact that the kids get to stay with the same teacher for a three-year period, allowing for a very stable relationship and structured environment. Since he's an only child, the Montessori school is a great opportunity to be with other kids in a very warm as well as educational environment. At the same time I'm proud to be a role model of a working woman for him.

THE IMPORTANCE OF STABILITY

What makes each of these two women's stories instructive is the relative stability they have provided for their children. A daily change in caregivers, as happened with Alex in chapter 2, can result in a very stressed-out, uncertain, anxious baby. The same is true if you change your child-care arrangement frequently in the early years and your baby or toddler isn't given the opportunity to bond with anyone for any length of time. Sadly, this is all too inevitable in the world of child care. Nannies can walk out at any time, and family day-care providers are often unstable operations. Even high-quality centers experience frequent staff turnover because the pay is low and the hours long.

One mother of a preschooler I spoke with put her son in a top-notch, corporate-sponsored child-care facility that was three times the price of other area centers. At first it was a pure delight to observe the "teachers," as they were called, and children in action, with every educational tool at their disposal. Yet, in the short eighteen months he was there, three out of the four teachers departed, including the head of the preschool group, who was by far the most experienced. Although the new teachers and the one remaining original were striving to do their best, and probably were better caregivers than most, they were quite a bit less experienced, and the mother felt that the overall environment was definitely impaired. Did her son suffer as a result? Probably not drastically, because he was three and four years old during this period and already securely attached and well adjusted. He also was attending the center only three days a week, from nine to four, unlike some of the other children who were there every day from eight to six and truly looked upon the teachers as surrogate parents. But imagine how it would have been if he were an infant who did not yet have a firm emotional foundation to draw on. Imagine also that this is the more typical mediocre-quality facility, with caregivers who have little if any training in child development and probably more babies than they should have to attend to. The possibility of secure attachment and a sense of stability grows dimmer and dimmer. Some parents, such as the one I am about to describe, may compound the problem because they do not understand the importance of constancy and long-term relationships.

Maggie, a mom in Chicago, has a two-year-old daughter who has had five different child-care experiences in her short life. Maggie went back to work when her daughter was twelve weeks old and put her in a day-care facility that impressed her greatly. It seemed that little Chloe was bonding nicely with her primary caregiver there. But when Chloe was seven months old, the family had to relocate and leave the facility and caregiver behind. At this point Maggie hired an in-home caregiver, but she found this situation distracting because she was also trying to work from home. After a few months she moved Chloe to a center, then another center, and then another center. Ironically, none of the locations was a real disappointment in Maggie's eyes—it's just that she wants the best for her child. Indeed, she says she's ready to move her yet again if a still better opportunity presents itself.

Now, I ask you: Could you, in a period of just two years, live in five homes or change jobs five times and not feel stressed? Maggie describes her daughter as highly extroverted and having a lot of fun being among her teachers and peers in these stellar facilities. Perhaps she is one of those incredibly resilient children we hear about from time to time, but the fact that she may be missing out on the opportunity to establish that critical connection with a caregiver is a concern. The well-connected child has a social and emotional advantage, and creating constant disruptions gives a child the impression that people come and go and relationships don't really matter. We know it is difficult for children who grow up in military families and are transferred from state to state and even country to country repeatedly during the course of their formative years. The same holds true for a constantly changing child-care situation, particularly if the parents are frequently unavailable as well.

Another popular child-care practice is the hiring of an au pair as a full-time caregiver. Au pairs are young women who are typically in their late teens or early twenties and often come from foreign countries to the United States as part of an exchange program: you provide them with room and board in your home and usually a small salary, and they help with your children and enjoy the cultural experience of life in another country. It's easy to convince yourself that this is a dream situation: it's very affordable as child care goes—you have live-in help, which means it's much less stressful getting out the door in the morning and you needn't worry if you run late getting home—and your child gets one-on-one attention. If a family expects an au pair to perform the traditional role of mother's helper, it can indeed work out well for everyone.

But the drawbacks come when parents expect them to be full-time nannies, as is frequently the case. Many of these young girls are not mature or experienced enough to handle the stress of tending to a young child day in and day out, and I strongly advise that parents not distort the role of an au pair into that of a substitute mother. They are typically given visas for short periods, usually about a year, so regularly hiring a new au pair involves annual upheaval for your child; they are often totally uneducated in child development and may not be interested in it as a career; and they may not have worked at any job for the eight-, ten-, or even twelve-hour days you will probably require. Bizarrely, I've even heard of parents who say they like this arrangement because of the annual turnover—they don't want their child becoming too attached to someone else!

Traditional nannies, or in-home caregivers as they are also called, offer the hope of one-on-one attention and a real bonding experience. How it really works out depends on the skill of the parents in choosing what could functionally be a surrogate mother. A hilarious and troubling picture of what can also go on in such a situation is presented in the novel *The Nanny Diaries*. The book details some pretty incredible exploits by modern-day, have-it-all parents in privileged Manhattan homes, and it serves as an amazing case history both of incredibly unattached and inattentive parents and of child victims of the epidemic. The very fact that the two authors, Nicola Kraus and Emma McLaughlin, collectively worked for some thirty families over seven or eight years is in direct contrast to the emotional goals of security and stability. These two women must have changed jobs an average of every six months! They seem generally fond of the kids they write about and well aware of the parental oversights (noting that absentee dads and overmedicated moms were quite the norm), but their account clearly illustrates that it's a mistake to assume that just because you have hired a nanny, your child will have the long-term bonding relationship he needs.

MAKING UP FOR LOST TIME

The right home environment can counteract many of the drawbacks of child care. So when and if you decide to work, you must ask yourself one more critical question: Do I have it in me to pull this off? Can I be deeply connected enough during the two or three hours in the morning and evenings when we are together to make up for the lost time? And will my employer be willing to support me in this endeavor?

In the early days of mothers joining the workforce, the main question on everyone's minds was: Will family life interfere with the ability of women to perform their jobs? As time has marched on, we've found the exact opposite to be true: it is more often the demands of work that interfere with employees' personal lives, not the other way around. Certainly the mounting evidence that we are working longer hours confirms this, as does the generally stressed-out nature of life today. I can't emphasize enough that it's becoming more and more difficult to do it all: to find that elusive nine-to-five job, an employer willing to say go ahead and leave early for the school play, and the time to make dinner, do homework, read bedtime stories, and nurse an infant.

Women's magazines, always eager to lend a helping hand, list clever shortcuts by the dozen: freeze casseroles or order takeout, mix up pancake batter and pack lunches the night before, tape yourself reading bedtimes stories for those nights away on business trips, get your dry cleaning delivered, quit cleaning, and cut your sleep time in half with the miracle energy diet. Oh, and by the way, don't forget to squeeze in that 5:00 A.M. workout and a lunchtime rendezvous with your spouse so your marriage doesn't go down the tubes. It's ridiculous to think that someone isn't going to suffer here.

WHAT'S A GOOD CHILD-CARE ARRANGEMENT, AND HOW DO I FIND ONE?

The current state of child care in our country is woefully below what we need, which makes finding the right environment for your child a challenge. Do your homework carefully and aim for flexibility in both your work situation and your spouse's so that you can minimize the amount of time your child needs to be cared for by someone else. Here's what else you need to consider:

- **TYPES OF CHILD CARE :** If you're going to use nonparental care, carefully evaluate the three standard alternatives: in-home or "nanny" care, in which one baby-sitter tends exclusively to your children; family day care, in which a neighborhood mom takes in a few extra kids in addition to her own; and day-care centers, for-profit businesses housed in classroomlike facilities with larger numbers of kids. Most parents tend to fixate on only one category of care—say, a center, because they think an in-home sitter is too expensive, or a family arrangement because they prefer a smaller group—but there are pros and cons to every option, and some might surprise you. In-home care can often be cheaper if you have several kids because family and larger day-care centers charge by the number of children you have. Additionally, a large center might sound impersonal, but since most have to be state-licensed and meet specific adult-child ratios, it may well have many qualified caregivers who are able to give their charges plenty of attention. (State-mandated ratios are usually in the area of no more than three infants to one adult, no more than five to one for toddlers ages eighteen months to three years, and no more than eight to one for preschoolers ages three to five. For specifics, you can contact your state's department of health, social services, family services, or human resources, or try the Department of Health and Human Services National Child Care Information Center website: www.nccic.org.) Consider, too, that family day care may seem like a cozy arrangement, but if the caregiver mom is spending most of the day on the phone, your child may end up more neglected than in a large group. The moral here: don't set up any one category of care as the "ideal"—it's not.

- **YOUR CHILD'S NEEDS:** When we think of good child care, we think of the kids' well-being first and foremost—are they safe? happy? well fed? well loved?—for obvious reasons. But what children need most from child care varies with their stage of development. Once you get past the fact that the situation is safe and sanitary, you need to look at the relationships and the structure of the child's day.

  - Infants needs someone to regularly hold, sing to, and interact with them; sensitivity to their temperament and sleeping and eating habits; and adequate stimulation, such as a variety of toys and an effort to change environments throughout the day.
  - For toddlers, physical activity is key. One- to three-year-olds need plenty of room to move inside as well as out, a broader range of activities (quiet reading corners versus noisy music rooms), and caregivers who are willing to help them negotiate issues of socialization (what's mine? what's yours? when can I have it?).
  - Older preschoolers need exposure to early learning (letters, shapes, counting, coloring) and patient caregivers who can help them help themselves when it comes to issues like getting dressed, tying shoes, and cleaning up toileting accidents.

Before you make your decision, observe and explore the child-care environment: How much individual attention do the children receive? What kinds of activities are they engaged in? Are the activities age-appropriate and stimulating, or are the children sitting around, sluggish and passive?

What are the energy and sound levels? The atmosphere should generally be lively and happy, but not too boisterous for a young baby, for instance. How competent, cooperative, and involved are the staff and the director? How stable has the staff been, and the business in general? Is it well established and respected in the community, with long-term employees?

- **YOUR NEEDS:** Leaving yourself out of the equation is a big mistake. If your child-care arrangement is a constant source of aggravation for you, then you and your family are all going to be more stressed. How much of a problem is it for you to drive twenty minutes out of your way for the drop-off and pickup? How much time do you spend packing lunches and diaper bags every night? How cranky is your caregiver if you're a half hour late? You may want to bend a little on your priorities if an arrangement is ideal for your child, but don't sacrifice your sanity in the process.

- **THE RIGHT RESOURCES:** It used to be that word of mouth (through friends, relatives, mommy groups) was the only way to go when lining up a caregiver, and you certainly don't want to overlook personal references. But as the need for child care continues to grow, so, too, does the access to it. In addition to the obvious starting points like the yellow pages and local newspapers, you can contact your employer (many now offer advice and referral services—after all, it's in their best interest too), child-care placement firms (but you may have to pay a fee), the Internet, and advocacy groups. Here are a few organizations to start with that offer advice and referrals:

  - Child Care Aware: 800–424–2246; www.child careaware.org.
  - International Nanny Association: 800–297–1477; www.nanny.org.
  - The Nation's Network of Child Care Resources and Referral: 202-393-5501; www.childcarerr.org.

- National Association for the Education of Young Children: 800–424–2460; www.naecy.org. While many states have government-mandated licensing programs that assess issues of health, safety, and caregiver ratios, the NAEYC is the one independent organization that offers a stringent accrediting process for child-care centers and preschools nationwide that also focuses on the developmental and edu-cational aspects of child care. Check the website for accred-ited facilities in your area.

HOW IS MY CHILD DOING?

You'll have two easy clues to whether your child-care arrange-ments are going well or not: your child's behavior and your relation-ship with the caregiver. Watch for these symptoms that something might be amiss and check into the concerns they indicate:

SYMPTOM:
Your child consistently resists being left with the child-care provider, not just on an odd morning.
CONCERN:
Your child may not like the caregiver or the environment, or may be telling you she's not getting enough time with you.

SYMPTOM:
Your previously well-behaved child's personality has taken a turn for the worse—she's become clingier, crankier, and less manageable.
CONCERN:
She may be insecure because she's not getting enough time with you, or the caregiver may have a parenting style (too puni-tive, too lax) that is at odds with yours.

SYMPTOM:

Your caregiver reports that your child naps much longer or more frequently than she does when home with you.

CONCERN:

Your child may be sleeping because she's being ignored or understimulated—in short, she's bored.

SYMPTOM:

Your caregiver complains frequently about your child's personality or behavior.

CONCERN:

She may have unrealistic expectations for your child's developmental level (which also means she may not know enough about kids to be in this business), or she may simply not like your child. Then again, she may be telling you something is amiss with your parenting style—perhaps that your child needs more limits.

SYMPTOM:

Your caregiver appears to be stressed whenever you drop off or pick up your child.

CONCERN:

She may be trying to care for too many children at once, or she may not be enjoying the experience of caring for your child—either way, your child is going to miss out on the kind of relationship he needs.

SYMPTOM:

The television is frequently on when you show up.

CONCERN:

Your child may not be experiencing enough human interaction; the TV may be the real baby-sitter.

SYMPTOM:

Your caregiver discourages visits from you, especially unexpected ones.

CONCERN:

Her caregiving standards may be lax when you are not around. What else may she be hiding?

SYMPTOM:

You have difficulty communicating with your caregiver: she becomes defensive when questioned, she seems unwilling to share information with you, or there's not sufficient common language between you to instruct her or find out what's happening.

CONCERN:

You are not going to get a clear picture of how your child spends his day or his true relationship with this very important person in his life. And a caregiver who is not a sharing, warm, empathic person is not likely to be the best nurturer for your child.

SYMPTOM:

You worry constantly about your child while you are at work.

POSSIBLE CAUSE:

Your gut is telling you the situation is not a good one for either you or your child—don't ignore it!

5

Whose House
Is This Anyway?

Parents wonder why the streams are bitter, when they themselves have poisoned the fountain.

—John Locke

A MOM PLEADS WITH her five-year-old daughter as she lies in the aisle of a toy store playing with some merchandise. "Get off the floor, Katie. We have to leave. I've got three more errands to run before we have to meet your sister's school bus." A short time later, "Okay, I'll buy you the toy if you'll just get up."

Naturally, Katie refuses. "I hate you! You never let me do what I want!" she yells, in spite of the fact that she is indeed doing exactly what she wants, and has been for quite some time. Her distraught mother proceeds to get down on the floor with her and attempts to explain, again, why it is that they have to go. "I still hate you, now leave me alone," Katie spits back.

Her mother's response: "Okay, I'll buy you the toy. Now please get up."

Many people would describe Katie as "spoiled," but for me that word has been used so long that it doesn't tell how bad the picture really is. Just what is a spoiled child? We tend to think of the spoiled child as one who has been overindulged, but I do not believe children are spoiled by acts of generosity. Relationships between parents and children become distorted when gifts are really bribes, placations, or bids for special influence. The child who has learned that oppositional behavior is a good way to get or obtain things is actually accepting these objects as a substitute for real love. Such a child is feeling lonely and abandoned even while receiving the gift. If you look closely at that moment, you will see that the child has no joy in this transaction. She has merely won the struggle.

Just as important, a spoiled child is also one who is consistently allowed to exert her will when it isn't appropriate. In fact, the power plays by the Katies of this world may well be a bigger cause for concern than their pile of possessions. All kids figure out how to pull their parents' strings to some extent, but Katie's parents are no more than doormats to her kingdom. Surely her parents' day-to-day existence is miserable. Surely Katie is in for a rude awakening when she realizes that the rest of the world won't cater to her whims and fancies. But there's even more than that. This child will go through life with her very close relationships centered on control rather than loving empathy.

Of course, there will always be times and situations when you can see that your child is right ("Mommy, you promised!") or has a special need—perhaps she just lost a soccer game and needs a little pick-me-up treat—and you will allow her to influence your parental behavior. But you should not give in just because you feel fear or guilt, are afraid of a fuss, or feel too tired and worn out. Giving in when you feel weak and tired is damaging to your child. But you'll also know when it feels, well, good to give in—you want to show your appreciation or excitement about an accomplishment, or see that justice is done, for instance.

Anthropologist Gregory Bateson was once watching a dolphin trainer. The trainer would throw the dolphin a fish whenever she did something the trainer wanted her to. But every once in a while, Bateson noticed, the trainer would throw a fish into the water for no apparent reason. "Why do you do that?" Bateson inquired. "Because dolphins need a free fish once in a while," the trainer replied.

Training human children naturally involves a few free fish now and then, but the trend I see among parents today is to give away all the fish and not bother with the training. Parents naturally tend to deny this is happening. My wife and I were vacationing at a coastal island recently and were able to observe one of these untrained children, about age three and a half, who was staying nearby with his family and appeared on the same beach in close proximity to us each day. Every time we saw this child he looked sullen and did not play as other children do but merely demanded things. On the beach, for instance, he insisted that his father be the one to draw pictures in the sand for him. There was no sense of comradeship between the father and the child; the child was focused only on controlling the reluctant father and showed no sign of play or pleasure. It was as though nothing was left to this child but to keep whining and controlling. He would whine, then cry, then get angry if the father indicated that he did not want to keep drawing the lines indicated by the child. The father looked uncomfortable and tried to get his son to join in the sand play and put aside his endless demands.

Every day the parents had a new excuse for why the child was behaving the way he was, even though no one had mentioned it—the first day he had jet lag, the second day he was hungry, the third day he was getting a cold—until they finally lapsed into silence about it. This is an extremely common occurrence. These parents will note that their child is joyless and controlling, but only as something to explain, not to address and change so that the child will thrive. Parents who get into this pattern are actually camouflaging the evidence of the underlying symptoms of the epidemic in their child—and allowing him to proceed down the path without help.

When parents fall into the habit of mollifying or placating a child, the child develops a need for more mollification and placation, just as a drug addict needs his substance. The more the child gets, the less it works, and the parents have to step up the dosage, so to speak. Whatever it is that they do to keep him happy, they intensify it, simply doing more of what doesn't work in the first place. If they started out a bit too permissive, they become more so. If they started making excuses for unacceptable behavior, they begin to come up with less and less plausible explanations. Eventually they snap and have an outburst of rage toward the child, which damages the relationship even further.

Meanwhile, their spoiled offspring may become angry and resentful when they realize that the world does not worship them quite so much as their parents do, and they may turn that bitterness to violence against friends, classmates, or coworkers. At a minimum, these kids are likely to become unmotivated and unproductive, since they've never experienced the rewards of earning or accomplishing anything on their own. I know you do not want this for your child.

THE TRUTH ABOUT THE CONSEQUENCES

As dreadful as these consequences all sound, parents today don't seem to recognize them. They know their kids are spoiled—two-thirds admitted it in a 2001 CNN/*Time* magazine poll—but they don't define "spoiled" as "rotten" or "ruined." If we say we have "spoiled" a dish we are cooking or a painting we've been creating, the listener knows that something bad and irreversible has happened to the item in question. But spoiling a child is treated these days by certain people as a badge of honor, or something to boast about ("I can't help but spoil my kid!"). Some parents are happy that they are able to bestow on their children the freedom and possessions they themselves may have been denied. It makes them look and feel important and loved. Doled out appropriately, such "spoils" are not necessarily a bad thing. But when they become a replacement for affection or attention, perhaps offsetting parental guilt, you and your child will both lose.

What is the damage to a child's development from such attitudes and behaviors? The first "injury" that I see coming from manipulative spoiling is a failure to develop empathy and a lack of desire to usefully fit into situations and relationships. If a child is endlessly indulged and never hears the word "no" or experiences limits, he never has a chance to learn that other people have lives, emotions, needs, and wills of their own. Without a well-developed sense of empathy, the child will not be able to love.

Another critical consequence is the distorted sense of power that a child develops when constantly catered to. Here's a fable for our time. A couple from Chicago were visiting their daughter, son-in-law, and grandchildren in Boston. The grandfather had organized a sightseeing trip for the family, and all the adults had agreed to go by train. As they were getting ready to leave, the four-year-old grandchild announced, "I don't want to take the train. I want to go in the car." The grandfather got annoyed, because this would require dividing the group into two cars and his intent was to make a family expedition. Instead of telling the girl that their plan was to go by train and they still intended to do so, the mother insisted on giving in to her child and changed the plans. In effect, she gave the four-year-old more power and status than the child's grandfather. A major blowup ensued, and for months the mother of the child did not talk to her father. His wife sided with the daughter, and the man suffered a great deal as a result of this wrath. All because no one could say no to a four-year-old! No one even thought about the consequences to the child of having the power to produce a family upset of this proportion.

In the current climate of child-rearing, parents have acted out their revolt against the rules and structure of the past by treating their children as they once wished they were being treated. Of course, as children we want to be cosseted and indulged. Even as adults, we love being in a sheltered environment, such as a spa, where the mission of everyone around us is to make us feel good and healthy. But could we really live indefinitely in such a place? I think not. What comes to mind for me are the Ludwigs of Bavaria, the tyrants and spoiled princes to whom no one would dare give disagreeable feedback and who were at risk of going over the top. Our rock stars and charismatic leaders run the same risk because the groupie response seduces them into thinking that their point of view is the *only* point of view and that everyone else will fit into their scheme of things.

I saw a couple recently at a workshop on the East Coast. They were two rather charming, well-organized, and purposeful people who came to me about an issue that was affecting their marriage. The issue turned out to be their three-year-old child. This little boy was eating dinner with them every night and monopolizing the conversation by asking questions, interjecting, interrupting, and essentially dominating the scene. (I'm sure if you watch the kids you see in public places you will find this behavior quite common.) The father was feeling as if he had no time with his wife, but the mother was afraid of "suppressing" the child.

This fear is sweeping the nation, the fear that somehow the imposition of limits will destroy some spirit in our children. We psychological theorists are more likely to think, however, that diverting children from unwanted behavior and teaching them better and more conflict-free ways of comfortably being able to pursue their intentions and motivations will lead them to be more expressive, more effective, and even happier.

As I discussed the issue with this couple, it became clear that their child had been dominant from the beginning. It had started around three or four months of age, when they began having a problem putting him to bed and spent more and more time soothing him and rewarding his demand for their company. Over the years their sleep had been continually disturbed because the child woke during the night and demanded a repetition of his mother's usual comforting routine. They also spent much time negotiating with this bright child instead of firmly saying what they needed him to do.

My advice to parents in this kind of logjam is to find a creative solution that will work for the whole family. I asked them why they felt they had to have dinner with their child every night. They hadn't thought about it. I suggested that one or both of them could sit with the child while he had his dinner; then they could put him to bed, and have their dinner together later. They both were excited at the idea. One would cook and the other would give dinner to the child; then the first parent would bathe him and read to him. They would take turns in each job, and then they would have their couple time afterward. I reminded them that a happy, intact parental couple was the greatest gift they could give their child. As you read further, you'll also learn how they could regain their authority with their child, who so far had managed to dominate the family in a troubling fashion.

As you can see, too much freedom is as fraught with danger as too much discipline. When we're afraid to say no, give our children too much benefit of the doubt, and abandon the structure that builds their moral backbone, then we're not giving them the code of appropriate behaviors necessary to grow and thrive and fit into society. Untrained kids are often out of control, unpredictable, unenjoyable, and ultimately dangerous. Structures of routines, obligations, and limits are not punitive measures, they are gifts—vitamins that protect children from the temptations of a valueless world. When you relate to your children on this level, moral behavior becomes natural. You don't have to train a dog not to bite his master—he loves him. Children who are guided and disciplined appropriately show love and respect for the parents who led the way.

In chapter 2, I wrote about the necessity for an attuned dance between parent and child. Whenever parents allow preconceived theories, closed-minded attitudes, or unrealistic expectations to get in the way of a conversation or situation with their child, they tend to remove themselves from the attunement dance. When parent and child dance together, anything is possible. Sometimes a "spoiling" treat is just what the doctor ordered, and sometimes a "No!" is appropriate. But when parents rule out the whole domain of corrective behavior, bad things start to happen.

As with everything we discuss in this book, the dance is the important part. Sometimes a baby needs to be picked up, but other times picking her up will only aggravate her if she's already overstimulated. Sometimes a preschooler deserves a hug and a candy kiss for good behavior, and sometimes he deserves a reprimand for breaking an agreed-upon rule, such as not going out in the backyard without asking first. Only the sensitive, truly attuned parent really has the best chance of knowing.

When this dance gets tripped up, what is truly spoiled is the development of positive connection and empathy. Children need our "no's," our insistence that our will matters, and our teaching that the moods of people around us have an effect on our lives. It is through dealing with difficulties that we learn to know and care about what happens with other people. It helps us feel that we are all in the same human boat, so to speak, and need each other to survive in a happy state. Parents who rob their children of limits hurt the development of something deep within their child: their capacity to care, to understand, and to show concern. From adversity, from limits, from "no's," and from expectations, children develop greater depths of empathy, compassion, and understanding. Without these experiences, they develop a one-dimensional view of the world as the provider of what they want, when they want it.

This leads us to the next loss suffered by the spoiled child: the ability to be grateful, the sense of being blessed by life and the people around us who love us and hold us dear. That loss is crushing. If we heard that someone had deliberately stolen this from a child, we would think it a crime. The loss of the sense of blessing and gratitude dooms one to a colorless life. A hamster on the treadmill. Living in black and white instead of Technicolor.

A man sitting next to me on a plane recently was returning home from a visit with his son and daughter-in-law and their two children. He said he was both sad to leave and relieved because it had been totally exhausting. "How so?" I asked. He replied that the way they raise children these days, the kids expect so much that four adults are not enough to keep two children happy.

He went on to describe how his grandchildren were in charge of the house. At mealtimes, for example, the mother would make dinner. The children would start complaining about what she had made and ask for other foods instead. She would quickly whip them up, and after two bites, they would say they didn't like those dishes either. His ten-year-old granddaughter, especially, was "very smart," the man noted, but "has no empathy for anyone else." She was concerned only with what she wanted to do or have and was indifferent to the feelings of anyone else. She did not seem to notice that her parents were unhappy about her constant demands and her lack of gratitude for their efforts.

Dan Kindlon, Ph.D., a professor of psychology at Harvard University, has an excellent discussion of what happens to such "spoiled" children in his book *Too Much of a Good Thing: Raising Children of Character in an Indulgent Age.* When we think of self-centeredness, he notes, it conjures up an egocentric toddler who believes he is the most important and special being in the universe. All children start out at this point. Indeed, responding to their every want and need as infants is what helps form that all-important bond of attachment we've been talking about. But the infant grows into a toddler who requires training from his caregivers to comprehend his realistic place in the family hierarchy and, ultimately, the rest of the world. Kindlon's position is that when a child doesn't receive this reality check, rather than evolving into the "haughty, arrogant peacock" we would expect, he takes a sadder turn, becoming self-conscious and anxious, developing poor body image and low self-esteem. Yes, he's self-centered, but from a negative, obsessive standpoint. Hence the problems with motivation, eating disorders, a need for material goods to prove self-worth. Anger is another paradox for parents: it evolves not from being told no or missing out on the latest high-tech toy, as modern moms and dads might fear, but from the feelings of abandonment that arise when kids don't have enough time with us, asserts Kindlon. All of these issues add up to what he terms an extremely "sad" generation of youth who are plagued with multiple psychological problems.

THE REWARDS OF TRAINING

The antidote to this problem-plagued generation may be a bitter pill for some parents. Right now the notion of "training" children is not in good repute in many circles. The many feel-good gurus bristle at the close association with the concept of obedience schools for pets. But for us, it is important to revisit this subject and clarify our thinking. It is important to understand that if you are raising a child—or almost any domesticated mammal, for that matter—you are always training, whether you intend to do so or not. Children are organized by evolutionary processes to be social and to want love, affectionate physical contact (hugs, kisses, pats on the head, a touch on the shoulder), the sense of being known, and the feeling that they have the personal power to influence others. Children will do anything to satisfy these deeply ingrained needs and seek to learn the behaviors that will bring them what they want. One could say that the lives of humans are determined by the decisions they make about what worked and what didn't work when they were very young. These decisions of the very young child tend very much to be unconscious processes based on misunderstandings. Nonetheless, the way the adult views the world and goes about seeking contentment and fulfillment is largely determined by the conditioning patterns established early in life.

Over the years behaviorists have made an excellent case for the notion that rewarded patterns of behavior tend to increase in almost any animal and the patterns of behavior that are not rewarded tend to disappear over time. And so goes the behavioral repertoire of children. That is why I say you are always training. At almost every moment you are either rewarding, ignoring, or actually punishing some behavior or emotional state in your child. Those people who are not comfortable with this idea will train their children unconsciously, and the patterns of behavior that arise as a result will look as though they have developed mysteriously. In the current climate of overemphasis on the relationship between genes and behavior, parents think such manifestations are genetic or even congenital—anything but the possibility that the way they are training (or not training) their child is producing the problem.

Thus, parents who are under too much stress, fatigued, or in need of more assistance in rearing their child may start to ignore the child when she is content. Conversely, they may become highly involved when the child is unhappy, angry, having tantrums, or making demands. Gradually the child will show less and less of the ignored qualities and more and more of the "rewarded."

Now, that is a curious statement. What do we mean by rewarded? A reward is anything that makes the child feel that his needs are being met. Even when we speak firmly to a child, we are giving him social contact and relationship. While a child appreciates kindly interest and attention infinitely more, if deprived of social attention, he will accept almost any form of it.

Most behavior is determined by rearing rather than genetics. Think about the example of dogs. Even though much of their behavior is instinctively predetermined, they are nonetheless very flexible and plastic and can be molded in a variety of ways. People who study dogs will tell you that a properly raised pit bull is a loving and reliable companion that will not show untoward anger or aggressiveness. It is clear that German shepherds can be brought up to be attack dogs, in which case they will tear out the throat of a designated target, or they can be raised as the loving, reliable companion to a family of parents and children. To bring out those qualities of heart that we want in our children, we have to understand that their behavior is resulting from the patterns of reward we are carrying out.

I want you to know that you are the potentially constructive agent who can transform your child at almost any time. It starts with asking yourself, "How do I act with my child? What draws forth my responses and attention? Do my actions and attention reward good behavior or bad?" It's essential for you to know that you have the means to affect your child deeply. Your presence, the social contact with you, being known by you, being loved by you, physical contact with you, murmurings, reading, experiencing stability in the home, all contribute to the inner security that lets a child grow and thrive.

In the early years, when the child behaves in a manner the parent doesn't want, saying "Please do not do that" or "No" is appropriate, along with giving a description of what the desired behavior is. Then when the child fulfills the parent's expectation for good behavior, the parent should show appreciation. For instance, if a four-year-old takes off his clothes at bedtime and throws them on the floor, the parent should say: "We don't throw our clothes on the floor. You're big enough now to put them in the dirty laundry basket. I shouldn't have to pick up after you, so please get them and put them in the basket now." And mean it! Stand over him until he does it, if necessary. When you check the next night to see whether the child has thrown his clothes in the laundry basket as requested, acknowledge the effort if he has done so: "I see you put your clothes in the laundry. I'm proud you remembered. You're getting to be so big and helpful!" If the child has thrown his clothes on the floor again, however, you must say, "Why didn't you follow the rule about putting your clothes in the laundry basket? What's up?" Then again stand over him until he does it. If on the third night you find his clothes on the floor, employ a natural consequence. Say, "If I find clothes on the floor, I will no longer wash them." Then stick to your statement until he gets to the point that he has no clean underwear or a favorite outfit isn't available to wear. Remember, consequences should be exactly appropriate to the misdeed.

It's good to talk often about values, "the way we do things," what is right, and what an understanding way of looking at a situation is. We talk about how things make other people feel and what they expect of us. It is of critical importance never to avoid dealing with a problem. That is the worst abandonment of all. A father of two very successful and very likable young men of college age spoke to me about some of his views of parenting. He shared two main points. First, he said that he is committed to holding his ground if he makes a ruling. One of his sons wanted to take a foreign trip. The father said no. His son, a college debater, came up with a million reasons why he should be allowed to go. The father replied that they were great arguments and made a great deal of sense, but that the answer was still no. He son asked, "Why?" "I just don't want you to do that, period," said the father. That was the end of the discussion. His second point was that sometimes he would get exasperated and simply tell his kids, "Do what you want," and walk away. His children considered that the worst outcome of all. They would have preferred being told no to such a dismissal.

One should expect a child to simply do what he is told most of the time. Yet children caught up in the epidemic are more likely to whine, complain, sulk, throw things, roll their eyes, outright defy their parents, and who knows what else, given the infinite creativity of children.

A whole other category of counterproductive parental activity is devising explanations and excuses for the child. Even if a child is tired or hungry, there is no excuse for rudeness or deliberately breaking a parental rule. If you feel put off by what I am saying, it may be because you would feel unsympathetic and guilt-ridden and are trying too hard to be fair, afraid of squelching your child's spirit, embarrassed at the thought of others seeing you be firm with your child, or caught up in some other counterproductive cultural pressure produced by the epidemic. You will need to put these notions aside in order to become a more effective parent, or risk turning your child loose in the world untrained and vulnerable.

My wife, Judith, and I were in a restaurant recently for lunch, and behind us I could hear a high-pitched voice talking in the kind of faux motherese that is so painfully common today: a saccharinely sweet kind of baby talk. When I hear that sound coming from the mother of a child beyond infancy, I know the mother is totally out of touch with herself, playacting how she should be, and essentially disconnected from her child. The restaurant had a container of crayons on the table and a big paper tablecloth for drawing and coloring. When I heard the mother ask, "Is it all right if I draw with the blue crayon?" I knew we would soon be witnessing a scene, because her question gave the child a degree of authority that was not consonant with any two people sharing a set of crayons at the table, let alone a mother and child. If he had been an adult, she would just have picked up the blue crayon and begun coloring. Naturally the child said no, and now the shared property was his. A few minutes later the demanding, angry whining we expected from this child began. After another ten minutes the mother had left her seat and was standing in a corner of the restaurant holding and rocking her son, who was quite big for this sort of soothing. (We later learned he was about two and a half.) She was treating him like an infant in a frantic effort to prevent an outburst. After another few minutes she picked him up and left, leaving her lunch behind.

I hear so many parents talking to children in this ridiculous way. False, saccharine, unreal statements create an artificial peer-like situation that puts the child in charge. You must avoid behavior that gives your child the erroneous sense that he is the grown-up. One behavior that always alerts me to this possibility is when a strong suggestion like "Let's go" has at the end ". . . okay?" There is almost no normal situation in which you should be asking your child's permission. These decisions are yours.

Another time I observed a parent carrying a rather large child of three or four years into a restaurant for lunch, and immediately my warning signals went up. I knew from my experience in "kid watching" that they would soon have an upset. This child was far too big to be handled this way, and I knew he was infantilized too. In a short time, sure enough, the situation blew up. The child dominated the entire meal, and his parents were reduced to coping with his insipient tantrum in a desperate attempt to keep him placated. After ten minutes of this, the mother, her meal untouched, was on the floor playing with him while the father ate at the table alone.

Yet another time I was standing in a produce market and heard a woman's voice saying in that affected manner, "We can't go there, come out, okay?" As I heard the voice rise in that politically correct, measured sound, I knew I would soon be witness to another scene from the epidemic. When I turned around, I saw the cashier coming out of her booth to help the mother corral the child. He, of course, immediately began to have a tantrum and ran around the small space near the register. The mother begged him to stop and come out. Finally a man across the store, who turned out to be the father, came over to help, and they each took one wrist of the now screaming and crying child and led him to the exit, leaving their goods behind. As they walked by, a lone adult near the front door said, "He must need a nap." This is the perfect response to help conceal what is happening—that this child is literally being tortured by his mother's indecisiveness.

> **CRITICAL MOMENT:** This mother acted as though it wasn't her responsibility to teach this child how to behave in a store. She was powerless, uncertain, and anxious. What kind of a picture of life is this to transmit to a young boy? If the mother had firmly said, "I want you to stop that and come here now," the child might have done it. If he didn't, she could have picked him up and said, "You cannot be in the store if you act like that." By not being firm, by not picking him up, by not telling him clearly how to behave, she injured that child and moved him a little way down the track of the epidemic.

I am sure these parents do not understand why their children are difficult, and how their own behavior is distorting their children's views of who they are, who their parents are, and the nature of the relationship between them. In the end the epidemic is a parental problem that can resolve itself rapidly if the parent will only wake up soon enough. The important point is that we can spot a child who has started down the epidemic track merely by hearing the mother's voice, without even knowing exactly what was happening or seeing the child. So can you now, if you will only look. The comfort level of the mothers around you will alert you to the coming epidemic moments. That is because *the mother's state is the epidemic, and the child's behavior is merely a symptom.* I have a friend who recently said to me that I "ruined his life" when I explained the epidemic to him. "I'm haunted by these kids everywhere I go. I can't even sit down and have a pleasant dinner in a restaurant without noticing this behavior," he told me.

If you are having problems with your child, it is because you are in some way not there for her. You disconnect, fail to be present, do not communicate a vision of how to live, do not communicate your love and how much it means to you that your child grow up to be a worthwhile and loving person. Whatever your children's ages, do not disconnect from them. Do not let yourself be governed by feelings of impotence. Do not walk away or pretend not to notice. That is the greatest crime a parent can commit. The parents of any of the recent school shooters could have made the contact, mustered the help, communicated the caring and love by paying attention and taking appropriate action—and stopped the process that led to their children's extreme violence. When a child asks "Why?" the response should be, "It's bedtime, period!" If he persists with the negotiation, you can then respond, "I am the parent and I say no!"

This process has to begin very early in the child's life. When a one-year-old child throws food from his seat to the floor, the parent has to react. Of course, you need to be sensitive to the intent of the child. Sometimes the problem is just inattention, and the child has to be shown how to hold the spoon or other utensil. But when the child deliberately throws food on the floor and looks at you defiantly, this behavior requires a definite "No," and if repeated, you should remove the food from the child's reach. When you have to go on to other tactics, you are now trying to repair the results of your previous neglect.

If you stay willing to deal with your child, things will work out very smoothly. I think it is possible for almost your entire time with your child to be composed of positive, productive interactions. An attentively reared child rarely has to be admonished, rarely sulks and whines, rarely defies her parents, and almost never speaks abusively to them. Threats should seldom, if ever, be needed. It is far more preferable to be lovingly firm about how you want the child to behave ("Honey, I just can't let you do this") and then move on to the consequences promptly, without the "threat" stage at all. Of course, you will need some guiding rules and principles ("no TV until homework is done," "no going outside to play until your bed is made") that may need to be invoked as reminders now and then, but imposing threats like "If you don't do what I say, I'm telling your dad when he gets home" is a symptom of your diminished authority. At their worst, impotent interventions such as "I am going to tell you only one more time after this . . ." have been humorously titled "penultimatums."

In extreme cases, threats or ultimatums may be necessary with an older, out-of-control child. If your child is under eighteen, it is still your responsibility to protect him or her from a dangerous lack of judgment. There is an increasing tendency to think of sixteen- to eighteen-year-olds as grown-up, when in fact they aren't. They are superficially mature-looking but don't always have the judgment to avoid drug or alcohol use, sexual promiscuity, violent gangs, vandalism, or other unsavory temptations. If you consider the consequences dangerous, you need to tell your child, "If you walk out this door, I am calling the police. You are not going to leave this house now."

I also do not recommend punishment that is designed just to make the child suffer, such as, "You were rude, so no dessert for a week." I like the idea of consequences that in some way are similar to what occurs generally in life. For instance, if she throws a tantrum on the playground, she should be made to leave. If he doesn't do his chores first, he can't go to his softball game. If your child commits an act of vandalism, he should have to save his money and pay for the repair of the damage he caused. Deterrence ultimately is best served by having the child join in your sense of values so that his conscience prohibits him from doing the act because he doesn't want to disappoint you. Remember, your child wants more than anything to please you. A child who behaves in a way contrary to this idea is always settling for what is second-best—the booby prize really. For instance, someone recently told me that the best part about her Thanksgiving was overeating. Permission to gorge for pleasure, in my opinion, is a substitute for being able to connect with family and friends in a loving way.

Thinking about consequences reminds me of an episode with one of my sons. When he was eleven, he was suspended from riding the school bus for a week because he got in a fight with another boy. Naturally we made all the expected inquiries about what had happened, and things seemed to be resolved. After dinner that night he asked me, "What time should I be ready to leave for school in the morning?" I said, "What do you mean?" He said, "I need a ride to go to school. I can't go on the bus." I responded, "Well, I wasn't the one punished, and I don't intend to take you to school. You will have to take the bus" (the city bus that stopped on the corner). And so he did. (One of the things I most appreciated about raising our family in Berkeley was the fact that schoolchildren could get city bus passes and were used to wending their way around town in this manner.)

I believed at the time, and still do, that natural consequences of this kind help children relate to the realities of life, not just to their parents. They need to learn that they shouldn't run into the street—not just because Mommy doesn't want them to, but also because they might get hit by a car. If I had yelled at and punished my son about the bus incident, he just would have been dealing with his father, but by having to get himself to school as a consequence, he had to deal with life too.

As you can tell, I am reluctant to negotiate with a child, or bargain, or reason endlessly. I don't believe that things have to be "fair." After all, whose opinion is going to carry the day anyhow? All these maneuvers are parental attempts at avoiding the bald truth: parents are in charge and responsible for the outcome. We all know that people have some concern about confronting children with the fact that children are sexual organisms, that they are mortal, and worst of all, that their parents are mortal. Many, I'm afraid, are also reluctant to confront their children with their authority.

A perfect example occurred as I was writing part of this book on the beach near where we live. A small child, four or five years old, was on the beach with what seemed to be a family group of some ten people. He was about thirty feet from them and engrossed in futilely trying to fly a small kite. He would run and pull, but there wasn't enough wind to hold up his kite. The family group was sitting in a circle chatting, and drinking beverages, and no one was paying attention to the child. This went on for a while, and then I noticed a tall man in his late thirties who looked and carried himself like a charismatic military officer and leader of men. He walked toward this little child, radiating assurance and command. I would have expected him to be a formidable, take-charge kind of guy.

He went up to the child and said, "We have to go now." The child looked right at him, turned around, and began trying to fly his kite again. The "colonel" watched the child raise the kite, run backward with it, then run forward to pick up the kite that had simply fallen to the sand and run back again, all the while not showing any sign that he knew his father was standing there.

CRITICAL MOMENT: This parent is in danger of having his authority usurped by a preschooler. He must remain firm and insist that the child come, or risk a tantrum when he finally does put his foot down.

After a few minutes the father turned around and walked back to where another man his age was standing holding a football, and they starting having a game of catch. This went on for a few minutes, and then the father seemed to summon up his resolve after a voice from the circle said again that it was time to go. He walked back to the child, and this time when he said, "We have to go," he took the child's hand and led him back to the kite. He told him to pick up the kite and then simply took the child's hand and started walking back to the family circle. The child at this point went without any complaint and seemed to know that leaving was now inevitable.

This scene seems to have resolved itself without major incident, so why am I bringing it up? Because, in my opinion, when a father or mother tells a child that they have to leave, they have committed a *speech act* that they have to deliver on. Otherwise, they impair their credibility, authority, and ultimately their command of the situation. This father was actually hurting his child when he said, "We have to go now," and didn't follow through. I could feel the tension in both of them as the child kept up the forbidden behavior while reducing his father to impotence. That the father also was damaged in this transaction was manifested in his regressing back to being a play pal with his friend instead of a father to his son, though he did recover by behaving more authoritatively in the end.

It is essential that children know that their parents are in charge, that when they say "now" it must mean now, or the children will get the idea that life is an endless negotiation with wishy-washy people. This issue starts extremely early, with bedtime, TV, meals, play dates, sharing toys, and the like. Once the line is drawn, it must be attended to.

Some children do better with warnings that a scene or situation is about to change. For example, this father might have said, "Son, we are going to have to go home soon. You can fly the kite for ten more minutes, but that's it." That kind of statement would have kept their relationship in order and given the child time to reorganize. Then the father could have followed up with, "We have to go now. Let me help you wind up the kite string. You know we will come back and do this again." Then he should have done whatever was necessary to enforce his position, including picking up the child and carrying him back to the family circle if necessary. (Of course, if he had maintained his authority all along, it's highly unlikely the child would have resisted.)

EVOLVING YOUR PARENTING STYLE AS YOUR CHILD GROWS

Many of these children we have discussed sound like out-and-out monsters, and they pretty much are. Plenty of their parents and even today's current crop of "experts" would chalk their behavior up to their being a "difficult," "oppositional," "high-need," "high-energy," or "high-maintenance" child. The labels are as common as the out-of-control behavior. But the fact is that these monsters were made, not born, and the process may well have been a subtle one. It can definitely be reversed if parents will only be responsible enough to take the necessary steps to do so. Whether in my office or over the phone, by e-mail or Internet, I find that reversals can be amazingly rapid.

Let's look at the story of Robbie, the four-and-a-half-year-old grandchild of a friend who came to visit. His mother, Peg, decided to stop working when she had Robbie because she wanted motherhood to be the commitment and experience she had always dreamed of. Her husband, Dan, a retail clerk, did not make a lot of money, and her not returning to work caused a great financial sacrifice for the family. They had to live in a smaller home than they would have preferred, and she tried to help out by taking in a neighbor's child for a few hours of baby-sitting. But Peg and Dan agreed that their family life was far richer this way.

And Robbie was clearly bonded to his mother. Peg had a sweet way of being with him that was not artificially saccharine, and he was open and loving to other people. He conversed with me easily about what kind of car we had or the stones he was collecting. His mother had also obviously read a great deal to him, as he was thoroughly familiar with many children's books and understood them. He appeared at first glance to be a blossoming child, ready for school and the world at large.

But as I watched him play, I saw a bothersome level of defiance from him, and a little too much softness on the part of his parents. For example, as he played atop a neighbor's pile of stacked firewood, he began to throw the logs onto the sidewalk. This was behavior that he should have known was undesirable, yet he continued, looking his parents straight in the eye as he did it. When his mother tried to get him to stop, her voice changed, becoming less sure and confident. She asked him to stop. He did for a second and then threw the logs down again. She then, in a very soft, unconvincing tone, said that he couldn't do that. She finally talked him out of it, but in the process revealed the family's inability to solve their relationship dilemmas with full communication. If she had known she wasn't willing to handle her son's reaction, she could have decided not to notice, or simply to walk away.

A more in-control parent would have said: "Robbie, these people piled up this wood and want it that way. You can't throw those logs around." Most kids would stop at this point, but if Robbie didn't, his mother had more options: she could have walked over, looked him closely in the face, and said determinedly, "Robbie, I don't want you to do that." If he again repeated the behavior, she should have said, "Okay, our outing is over. I'm taking you home." And followed through. The pace would have been accelerated, without the time delays and hesitations that usually started to excite his resistance. Opening the subject and not following through had taught Robbie to be defiantly oppositional.

Another time the same family vacationed near us, and these parents, who were so good at bonding, again appeared not very comfortable in maintaining their place as heads of the family. Robbie interrupted us repeatedly, and they abandoned their conversations in midsentence and turned immediately to him.

When he started picking a leaf off a plant, his father said, "Robbie, please stop that." Instead of listening, he looked his father in the eyes and pulled the leaf off anyhow. The father looked away, and Robbie played with the plant until he tired of it. Robbie's father quickly backed down at the slightest resistance; he let himself be disregarded and put to the side by his child. It would have been better to not have mentioned the leaf if he wasn't prepared to follow through. And Robbie's mother, involved in conversation, did not appear to notice the incident.

When the time came for them to leave, they encountered more resistance and gave in to their child again. Instead of telling Robbie matter-of-factly that it was time to go and he should gather his things, his mother began a negotiation: "It's getting dark and we should be going in a few minutes. . . ."

Robbie glanced briefly at her, then turned back to what he was doing.

"Let's get our things together, Robbie. . . ."

No reaction at all from the boy.

"Okay, five more minutes."

Five minutes later, "Okay, we have to go now. It's really time. . . ." Robbie just sat and glared defiantly at his mother as she began to search for his jacket. Peg was essentially avoiding making a scene to obscure the fact that this battle of wills even existed. She was afraid that it would have been quite clear to us that there was trouble if she had put her foot down and he had made a scene in response. A mother or father doesn't need a child's agreement or acquiescence to decide it's time to go. The notion that a child can say no arises either from the parents' fear of confrontation or from the political beliefs that lead them to think that even a very small child should have an equal voice in such decisions.

Now, this is hardly one of those monstrous scenes of misbehavior that pepper articles on spoiled, out-of-control kids. But I chose it because it's a perfect example of the subtle negotiating and fear of asserting parental authority and responsibility that is so prevalent now. The behavior of Robbie's parents is problematic because it denies the truth of the situation, confuses the child, and leads him to think that he is deciding things he has no business controlling at his age. He is left without parents who manage his world while he safely plays, and he is given a false feeling of omnipotence attained by oppositional behavior. In other words, these tiny, almost insignificant moments put the family on a path that is likely to lead to this child's becoming increasingly more difficult, more imperious, ruder, more willful, and highly unpleasant when confronted. The parents don't notice what is happening because they are reacting without considering the message they are sending about the nature of power, control, and the relationship between child and parent.

Some people would offer the excuse that these parents were inhibited because they were being observed. Sure, that is true. However, there are many difficult situations—sitting in church, at a restaurant table, on the bus, in the grocery store—in which kids are likely to act up, and parents have to get comfortable with the idea that the education of their child is more important than the opinions of onlookers. Besides, chances are that their opinion is going to be that you're not in control of your child anyway, so you might as well take control!

There will still be people out there clinging to the anti-authoritarian attitudes of recent decades, but more and more, our culture is recognizing that we have let our kids go too far, and it's time to rein them back in. It's time to topple the myth that it is stifling for a child to be controlled. The well-behaved children of previous generations were a source of pride for their parents; the difference between then and now is that we know how to encourage such behavior without also being oppressive or dictatorial.

There's another reason that the story of Robbie is so relevant: it illustrates how parents must develop along with their child. Their parenting practices must be appropriate for each stage the child goes through in order to be effective. Robbie's parents, Peg and Dan, were terrific at bonding, support, encouragement—all critical for infants and young toddlers who are searching for security in their world. But once that early bond was established, Robbie needed to learn that there were boundaries in his universe and that no meant no. By not evolving with their growing child, whose very nature it was to test limits more and more, their effectiveness was diminished, and Robbie was beginning to take over in the power struggle. The bigger he gets, the harder it will be on everyone, particularly as the school years approach, if he has not learned appropriate behavior for his age. Peg and Dan had a beautiful child early in life, but he's not going to be so beautiful as an adolescent if they don't make more of an effort now to establish just who is in charge.

In fact, when I ran into Peg again about a year after the incident, she made a dramatic gesture and looked really upset when I inquired about her son, who by then was five and a half. "He's gone into a terribly difficult stage—I just can't control him," she replied with exasperation. She actually did think of it as a stage and was waiting for resolution to occur spontaneously. She hadn't even considered the fact that Robbie's difficult behavior was a natural outcome of the behaviors I had observed at ages three and four. Peg didn't go into detail in this public scene, but her pain and consternation were quite obvious. I felt that all I could do, despite my concern, was to listen and empathize with her shock.

The fact is that age five ushers in what is typically a really delightful stage. Early psychoanalysts called the years between five and about eight the latency stage, because the child's instinctual drive to test and push limits is buried by more affiliative attributes of his personality. By kindergarten, children are usually happy, pleasing, very rule-oriented, curious, and eager to learn. If parents like Peg were more aware of this normal progression of development, they would quickly recognize when their child is deviating from it. If you are having trouble managing your child at an age or stage when other parents you know are not, by all means, do some research as to what the expectations for your child's behavior are, and seek professional help if necessary. It may simply be that your parenting style has veered off in an inappropriate direction and that a few changes in your interactions can steer your child back on course.

Even if parents do manage to wield authority over their children when they are young, it's common for them to abdicate the critical role of authority figure as the children get big enough to interact on a more friendly and enjoyable basis. They try too hard to be friends with their children and become fearful that being firm and clear will damage their relationship with them. How ironic it is that our children end up loving and respecting us even less as a result. Katie in the toy store does not look up to her mother; she looks down on her as she crushes her with her willfulness. Chances are that she'll grow up resenting the fact that her parents didn't adequately prepare her for the world and will blame them when she has trouble coping.

We don't need research to tell us that if you have problems with relationships in childhood, they are likely to continue into adulthood as well, but there are endless studies confirming that commonsense statement. Chris Knoester, Ph.D., a former Pennsylvania State University researcher, now at Ohio State University, analyzed data from a longitudinal study of married couples and found that their children who experienced behavior problems such as temper tantrums, bullying, or destructiveness were more likely to have emotional trouble as young adults. "Compared to their better-adjusted peers, children with a history of behavior disorders, once they entered adulthood, achieved significantly lower levels of overall happiness, life satisfaction, and self-esteem," Knoester notes. "They also report weaker rapport with relatives, poorer relations with their parents, and in general more difficulty establishing intimacy." Interestingly, Knoester found that these negative traits were more prevalent in children from smaller families, in which one would expect the parents to have more time for their children and less financial strain.

It sounds like a wildly radical idea: kids want to have limits on when they go to bed, when they do their homework, when they watch TV, what they eat, who they play with. And they thrive in tightly managed environments. We're depriving them when we don't say no, not when we do. Consider another recent study about children and bedtime: a research team from Rhode Island Hospital, Brown University School of Medicine, and George Washington University compared eighty children from a sleep disorders clinic with fifty-two others at a primary-care clinic. The researchers asked the parents of the children about sleep disturbances, child temperament, behavioral problems, and parenting styles. They found that lax and permissive parenting was strongly associated with sleep disturbances. Lax parenting was described as parents giving in, allowing rules to go unenforced, or providing positive consequences for bad behaviors, such as letting kids stay up when they resisted bedtime, or giving in when they threw a tantrum. To me, it seems clear that the message these children got was: the worse I act, the more likely it is that Mom and Dad will give in. Other research has found that TVs in children's bedrooms contribute to sleep problems and that preschoolers who sleep less have greater behavior problems during the day.

It's a vicious cycle that contributes to one big messed-up household: the kids are out of control, and the parents can't get them to go to bed. The kids end up overtired and out of control because they're sleep-deprived. Then the parents buy a TV and put it in the bedroom to keep them pacified during those frustrating evening hours, which complicates the problem further. The kids get bigger and end up with computers in their rooms, doing who knows what on the Internet all night long while their increasingly out-of-touch parents sleep across the hall. The next day they go to school in a zombielike state and fail their tests, or come home and nap instead of doing their homework. Then the cycle repeats itself.

OF EMPATHY, ANGER, AND CONTROL

The very difficult problem for many parents is being able to enforce boundaries without becoming angry. By that I mean being able to tell their child, "This is how I feel," or "This is what I want," or "These are the rules," without having to become angry in order to express themselves or press through inhibitions about such expression. Often when parents can't do this they simply give up and allow their children to do or say things that should be forbidden.

The best atmosphere in which to raise a child is in a climate of love, of high regard for each person, all the while maintaining very clear expectations of what the child must do and not do. The presence of absolutes in no way has to dilute the climate of love and acceptance. It is a loving act to stop a child from doing forbidden things and to teach her how to behave in the world.

We all get overwhelmed at times and then to some extent lose control. Nevertheless, you need to recognize that in your child's body is a little human soul that wants so much to be close, to love, to be loved and accepted. When she forgets this and acts in an unacceptable way, her coping skills have been overwhelmed. Now, that does not mean that she should get her way. It does mean that you should get interested in exactly what things mean to your child, and that you should show her empathy even while talking firmly about not giving in to her demands. This combination of empathy and firmness is what really heals that place in the child that is responsible for the breakdown. All children have to learn to experience the pain and frustration of not getting their way and still stay in emotional connection with those they love.

The danger is that the parents' own coping systems are threatened by the child's anger and behavior. When that happens, they lose for a moment their ability to approach their child secure in the knowledge that he is still this good little human being who loves them no matter what he says and is desperately coping with his own life. When the good and loving side of their child remains clear to them, it is easier to be curious, to ask, "Why did you do it?" with interest instead of negativity. This is the approach that really heals and really works—not losing yourself in your rage over the child's behavior, or copping out because you can't deal with it.

The bottom line is this: when we don't train our children to behave, they train us to be their servants. One of my favorite examples of how out of whack things have become is a product called a "splat mat." When my kids were little and they threw things off their high chair, as all children do, I'd laugh the first time and tell them no. They'd repeat the behavior, of course, and then I'd take away what they were throwing. Eventually they learned not to do it. Now parents buy splat mats, kids throw what they want, and the parent cleans it all up when the kid tires of the game. As with Robbie's endless struggle for control, it may seem innocent enough when your child's an infant, but eventually those messes are going to get bigger and uglier and won't be fun to clean up.

Parents must understand that these early errors lead them to treat their children as younger than they really are. If children are not expected to behave in more and more grown-up ways, they maintain their same infantile patterns. And parents help keep them that way by treating them as if they are in fact immature and developmentally lagging. If your child is very young, these mistakes will be easier to fix; if she is older, you may need professional help to break heavily ingrained patterns—hers and yours both.

Throughout this book I've sought to make one thing clear: raising children should be a pleasure *almost all the time*. It's an enjoyable and fulfilling role, and the benefits we derive from doing it well are incomparable. When life with your child ceases to be fun and pleasant, something is wrong with the way your family is functioning. And if we resort to making excuses and putting labels on our kids, we have no hope of improving the situation. The responsibility for their behavior is ours—while parenting should not be a dictatorship, it is also not a democracy. There's a loving, happy medium you can achieve that will produce productive, well-adjusted children and peaceful relationships.

HOW IS MY CHILD DOING?

Watch for these signs of an out-of-control kid:

- You find yourself giving in to your child whenever you see a tantrum brewing.
- Your child frequently talks back, insults you, or curses at you.
- Your child has a habit of hitting, kicking, spitting at, or otherwise physically assaulting you when he's angry.
- Your child misbehaves only in certain situations—he may be perfectly cooperative with his teacher, for instance, but throws tantrums or behaves defiantly for you.
- Your child resists coming to the table for family meals.
- Your child outright refuses to do schoolwork.
- Teachers frequently complain about your child.
- You find yourself frequently embarrassed about your child's behavior in front of others.
- Your child seems unable to make or keep friends.
- Your child has persistent feelings of unworthiness and inadequacy.
- Your child has a total lack of understanding of your needs. Telling her she has to wait a minute for a drink or a ride to the mall results in that cold, dead-eyed stare we saw in Meadow Soprano week after week on the first season of *The Sopranos*.
- You find yourself frequently feeling frustrated and unappreciated, no matter how hard you try to please your child.

6
Raising Moral Children in a Valueless World

To educate a person in mind and not morals is to educate a menace to society.

—Theodore Roosevelt

OUR CHILDREN ARE BEING brought up in a morally indifferent society in which they are barraged with sadistic, grossly sexual, and violent television, music, video games, and Internet activities. As of this writing, they can type in "whitehouse.com" on the computer while doing a homework project and end up viewing pornography instead of a government-sanctioned website. We have shock rock and cringe radio, which manage to combine the worst aspects of rap and TV. Just listen to some of the lyrics of the unbelievably successful (given the gross obscenity of their material) musical group Insane Clown Posse. They recount stabbings and sexual violence and advocate drug use to twelve-year-olds. Recently on *The O'Reilly Factor,* host Bill O'Reilly suggested that they were harming children by exposing them to such corrupting material. The group's response: "That's not our job—it's their parents'. We are just entertainers. They listen to us because they are just like us."

I don't think you want your child to be just like them. But if you don't stand between your child and a society that doesn't share your values, you may lose control over what values he ultimately adopts. We live in a society that has in great measure drifted into a moral relativism in which there are very few things that are categorically wrong to do. Almost no matter what people do these days that is nominally "against the rules," they can find extenuating circumstances that make it acceptable: "Everyone else is cheating, and it's the only way I can get high enough grades to get into college," or "Everyone is smoking grass, Mom."

"Is it legal?" is being substituted for "Is it moral?" We no longer are naively trusting enough to believe our politicians mean what they say, or even that they base their decisions on what they deem to be good for our nation and their constituents. The Enron scandal has brought our attention to the widespread use of subterfuge and downright misinformation in order to become rich and successful.

This chapter is intended to make you aware of how far we have gone in abandoning standards of caring and even decency. As there is less devotion to moral and ethical issues in our society, there is less support for, and in fact a greater assault against, your child's developing values system. We have to be very careful to protect our young children until we have instilled in them a sense of values, they have come to an understanding of the destructiveness of a great deal of what they see around them, and they are mature enough to hold their own and make wise choices.

I think it is important to document these problems because I want you to become aware of how desperately we need to change the way we are bringing up our children. Only you can intervene to save your child. You need to be alert about your children's friends, their parents, the school, even the library. Pushing for information can be difficult and at times embarrassing or even frightening. People may think you are fussy, perhaps even self-righteous, when you ask questions like, "Does this library screen out pornography on its computers?" I have asked a number of librarians their feelings on this issue and was rather shocked that most of them said their biggest worry was limiting children's access to the world. If society is in a sense going mad—and I believe the school shooters are telling us something like that—the effort needed to raise your child is going to approach the heroic. It will be so easy to give in and agree that such and such a practice is the way we do things now, or even worse, that there might be some merit or wisdom in what is being practiced. If you have any doubt, think about what you see all around you. Ask yourself if kids are looking happier, more wholesome, more buoyantly energetic these days. I think they are not.

When I refer to moral and ethical training, I am speaking of the process by which a family passes on the values that they hold dear. The passing on of values takes place at every level of development that we discuss in this book. You do it when your baby throws his cup from the high chair and you make it clear that such behavior is not appropriate and take the cup away. You do it when you establish routines ("bedtime at eight o'clock") and limits ("no TV until your homework is done"). You do it when you praise people for behavior that reveals their valor, caring, or generosity. You do it when you spend hours reading and conversing with your child and your special dance of connection takes place. You do it when you give your child first a warning, then a disapproving look and a firm no as he reaches for a forbidden object. Then, if he persists, you remove him from the scene; you don't just keep saying no. Remember: your young child doesn't think in terms of abstract values but is concerned with whether you smile, frown, or stop him from doing something. Your child will internalize all these signals, even if he goes through periods of resistance.

THE NASTY GENERATION

Talk to any teacher about the children he or she sees every day, and you will probably hear that the current generation, even those from comfortable homes, receives little effective ethical training. Children's behavior both in and out of the classroom is more aggressive, less respectful, and increasingly selfish and uncaring. Some of these kids are meaner, nastier, more venomous and vengeful, and it's far tougher for teachers to control a class than it used to be. There is an association between these qualities and impaired literacy acquisition. More and more, children from homes and neighborhoods that would routinely be expected to do well are severely impaired in their ability to learn and be educated. Increasingly, our schools must focus on discipline at the expense of education.

Front-page headlines declare that teasing, bullying, cheating, stealing, lying, and other undesirable behaviors have increased right in proportion with the rest of the problems in our society. Of course, it's always been true that kids occasionally commit such transgressions. Time was when there were one or two bullies in every school, and all the other kids knew never to be caught alone in the hall with them or cornered by them on the playground. This sort of bully was different, though—he stood alone in a crowd. You knew he didn't have the same values as everyone else, and there was no hope in talking or negotiating or trying to win him over. Bullies in the past weren't cool; they may have been feared, but they weren't admired.

Now almost everyone's a bully or a victim, it seems—even so-called good friends regularly hurl insults at each other. But it's not just manners and tact that have been abandoned. Clearly the understanding of how someone feels when denigrated or treated contemptuously, and the loyalty one would be expected to show a friend, have ceased to exist in all too many childhood social circles. In "The 2000 Report Card on the Ethics of American Youth," a survey of preteens and adolescents conducted periodically by the Josephson Institute of Ethics in Los Angeles, California, children had no hesitancy or shame when admitting that they stole, cheated on tests, and lied to their parents. Although many of us as children may have done things such as shoplift a little candy or take money from our dad's wallet, we weren't about to admit it to adults. We knew it was wrong.

Many of today's school-age children and teens tend to act as though they're entitled to what they want regardless of how they get it, that the high test score is worth just as much with a crib sheet as without it, and that it's okay to lash out at peers if they annoy you. Frequently these days children start out as sandbox bullies in their toddler years and go on to become school bus and playground bullies in grade school. The flip side of this development is that the bullies can become victims in turn, as their violence leads to retaliation from those they've bullied, those kids whose sense of alienation turns into dangerous rage.

Many journalists reporting on the Columbine tragedy suggested that Eric Harris and Dylan Klebold were retaliating for being teased. Although not all such youth explode violently, school shootings do give us the opportunity to understand what factors in our culture lead some kids to kill. I want you to understand the parental practices that would have made such an outcome impossible, so that you can save your child from such a fate. Teaching children values like empathy and compassion and loyalty and responsibility is the only way to prevent such episodes.

GROWING UP WITHOUT A MORAL MINDSET

The evidence of what can go wrong in a valueless society is hardly limited to children. The collapse of the corporate energy giant Enron in 2002 was much more than a financial disaster: it captured with remarkable clarity the essence of the epidemic. Certainly financial crimes have been committed in the past, such as the famous and extraordinary nationwide Ponzi matchbook pyramid scheme. But these other large embezzlements and price-fixing scandals involved one or two people in charge who knew they were doing something wrong and shared that knowledge only with their criminal associates. They knew well that their behavior would have been abhorrent to most people and that they were risking their reputations, their honor, and their freedom by engaging in it.

The Enron fiasco, on the other hand, required the knowing participation of hundreds, possibly even thousands, of people at the level of company executives, accountants, stock analysts, brokers, government officials, politicians, and maybe even the news media. It could only have happened in a morally relativistic culture in which a quest for power and money held sway over considerations of goodness, honor, fiduciary responsibility, and fundamental caring for the welfare of others. The act of urging employees to fill their pension plans with the stock that Enron executives were selling constitutes an act as devastating as any I have known. These executives acted consistently with the kind of upbringing that encourages the development of cognitive power and cunning but not real emotional intelligence, not compassion, not empathy. They may have ruined the lives of more people than did the attacks of September 11. The victims of Enron are at risk of spending their old age pensionless, struggling with the bitterness of having been so deeply betrayed by those to whom they had committed their vocational lives and their retirement funds.

The participants in the Enron scheme had no previous criminal record; they were regarded as relatively normal people. The true horror is that their behavior has come to be considered normal as well. The extent of moral collapse in big business is neatly documented in Arianna Huffington's book *Pigs at the Trough: How Corporate Greed and Political Corruption Are Undermining America*. It is clear that the epidemic doesn't stop when our troubled adolescent boys grow up. They become executives because of their superior cognitive development but remain as equally damaged emotionally, socially, and morally as the teenage shooters. That is, they have the same diminished sense of the connection between themselves and the consequences of their actions, a lack of compassion and empathy (their victims are the equivalent of video game characters, vague and unimportant), and the misguided notion that they can define morality at their own whim.

It is not just the retirees and investors who are hurt. Just think of the damage to the families of these white-collar criminals. Children have lost respect for their parents. Often assumed to be complicit, spouses have had to go out and face widespread disapproval, condemnation, and even legal difficulties. Because as a culture we are normalizing so much disturbed development and behavior, it may look to observers as though nothing out of the ordinary is going on: of course our spouses fake earnings reports, and the heads of the world's two greatest art auction houses are meeting to fix prices. That's what you have to do to get along.

Yet in spite of all the horrifying headlines about teenage criminals, substance-abusing athletes, perverted shock rock musicians, and deceitful businesspeople and politicians, there is also a source of inspiration for parents and children alike. When we watched the aftermath of the September 11 terrorist attacks, society collectively wondered where all the instant heroes had come from—the firefighters, rescue workers, and average citizens who put their lives on hold to help the victims, their families, and the residents of New York and Washington, D.C., recover and regroup. Raising children to be caring, giving, empathic, and good of heart began to be talked about. It was a welcome contrast to what we've been used to seeing.

The fact is that there is still a large segment of our society that raises its children to live lives informed by moral and ethical values. Such a firm ethical mindset will always transcend the pressure of popular culture, and I hope it will hold our society together in the face of difficult circumstances. But most of the time we don't hear much about these people. They are the ones just doing their jobs, going to church, volunteering in their community—but not making headlines. These are the kids who grow up and become rescue workers, Peace Corps or Teach for America volunteers, and PTA parents. They serve on our police forces, in our fire departments, and in the military; they teach in our schools and nurse in our hospitals. They run worthwhile businesses and treat their employees fairly. Again, the choice is yours: Will your child be more likely to become a white-collar criminal, terrorist, or teenage shooter or a good, decent human being who contributes to society? The values you demonstrate in your day-to-day interactions will make all the difference in the outcome.

WHERE DO WE GO FROM HERE?

Humans come into existence with few built-in instructions for how to behave. Cultural evolution has transcended biological evolution as the agent of change. This allows upbringing to be the critical determinant of how children turn out. If children's minds are like computer hardware, children's interactions with their parents (and indeed, with the world) are the software. Of course, children come with their own temperaments and reactions, but fundamentally, if a child is raised by cannibals, he will in all probability be a cannibal too. *Everything* we do teaches our kids something about the nature of life and how to be a human being. As parents, we should constantly ask ourselves, "What does my action in this situation teach my children?" What conclusions will they draw when we give in to their tantrums? What will they conclude when we are inconsistent in our positions regarding homework or bedtime or truthfulness? What conclusion about life will they draw when their existence is all about entertainment or expensive gifts that substitute for loving attention?

Constantly questioning ourselves in this way may sound overwhelming or even impossible. And yet, as is true for every other animal, we *know* deep down exactly what's required to raise good kids if we bother to pay attention to our instincts and tune out the distracting, conflicting messages our toxic culture is sending.

There are critical steps parents must take to teach their kids how to live in the world at large. Children learn these lessons when we:

- **ESTABLISH BOUNDARIES:** Every child needs a code of appropriate behaviors to grow and thrive and fit into society. But contrary to what many parenting gurus are trying to tell us, rules and routines support our children's development. Parents must know their child, know themselves, and experiment to find the boundaries that work. The cardinal rule: if it doesn't feel right, don't do it. And especially don't let your child do it. If you are in touch with your real feelings and convictions, you will feel confident and good about your decisions and you won't need to explain them unless you want to do so for teaching purposes. You must create structure for your child, make rules for him, and establish his position relative to yours. *If bonding transmits the germ of humanity, boundaries allow children the safe space in which to explore and begin to understand and fit appropriately into their world.*

- **MAINTAIN DISCIPLINE:** There's an easy way to tell if you're caught up in the epidemic yourself—the very word "discipline" will sound cruel to you. Disciplining children is out of fashion in American culture today, but children need it in order to be psychologically healthy and happy. Discipline is as much an act of love as cuddles and kisses. The psychological structures that develop from dealing with frustrations and limits teach children to focus on a goal and carry out activities consistent with those goals. At the same time discipline helps them learn how to fit in and accommodate the appropriate demands of life by being able to understand others' points of view and developing enough of a sense of responsibility to hold down a job.

When these traits don't develop, children become cold, disobedient, and easily disappointed and are more prone to addictions to media or substances. The ordinary pains and frustrations of everyday life overwhelm them, and they are temperamentally unable to meet new challenges.

- **TEACH SELF-CONTROL:** The virtues of self-control and the ability to postpone gratification are fundamental to living in the world, but many parents today simply don't work to pass them on to their children. Frankly, skimping on this aspect of parenting is as neglectful as skipping the polio vaccine. And yet, among many educated, affluent, and concerned parents, placating has taken the place of teaching self-control. A child who gets what she wants by throwing tantrums when young won't develop the emotional resources to deal with her frustration and boredom and will only become more explosive with time. How will such a child say no to inappropriate behaviors or substances when her peer group invites her to participate?

- **INSTILL RESPECT FOR OTHERS:** If children don't have respect for those in charge at home, they may not have respect for teachers, which compromises their ability to learn, or their employers, which compromises their ability to succeed in the work world. If they don't have respect for peers, they won't be socially competent and instead will use destructive strategies like bullying to get their way.

- **INCULCATE MORAL VALUES:** We're on the far side of the spiritual parabola, where it isn't politically correct to consider moral training as central to child-rearing. As a result, children today don't deeply internalize the distinction between right and wrong, don't respect the rules, and don't understand the consequences of immoral, unethical, or illegal action. Parents must find the courage to live *every day* the values they feel their child should have.

- **PROMOTE A HEALTHY DEGREE OF SEPARATION:** The inculcation of morals is a long process that begins in infancy and continues throughout childhood. As a baby, a child learns to be content alone in his crib, then to play in a safe spot on his own with minimal supervision; eventually he learns the self-control and focus to be allowed to cross the street by himself, to ride his bicycle out of the neighborhood to a friend's house, and to establish his position in school. The child must learn that rules are part of life and don't mean he is unloved or unfairly treated. Yet it certainly feels that way to the unsocialized and untrained kid.

- **ESTABLISH APPROPRIATE ACCOUNTABILITY, PRIVACY, AND TRUST:** It seems natural to think that kids should enjoy privacy and trust as inalienable rights. These are most definitely not rights, however, but earned privileges, meted out appropriately to the gradually maturing child and maintained by behavior that conforms to family mores. Parents today need to learn the trick of doling out responsibility in age-appropriate ways and rewarding children with trust when they prove they can handle it and understand that they will be held accountable for their actions. For example, when a toddler spills milk accidentally, Mommy smiles understandingly and says, "The milk spilled, let's clean it up." But when the child is a little older—say, age four—and breaks a bowl you have forbidden him to touch, he should be taught that:

1. He misbehaved.
2. He did damage.
3. He created a mess that has to be handled.
4. It is his job to clean it up.

Depending on the child's age, you may help him clean up or not, but you should supervise and see that it is done appropriately so that the child recognizes that his behavior calls forth certain responses from the environment. When a child can make the connection between his behavior and your responses—an ability he will acquire when you respond honestly, promptly, and appropriately—he will learn to control those responses by behaving in accord with the moral and ethical values of his family and society.

GETTING CLEAR ABOUT YOUR FAMILY VALUES

The first step in imparting these critical lessons is to understand what you yourself believe and want to convey to your children. I urge you not be haphazard, because these values are going to come out in your daily exchanges, whether you've consciously decided to teach them or not.

The very definition of values is highly subjective. Consider these issues:

- Will your value system have a secular, philosophical, or religious basis?
- Which takes priority: strong character or success at any price? Is being a good friend as important as being class president? Does volunteering in a soup kitchen score as many points as a high grade point average? Are both important? Are neither?
- What is your definition of a "good life"? What are the paths that you think lead to satisfaction? Whom would you consider a good role model for your child?
- What characteristics do you want your children to have: loyalty, honor, dignity? A devotion to community, family, and duty?
- Do you make time for the kind of pointed discussions that teach relationship skills? This takes a lot of work, but it's a good idea to help your child deal with her feelings. When she comes home from school upset, for instance, you first need to find out exactly what happened that upset her and help her feel secure again. If you feel she behaved inap-

propriately, then teach an appropriate response. You may say, "In our family, we don't do that," then "This is what we do."

- How else will you convey your values? Some parents choose to post their own set of golden rules on the kitchen refrigerator, as black and white as the grocery list. All parents must teach by example.

A significant memory from my childhood is of a conversation I had with my father about a friend's family. My father would come home from work early, and we would both head for the den, where we played checkers and talked. It was during World War II, and everyone knew there were people engaging in black market activities. I remember telling my dad about my friend Joey, whose family seemed to be getting richer by the day. They had a new Cadillac, went on impressive vacations, and bought lots of expensive toys. Of course, I was envious, but what I remember most is my father's response: "I wouldn't do that. I prefer to sleep well at night." And I knew exactly what he meant—he wouldn't do anything that would give him a guilty conscience or interfere with his sense of well-being. I saw that my father stood for something. That phrase became a shorthand reminder throughout my life that I, too, wanted to "sleep well."

Those kinds of subtle comments, behaviors, and examples are frequently what hit home with children, for the simple reason that when parents are secure in their values, their children are too. The children have less need to derive their self-worth from showy possessions or boastful comments or to gain attention by being the clown at the party or doing daredevil stuff wildly beyond their ability. They learn what's really important from their parents' behavior, then internalize it for themselves. A toddler needs to receive a great many "no's." Eventually he starts following the rules because he doesn't want to hear "no" again, then because he wants to please us. Finally he internalizes the fact that a behavior is wrong, and he says "no" even when there's no parent looking over his shoulder—when a friend tries to entice him to shoplift at the mall, for instance, or smoke a joint behind someone's garage. In college he refrains from cheating on tests; in the office he doesn't fudge his expense reports. For those parenting gurus who say that early moral guidance and discipline is demeaning and stifling, I say that's ridiculous. Disciplining the toddler is the foundation for transmitting morals and appropriate behavior, and if you have a strong bond with your child, that becomes a loving, empowering task, not a punitive one. On the other hand, children who have unchecked behavior disorders lose their empathic ability.

This is borne out by a study conducted by Paul D. Hastings, Ph.D., and Carolyn Zahn-Waxler, Ph.D., of the National Institute of Mental Health, in conjunction with researchers at the University of Colorado at Boulder. The researchers followed three groups of children—from preschool into the elementary school years—who had low, moderate, or high levels of aggressive and disruptive behaviors. In the preschool years the aggressive, disruptive children showed just as much concern in response to an adult's distress as did children with fewer problems. But by age six and a half, the level of concern for others had decreased markedly in the most aggressive and disruptive group, and they were the least prosocial (sociable, cooperative, and connected) children, displaying more active disregard for others, including anger, avoidance, and amusement at others' distress. Conversely, those children with the highest level of concern for others were aware and distressed by the fact that their actions harmed others. Concern for others may well make it possible for children to take responsibility for their actions, these researchers noted.

Parenting styles also played a role in the children's empathic development. The study noted that children had greater concern for others when their mothers were warm and used reasoning but also reacted appropriately in situations that required firm interventions. Mothers who were overly strict and harshly punitive, who did not tend to reason or establish reasonable and consistent rules, and who reacted to problem behavior mainly with anger and disappointment were likely to impede their children's prosocial development.

Appropriate guidance and limits help to teach a child how other people feel. When parents let a child run wild, they are in fact abandoning him. A lack of social structure is painful to a child; he will dampen his emotions and sense of empathy to spare himself the feeling of abandonment.

Children who are joyless and selfishly aggressive in their preschool years are at risk. They urgently need training and support, and I would assume that they are not getting what they need in the way of love and connection. When someone starts lovingly training them, they will connect and start to feel again. Being empathic is the natural state of human infants and children. We see this clearly in a pure culture, such as developing puppies, which automatically love and show affection toward their owners. Loss of empathic feeling is the result of injury and leaves a child damaged. A child with diminished capacity for empathy has not been given the love, bonding, and training she needs to thrive.

The single best book I know that is designed to help parents communicate with their children, especially daughters, but in spirit all youngsters, is *All That She Can Be* by Carol Eagle, Ph.D. She presents practical and detailed conversational exchanges that illuminate the life of the young person and the issues that arise for their parents. This book will empower you to create more productive and warmly empathic relationships with your children.

CULTIVATING STRONG CHARACTER TRAITS

Parents today certainly have varied ideas and goals for their children, but certain admirable traits are always in style. A friend of mine in the magazine business recalls a cover line on a parenting publication she worked for that boasted: "How to Raise a

Nice Kid." The magazine flew off the store shelves, and it's no wonder. It's a promise we all want to fulfill, for our kids and for ourselves. As we saw society take a turn for the worse in the past decade, raising nice kids has become ever more critical.

What are the traits that make a "good" kid? We've already emphasized empathy, the ability to put yourself in someone else's shoes, to feel their emotions and respond in a caring way. Feeling empathic also promotes respectful behavior: you're far less likely to bully or tease someone if you understand that those behaviors hurt his or her feelings. Loyalty, honesty, responsibility, and perseverance are also key. The Harvard psychiatrist Robert Coles, M.D., offers his definition of a "good" child in his book *The Moral Intelligence of Children:* "Good children are boys and girls who in the first place have learned to take seriously the very notion, the desirability, of goodness—a living up to the Golden Rule, a respect for others, a commitment of mind, heart, soul to one's family, neighborhood, nation—and have also learned that the issue of goodness is not an abstract one, but rather a concrete, expressive one: how to turn the rhetoric of goodness into action, moments that affirm the presence of goodness in a particular life lived."

"Nice" kids think of others as well as themselves ("It's your turn now") and offer friends support ("Good hit, Joey!"), loyalty ("You can't call my friend names!"), and compassion ("Ooh, that hurts. Let's get a bandage."). They're polite not just when Grandma comes over, but as a rule, and they remember to pitch in by doing things like taking their dinner plate to the sink when they're finished and putting their dirty clothes in the laundry basket.

Yet many kids today demonstrate such a startling lack of these character traits that schools now resort to a regularly scheduled moral curriculum. The Josephson Institute sponsors the "Character Counts" coalition, a training program for teachers, coaches, and other community leaders that helps them instill what the institute refers to as "the Six Pillars of Character": trustworthiness, respect, responsibility, fairness, caring, and citizenship. Other schools have introduced programs espousing what are known as the fourth and fifth R's: responsibility and respect. And there's even a Washington, D.C.–based clearinghouse for character education information known as the Character Education Partnership. How sad it is that the much-too-limited funding for education has to pay for the moral training that children should be getting at home.

These are all admirable efforts, of course, but they are too little too late, and they come from substitutes for the people who could have done it more effectively. If parents were doing a better job in this area at home, schools could focus on the academics they were designed to teach. Indeed, parents get upset when budget constraints limit the more creative aspects of curriculum, such as art and music, but if districts have to pay consultants and outside firms to help instruct kids in being civilized, it shouldn't surprise us that there's little money left. Such precious resources should be dedicated to the schools' essential mission.

Helping their children develop a moral mindset will always remain foremost a parent's job. As with the drills and practices it takes to help your child learn math and spelling, if there's no moral "homework," so to speak, lessons will easily be forgotten, particularly if they're not also enforced in the lunchroom, on the playground, or by the teacher the next year. Consistency at home and at school is what counts for character development, academics, and pretty much everything else regarding raising children. We can't expect schools to be all things, or to "fix" our kids.

BEING THERE

It's easy to see how parental communication and example-setting are so paramount with children. A mother told me the story of her first-grader, a child who appeared to be well grounded, empathic, and conscientious. Yet this child came home from school one day and told the story, laughing, of a little boy in her class who started to cry when he didn't pass a "sight word" test. "Isn't that funny—he started to cry right in front of everyone," she giggled.

"Well, he must have felt really bad and embarrassed," replied her mother. "What were you feeling when this happened?"

The little girl replied that she didn't know what to do, so she just laughed along with the other children.

"I see why you giggled—it must have been very uncomfortable," said the mother. "But just imagine how hurt you would feel if the kids laughed at you. If he gets upset because he's having trouble again, I think it would be nice of you to say something when you have a chance, like, 'Don't feel bad, Matt. You'll get it next time. You're just learning.'"

> **CRITICAL MOMENT:** This parent was luckily on hand and observant enough to demonstrate an ethical response for her child. It's what educators like to call a "teachable moment." In today's homes, where the pace is frantic, schedules are tight, and parents are physically or emotionally unavailable, there may be no one around or involved enough to impart such lessons. Without her mother's example to fall back on, this six-year-old would not have learned to respond with empathy the next time a peer was in such a position. And as kids get bigger, the issues that estrange them from each other become increasingly more complicated, from not having the right jeans to being overweight or having a different color of skin.

SELF-ESTEEM IS THE NATURAL BY-PRODUCT OF GOOD CHILD-REARING

The whole issue of confidence, popularly known as the self-esteem movement, has attained a trendy, almost cultlike political status. Parents want techniques to bolster their children's self-esteem, but you can't produce self-esteem with "techniques." Self-esteem is a natural by-product of a healthy, productive life lived by fully developed children. Give children the emotional underpinnings necessary to grow and thrive—a solid bonding experience, loving limits, the opportunity to be productive and contribute to the family—and self-esteem will evolve effortlessly. It's really the last thing parents have to worry about when they are doing their jobs. And when it's not there, we have to look at the true cause, not try to fix it with the latest trend, such as lavishing excessive praise on everyday good behavior. Having realistically high self-esteem is far more complicated than just thinking you're good at everything—it's also a matter of knowing your limits and managing them without becoming undone. Self-esteem as portrayed by the current generation of pop psychologists is nothing less than self-worship, narcissism. As the self-esteem movement marches on, we can begin to see that the problems of American children—disaffection, delinquency, poor academic achievement—have multiplied along with it.

Not that indiscriminate gold stars and posters that say "You're Special" are totally to blame for our ills. But in all likelihood, we have set up a generation for failure. According to Maureen Stout, Ph.D., author of *The Feel-Good Curriculum: The Dumbing Down of America's Kids in the Name of Self-Esteem* and a professor of education at the University of British Columbia in Vancouver, the self-esteem movement has been a massive act of self-destruction. Somewhere along the line, social and emotional development has trumped academics.

Stout's pet peeves about the self-esteem movement: sugarcoating assessment, social promotion, lowering expectations, and eliminating competition, not to mention grades. According to the self-esteem movement, we shouldn't assess children's abilities, because if you can't give a child an A, it's going to terrorize her. But grades are not a punishment. They are a helpful and productive tool. And there are ways of doing ongoing assessment—with discussion and reports and portfolios of work—that are less stressful and pressured. Let's not forget, too, that dumbing down curricula has become necessary in many schools because children today are not prepared to meet the academic standards that were the norm thirty years ago.

But once again, it's not just about what's happening at school. We can't dismiss the effect of today's family life. When we work long hours and then, guilt-ridden, try to compensate our children with pointless praise and empty pats on the back, these gestures are not in the best interest of the child or his future. "There is no self-esteem movement in the work world," one shrewd dad told me. "If you present a bad report at the office, your boss isn't going to say, 'Hey, I like the color paper you chose.' Setting kids up like this is doing them a tremendous disservice."

The older the child, the more damage lame encouragement and shallow praise will do. Young children eat up praise of any kind because they don't have the ability to really evaluate their own work, and in the short term it's an effective way to temporarily make them feel good. But by the third or fourth grade, most children start expecting more credible comments. A preteen will suspect you're kissing up or trying to manipulate him in some way.

Praise that rings true to children requires certain characteristics. It must focus on effort and accomplishment ("I noticed you studied really hard for your spelling test, and it paid off— you did better than the one last week"). Never evaluate the self ("You're such a good boy/bad boy"), or you'll push your child further toward yet another aspect of the epidemic: slavish devotion to image. Be real and specific in your praise. Avoid full-throttle pronouncements like, "You are the best helper in the world." Perhaps try something like, "That was a good idea to sort the clean laundry by owner. Now we can put everyone's clothes away faster." Praise also has more impact if it's selective in terms of what is praised and conditional in terms of expecting a certain level of achievement. When it's unexpected, it becomes something really remarkable. In contrast, given too freely, it can produce a "praise junkie," a kid who expects to be complimented for everything, all the time.

If we've learned anything in this theoretical tug-of-war, it's that self-esteem comes from feeling like a worthwhile person, not just from being flattered. It's a by-product of competence, built upon independence and functioning. The catch-22, however, is that those skills are harder for kids to come by today. There's far less opportunity for a pickup game of softball or kick the can, which taught skills like sharing, turn-taking, refereeing, diplomacy, watching out for the little guys, and dealing with the big guys, all matters handled by the kids themselves. You don't get that in the organized team sports and activities children participate in today. The coach tells them what they'll play and when, on a team chosen for them and made up of kids their exact age. Nor, for safety reasons, can most parents just say, "Go out and play and be home for dinner."

Parents today have to create other ways to teach their kids the same skills without that natural framework that once existed. That means returning to regularly scheduled family dinners as often as possible, where kids can learn to set the table or help prepare a meal, and then enjoy the civilizing effect of the give-and-take of dinner conversations. It means playing board games that teach negotiating, sharing, rules, and the etiquette of winning and losing, all features of the larger world they will be entering later. It's the oft-repeated antidote: more family time, more activities like crafts or skating or biking—whatever you and your children enjoy. And certainly less mind-numbing media exposure—when the TV is on, you aren't interacting with each other.

Helping kids set small goals is another critical part of the process. Don't push your first-grade child to read like her best friend, who's already at third-grade level. Get through the beginning books first so that she can gain a sense of personal mastery by being able to compare what she achieved this month with last month.

A father I know named John has firsthand experience with the motivation of success. His ten-year-old daughter, Rebecca, lives with her mother and stepfather in another state and has been afraid to fly by herself when she comes to visit him. John has to fly to her home, collect her, and bring her back. "Rebecca is very shy and has no confidence about trying new things. I've left her alone at a basketball game so I could go to the bathroom and have come back and found her in tears," John notes. "But when she came to visit me last summer, I took her on a hike. She got tired and was really reluctant to finish. I encouraged her to push on, and she did, with great effort and courage. When we got to the top of this mountain, there was a breathtaking view, like being at the top of the Empire State Building. I could see that she was so proud of herself. A short time later she turned to me and said, 'Daddy, I think I can fly home by myself.'"

Therein lies the true secret to emotional growth and high self-esteem: when you achieve something worthwhile, you feel really good. Given the skills to succeed, children will do so without us propping them up, and their self-esteem will develop naturally and obviously. You'll see it clearly when your child is centered, confident, productive, and generous.

LET KIDS CONTRIBUTE

How do you get your child to pitch in? By making the time to let them help at a very early age. You don't have to push preschoolers to pitch in—they're just dying to "help." It begins with pretend play—when they cook in their toy kitchens, toddle around behind plastic vacuum cleaners, hammer away on child-size workbenches. Doing what you do is playtime to them. The trouble is that we have a tendency to spoil their fun when they get excited about a real task: "Not now, honey, I'll do it," is the typical hurried response. But four-year-olds can set the table and transfer laundry from the washer to the dryer, and they just love cleaning lower panes of sliding glass doors (where all their fingerprints are) with a squirt bottle and roll of paper towels. Find the patience for these activities and they quickly grow into making their own beds and picking up their dirty laundry. It's just a matter of exercising their productivity muscles so they don't atrophy. Give in to the pleas of "I hate taking out the garbage," and you'll raise a whiner with a bad attitude. Tell him instead, "Well, we can't live with it piling up; it's your turn this week, so go to it," and you'll be teaching your child to work with the circumstances life doles out. Remember, your child's natural inclination is to bond with you. Helping out is another way to do that because it involves spending time with you and earning your appreciation.

The best motivation is to structure situations that encourage children's naturally occurring positive behaviors, then reward them for acting appropriately. If your child keeps complaining that he's too tired to pick up his room and you let him get away with not doing it, he's going to whine the next time you tell him to do something. But if you encourage the child who helps out, he will want to help. Let's say your son is hungry for dinner. You might tell him, "If you help me set the table and clean the lettuce in the salad spinner, we will be able to eat sooner." He's likely to do so, and you can then respond, "You were such a big help this evening, I think we should have an extra bedtime story!" (And if he doesn't want to help, the natural consequence, of course, is that he remains hungry longer.) That's how those dolphins in the last chapter learned to do incredible stunts. And, yes, a free fish now and then helps too.

THE PROS AND CONS OF ALLOWANCES

As kids get older, the subject of money naturally enters into family transactions. They need it, you have it—do you give it to them or insist that they earn it? This is a complicated and contextually sensitive question, and one that should be given careful thought by every family. Children need to learn the value of money and how to manage it. But they also should be expected to make certain contributions to the family *without being paid.* My personal feeling is that parents should require chores starting at a young age, *and without payment,* so that children can view themselves as active participants in the family. Even preschool-age children can pick up their toys, put their laundry away, help clear the dinner table, and sweep a floor with a broom. As they grow bigger and you are ready to impart some lessons about the value of money, begin to provide a reasonable level of allowance for your particular community. But avoid characterizing it as a payment for chores.

It's also important that you be very clear about what your child's allowance is to be used for. Explain that you will no longer fund items that everyone agrees should be paid from the allowance, such as those extra snacks she wants from the cafeteria vending machine, or those Saturday trips to the batting cages, or a trip to the movie theater. If your child is interested in a bigger purchase—say, a clothing item, a new CD player, or even a pet hamster—use it as an opportunity to teach about savings. You may set up an arrangement with her whereby she puts aside a little each week until she has enough, or you can allow her to earn some extra money by doing additional jobs beyond the call of duty. Then, after she saves up enough for, say, the hamster, you may feel like rewarding her achievement by supplying the cage and water bottle. When children have to use their own money for expenditures, they come to understand that the allowance is not free of attached responsibilities. They learn from allowance the value of money management and quickly learn to budget purchases.

Of course, the day will come when your child asks how he can earn more money for bigger purchases. Offering your child the option of doing beyond-the-call-of-duty jobs—such as taking over the lawn care instead of hiring an outside service to do it—is one way to handle this. You might suggest: "I was going to hire someone to mow the lawn for the summer, but if you want to earn the money by doing it yourself, you can. Just be aware that I expect the same frequency and quality of work." In such a situation you should also set some ground rules for what your child will be permitted to spend the money on, since making a larger purchase is a great way to teach responsibility. Explain to your child the value of shopping around for the best price, watching for sales, and saving up for bigger purchases rather than repeatedly spending small amounts at the candy store. Such role modeling will condition your kids to not spend their earnings frivolously.

After you've dealt with this for a while, you'll be an old hand at allowance issues, and it will be easier to see when exceptions can be made and when you should toe the line. I have heard of parents who offer incentives to their child—for example, not to smoke: "If you never smoke a cigarette, I'll buy you a car or pay for a trip when you turn twenty-one." (Research shows that kids are far less likely to take up smoking if they have gone this long without trying it.) And, you know, it can work beautifully.

Be sure you avoid creating an inflated sense of entitlement. Children shouldn't think they will automatically get the hottest high-tech games as soon as they come out, or a new car the minute they turn sixteen. It's one thing if your child needs and is capable of earning the money for a big share of a used car that will make a better job possible. When your child insists that everyone else has a new and sexy car, you might reply, "I don't care if everyone at school has a Rolls-Royce." Remember, some children will naturally try for everything they see, but don't necessarily expect to get it. When you give in easily to every whim, you create expectations rather than appreciating an occasional and delightful treat.

The following "Real Rules of Life," perhaps apocryphal, are attributed on the Internet to a speech given by Microsoft founder and CEO Bill Gates to a graduating class of high school students. I found them amusing and worthwhile.

RULE 1
Life is not fair—get used to it.

RULE 2
The world won't care about your self-esteem. The world will expect you to accomplish something *before* you feel good about yourself.

RULE 3

You will *not* make $40,000 a year right out of high school. You won't be a vice president with a car phone until you earn both.

RULE 4

If you think your teacher is tough, wait till you get a boss. He doesn't have tenure.

RULE 5

Flipping burgers is not beneath your dignity. Your grandparents had a different word for burger-flipping—they called it opportunity.

RULE 6

If you mess up, it's not your parents' fault, so don't whine about your mistakes—learn from them.

RULE 7

Before you were born, your parents weren't as boring as they are now. They got that way from paying your bills, cleaning your clothes, and listening to you talk about how cool you are. So before you save the rain forest from the parasites of your parents' generation, try delousing the closet in your own room.

RULE 8

Your school may have done away with winners and losers, but life has not. In some schools they have abolished failing grades, and they'll give you as many times as you want to get the right answer. This doesn't bear the slightest resemblance to *anything* in real life.

RULE 9

Life is not divided into semesters. You don't get summers off, and very few employers are interested in helping you find yourself. Do that on your own time.

RULE 10

Television is *not* real life. In real life people actually have to leave the coffee shop and go to jobs.

RULE 11

Be nice to nerds. Chances are you'll end up working for one.

HOW IS MY CHILD DOING?

Children pick up on ethical behavior remarkably early when it's role-modeled for them. Here's a timeline to guide you—and them—in values development.

- *Six to twelve months:* Your baby should enjoy smiling, interacting, and sharing positive exchanges with you. She's learning that making you happy makes her feel good too. A willingness to accept routines is also indicative of a secure sense of self, the basis from which all value judgments will stem. She will begin to aggressively explore by touching, poking, pulling. When she goes too far and becomes inappropriate or destructive, she should be gently stopped.
- *Twelve to eighteen months:* Your toddler should be learning to demonstrate kindness to others, like offering you one of his animal crackers or patting you gently if you are hurt. Again, he may get aggressive when excited or curious, and should be stopped, a little more firmly, when kicking, pulling, grabbing, or the like. Demonstrate for your child how to pat, rather than hit, someone or something he wants to touch.
- *Eighteen months to two years:* The ability to demonstrate empathy continues to expand as your child finally grows to realize that even though pulling hair or grabbing your glasses is fun for her, it hurts or is irritating to you. Unprovoked manifestations of hostile behavior should not be tolerated with siblings or strangers at

the playground. When you show dissatisfaction with her behavior, she may start to cry or look forlorn. Your discomfort, in essence, provokes her distress. Early manners (saying "please" and "thank you") should be inculcated and expected.

- *Three to four years:* Preschool children should be developing an increasing ability to share their toys, wait their turn, and listen respectfully, at least most of the time. They should also be able to control their urges to hit, grab, kick, or engage in other antisocial behaviors when they don't get their way.

- *Four to six years:* As children enter school age, they should be expected more and more to take care of their belongings (hang their coats up, bring their toys in after playing outside, cap their markers so they don't dry out, and so on). They should also know the Golden Rule ("Do unto others . . .) and be reminded of it as necessary.

- *Five to seven years:* Yes, this age group still breaks rules, but in general they should be very aware of expectations and happy to comply with them, and in fact proud of themselves when they do. They're also chagrined when caught. They understand that it's wrong to lie and can accept the justice of their parents' indignation.

- *Seven and up:* Your school-age child should be learning tact and should care about her impact on other people when dealing with both peers and adults. It's time to call your child's attention to callous comments or teasing. Conversely, these children are starting to develop strong feelings of loyalty to friends and to stand up for them if they are being ostracized or bullied. Children this age who have a sound moral foundation want to be good because they know it's the right thing to do, not just out of fear of being caught. They should be interested in helping out others less fortunate and willing to perform small acts of community service, such as collecting for a food drive or cleaning up a park. Preteens and older children should demonstrate a sound work ethic, looking forward to baby-sitting, lifeguarding, or mowing lawns to earn some money and save.

7
Don't Touch That Dial!

Knowing is not enough; we must apply. Willing is not
enough; we must do."

—Johann von Goethe

YOU MAY FEEL LIKE skipping this chapter, and for good reason: it will
be downright painful at times, because what I am about to say
could well require as big a change in your lifestyle as any other
aspect of parenting we've covered so far. The fact that television
and children are a toxic mix is hardly news. What is news is that
children are watching and interacting with TV and other media
even more hours per day in the face of mounting, indisputable evidence that it interferes with their neurological, psychological, and
emotional development. We know that passive watching is nothing
less than poison to their impressionable minds, yet no one seems
willing to pull the plug. The real question is: How much media
exposure can children endure before it becomes detrimental, and
how can we improve the context and quality to make it more consistent with children's growth and health?

Watchdog organizations—such as the American Academy of
Pediatrics and the Center for Media Education—provide their
own "media dosage" guidelines, but these organizations do so

with certain limitations: their decisions are reached through consensus and are designed to offend the least number of people. Yes, they have the interests of children at heart—but they must also consider the businesses that support them financially, and government representatives are influenced by lobbyists.

The media management plan I lay out for you here will be challenging, perhaps even brutal at times. It is presented only in the very best interest of your child's future development, as well as your family relationships. By being aware of the risks, you and your child will learn to enjoy and benefit from the media, without the risk of mental and physical damage that is the inevitable result of media addiction and abuse.

A BRIEF HISTORY OF TV AND THE FAMILY

Let's begin by taking a hard look at the history of television in family life. In the late 1970s an advertising executive named Jerry Mander wrote a very impressive, thoroughly researched, scholarly book entitled *Four Arguments for the Elimination of Television*. Mander claims that excessive TV watching deadens the mind by bypassing the thinking process and leaving viewers in a hypnotic, bored-yet-hyperactive state. At that time television was on for a shocking eight hours a day in the average American home with children, and studies were already beginning to emerge that pointed to a decline in children's memory and verbal skills.

Around the same time journalist Marie Winn made similar accusations in her groundbreaking book *The Plug-In Drug: Television, Children, & the Family.* Winn and Mander were the first critics to awaken parents to the fact that the problem is not just *what* programs children are watching, but also the very *act* of viewing. The *Christian Scientist Monitor* declared, "If you have children who watch television, you owe it to yourself—and them—to read this book." The *Washington Post* said, "She must be listened to. She has got hold of something so big that it has escaped the rest of us."

But did many people actually do anything about the prevalence of TV in their lives, not to mention the mediocrity of the programming? Hardly. The tentacles of cable were groping their way into the American home. This was the era of *Charlie's Angels, Dallas,* and *All in the Family.* By the mid-1980s, *Dynasty* ruled the airwaves, and soon baby boomer parents were planning their week around angst-ridden episodes of *Thirtysomething.* Preschoolers had become the largest viewing audience of all, according to Winn's research, spending anywhere from twenty-two to fifty-four hours a week in front of the TV. Still, parents were quick to rationalize this orgy of watching because they were "educational" programs, such as *Sesame Street* and *Mister Rogers' Neighborhood.*

The TV activists who were most vocal in these days—a grass-roots organization known as Action for Children's Television (ACT)—also focused their efforts on requiring the media industry and government to mandate quality children's programming. In 1990 they succeeded in getting the Children's Television Act passed. This federal legislation required stations to demonstrate how they were serving the educational and informational needs of children. Under the Children's Television Act, some of this programming had to be "specifically designed" to educate. Stations were obliged to inform the FCC, as part of their license renewal process, how they were fulfilling this new mandate. Another part of the Children's Television Act placed some limits on the number of commercials that could air on children's television.

The less-than-objective media portrayed the Children's Television Act as a major accomplishment at the time, but it was really nothing more than a smoke screen that allowed parents to continue their excessive use of TV as baby-sitter. In wisely noting in her book that ACT's premise was fallacious, Winn quotes one of the organization's founders: "We came to the realization that children watch a great deal of television that is not particularly designed for them, that parents have a perfect right to ask those responsible for such programs aimed at the young to meet the specific needs of children, for at least a couple of hours during the day or evening."

Winn then goes on to ask: "But is it the specific needs of *children* that are at stake when parents demand better programming? Surely the fact that young children watch so much television reflects the needs of *parents* to find a convenient source of amusement for their children and a moment of quiet for themselves. When parents work to improve children's programming, it is their own need that underlies their actions, to assuage their anxieties about the possible effects of those hours of quiet, passive television watching on their children. It makes parents feel less guilty, perhaps, if those hours, at least, seem 'educational.'"

Let's face facts here: if industry executives and children's television activists were truly planning for the best educational interests of children, they would take kids' programming off the air altogether. What's really in their best interest is to not watch TV at all. Why should we believe that anyone who is making money by generating addictive entertainment for children has their best interests at heart?

Believing its job done, ACT disbanded in 1992, but the law it helped to pass was practically unenforceable, as loophole after loophole was added. In another bow to parental and political pressure, the television industry, already proven incapable of policing itself, created a rating system in 1997. Participating networks now flash a rating symbol in the first fifteen seconds of a program in the upper left corner indicating age level (TV-Y is appropriate for children as young as two, TV-Y7 means it's suitable only for children over age seven, and so on) and whether the content contains sex (S), violence (V), or crude or inappropriate language (L). Of course, this rating system assumes that the parent is watching in those first fifteen seconds and will flip the channel when necessary. That's not terribly likely when you consider that the Henry J. Kaiser Family Foundation, a public health group that monitors the news media, has found that children ages two to seven watch TV without their parents present 81 percent of the time; that figure skyrockets to 95 percent for kids eight and up.

The same survey did find that more than 54 percent of parents said they were using the content ratings to determine program suitability for children, but that still leaves close to half of all children in this country pretty much watching whatever they want. And that's if you can even believe the parents. When the Kaiser Family Foundation surveyed the actual children doing the watching, they tended to report much less supervision than their parents claimed. In fact, the kids themselves reported spending close to five and a half hours a day—six and three-quarters for kids over age eight—using media outside of school, which includes TV, computers, video games, movies, music, and print media. And I'd certainly be willing to bet that reading books, newspapers, and magazines comes dead last in forms of "media usage."

As part of the sugarcoating of what was really a terrible situation, Congress also passed a law requiring that all new TVs be equipped with a "V-chip," a device that allows parents to block inappropriate programs. The idea behind all this activity was that parents could watch for the ratings and then block out shows they deemed inappropriate for their family. But again, according to the Kaiser Family Foundation, most parents aren't using the V-chip either. Approximately 40 percent of all households now own TVs containing V-chips, yet half the owners don't even realize it, and of those who are aware of the V-chip, only about one-third use it, the foundation's nationwide survey estimates. That means that fewer than 10 percent of all parents nationwide are bothering with the V-chip, the group estimates.

Movie ratings are equally unreliable. I recently rented a film called *Focus* that had a PG-13 rating. This movie opens with the most brutal rape and murder scene that one can imagine. I couldn't believe the rating. It was a very good motion picture; I do not in any way want to disparage it. But I cannot understand why anyone would think it a good idea to have a thirteen-year-old see this sadistic scene. The point is that ratings from the movie industry cannot be taken seriously, and I suggest that you talk to someone you respect who has seen a movie before you turn your kid over to it.

In addition to the programming columns published in local

newspapers everywhere, a credible source online for reviews of children's TV, movies, videos, and software is www.parents-chice.org. This is the website of the nonprofit Parents' Choice Awards group, which has been evaluating toys and media for children for two decades now. To investigate video games, websites, and software, try www.esrb.org, the website for the Entertainment Software Rating Board. The Parents Television Council also provides a website (www.parentstv.org) that gives thorough descriptions of content on primetime network shows, with an overall red-, yellow-, or green-light rating.

While the descriptions are generally accurate, you will have to consider the appropriateness of any media offering for your children in view of your individual family value system. For instance, one mother I know was surprised to find that a "family show"—so considered because it was free of violence and foul language—had an episode in which a teenage pregnancy was treated as a normal occurrence, and she found herself having to explain to her eight-year-old something that she knew the child wasn't ready for.

MAXIMUM MEDIA, MINIMAL PARENTING

What it comes down to is this: government-mandated tools like the V-chip are nothing but bureaucratic attempts to solve the continuing problem of absent and inattentive parents. They're designed to make parents feel okay about what they're doing to their children. Yes, parents complain mightily and worry incessantly about the effects of the media on their kids, but most are unwilling or afraid to turn it off. We don't need research to tell us about the popularity of home satellite dishes and cable services that provide access to literally hundreds of channels. Or about the morphing of TVs from little black boxes into wall-size screens of movie theater proportions. And what's the latest remodeling trend? The "home theater," complete with stadium seating. Do you even know a middle- or upper-middle-class child who doesn't have a home computer or video game system? Both the TV versions of Nintendo and PlayStation and the portable handheld models are de rigueur by the time kids reach the age of four or five.

It's almost as if the more bad news we get about media influence in children's lives, the more lax parents become about allowing kids to overdose on it. What possesses these parents, who most definitely know better? The simplest explanation, as Winn said more than twenty years ago, is that they need to keep kids busy. But watching TV is hardly the only way to keep them busy. Why are parents choosing it, then? Because it's easy, because cultural pressures push it, because they feel the need to conform to the lifestyles around them. They are unprepared to parent in the way that is best for their children—the harder, more demanding, more involved way—so they rationalize taking the easy route. They've been assured by our toxic society that it's okay, everyone is doing it. It's similar to how we once viewed smoking—everyone knew it was bad, but no one stopped. Yet as we look deeper into this issue, we can see that it's also about diminishing and obscuring the very need for parenting. All that electronic entertainment replaces the need for Mom and Dad and—most unfortunately—that loving, communicative dance in which children grow, develop literacy, and become able to learn and manage themselves in a productive way.

This situation is very clearly illustrated by the current trend toward putting TVs and entertainment systems in vehicles. When my children were young, we used to go on camping trips to Idaho and Montana. The ride from our home in Berkeley, California, would take as long as fourteen hours, and to get through some difficult moments my wife and I would spend some time in turn-riding in the backseat with the kids. It was clear to us that we had to establish a family scene that was worthwhile. If we left the kids alone back there, they would gradually devolve into bickering and annoying each other. So there were periods of time when we would chat, involve them in singing and word games, or read a book with them. Then for a while we would leave the kids to themselves, coloring or dozing or whatever, and later we'd get involved again.

Sometimes one child would sit up front. As the trip went on and on, the kids would need more support, and we had to improvise more intensely. Periodic pit stops helped break the tedium of the confinement. But overall they were participants in the trip—rather than just passive baggage—and they benefited from being part of it.

What is the point of describing this scenario? The introduction of electronic entertainment has made it unnecessary to do the hard but important work of parenting. Without the boredom of a trip, parents are spared having to find creative ways to deal with an uncomfortable and unusual circumstance. This captures the essential problem of overreliance on media: it helps us avoid the uncertainty and the frustration of challenging situations. Parents are being helped to become so isolated that even in what should be an intimate family scene, each sits in his or her own bubble—the child immersed in media and the mother or father on the cell phone or listening to talk radio or music.

Why we do this now is not clear. Yes, our lives these days can be frantic, but driving in a car offers one of those few times when we don't feel we have to be running around—when we have minutes or hours together with our families with no other obligation than to get from here to there and enjoy one another's company while we're doing it. This is a time when families could be cozy and close. But we have become so afraid of tension or discomfort that it's just easier to anesthetize our children and often ourselves. As children are left more and more alone to improvise their lives in day care and various extended school experiences, there's often no chance to build up that body of association that leads to shared memories of good and bad times, family jokes, favorite songs and word games, and an atmosphere in which fantasies and news can be shared. We are reducing family life to the point that parents and siblings are physically sharing the same space but otherwise having no real relationship with each other.

The situation gets worse as the children get older. TV watching starts as an excuse for parents to carve out a little precious time for themselves or as a convenient baby-sitter when parents are trying to field e-mails from the office. Then they don't have the energy to say no when the child balks at turning it off. Eventually more sophisticated electronic entertainment becomes an easy way for parents to avoid interaction—especially the negative kind—when they're just too tired to handle it. And don't forget that they are trying to deal with difficult children who are not fully attached and trained; it is much more difficult for them at this stage than for parents who have been committed from the beginning. They give up when they can't get along with their kids, then drown out their discomfort by hiding in front of their own bedroom TVs, leaving the kids to their own devices, literally and figuratively. Just when parent-child communication becomes the most critical, it breaks down, and children listen to the confusing messages of a toxic culture instead.

MEDIA MIND GAMES

The messages children begin to view over and over in both programmed content and advertisements are:

- It's okay to use fighting and other forms of aggression to deal with conflict.
- Using slang, bad grammar, and even curses is the acceptable way to communicate with peers.
- Cigarettes and alcohol are cool and attractive.
- Thin is definitely in, but fattening snacks and fast food are the most delicious.
- Everyone is having sex, and there are no negative consequences, such as disease or unintended pregnancy.
- Behaving disrespectfully toward adults and peers is both acceptable and another way to look cool.
- It's okay to pretend to be someone you're not when you're just a screen name and no one can really find out.

The underlying intent of commercial interests is nothing less than to kidnap your child, to trap him in the world of consumerism, triviality, and passivity. If you don't fight, they will win. They operate through the media and use computers so they can have their message beamed twenty-four hours a day: be the first kid on your block, don't miss out, every kid will want what you have, you can look and feel important by buying and eating or wearing this product.

Creators of programs thinly disguised as "educational" bombard children with commercials for products based on the characters featured in the programs themselves. Even the public television programs are big money earners for their stations, with prestigious donor corporations playing the pretend game of being good to children when they're really buying the goodwill of parents for products. These executives are no different from those at major networks and movie studios. They get rewarded if they produce programming that captures your children for more hours a day. They are vampires preying on children.

The worst part is that they use TV to enroll your child in consumerism behind your back. When they are advertising junk food to your child in shows that they know you will not see, they don't want you to have a free selective choice. When you go to the store, they want you to be confronted by a begging, whining kid who will make your life a misery until you buy what he wants. If you are a wishy-washy parent who can't easily say no, you're in big trouble—and so is your kid.

Parents need to strike back. If you understand that producers of programs for kids are more akin to tobacco company executives than child welfare professionals, you will find it easier to stop buying their products no matter what your kids say. Look how consumers brought the powerful Nike corporation to its knees by refusing to buy their shoes when it was revealed they were being made in sweatshops. You can strike a blow for decency toward children by boycotting this sort of TV programming and all the related merchandise.

Incidentally, the Parents Television Council website I mentioned (www.parentstv.org) also rates the best and worst advertisers in terms of their sponsorship of good-quality family programming. Companies are given points when their ads appear on wholesome, family-friendly shows and lose points for advertising during what the group calls "raunchy" shows—those that have the worst ratings by the council. Some companies, such as Wal-Mart, appear to go out of their way to advertise only during family-friendly programming. Others, like Disney and McDonald's, run their ads equally during good and bad programming. And perhaps most tellingly of all, big media companies—Sony in particular—tend to spend much of their advertising dollars on the raunchy programming. But don't be taken in by any notion of "better." TV-watching is not beneficial for your child unless you are doing it together as a social experience on a special occasion. A little entertainment is fine—just don't kid yourself that it's educational.

THE EFFECTS OF MEDIA ADDICTION ON DIET AND HEALTH

Childhood obesity is another side effect associated with overuse of media. There's more than enough research to document that excessive participation in sedentary activities like watching TV and playing video games leads to weight gain, and obesity among American children has reached epidemic proportions largely because of these pastimes. Weight gain around the abdomen is a symptom of a dangerous metabolic condition called insulin resistance, which is often a precursor to type 2, or adult onset, diabetes. This disease had previously been found only in older people, but alarmingly, physicians are now diagnosing it in children. Not surprisingly, it is aggravated by large doses of carbohydrates, candy, soda, and trans-fatty acids derived from the shortening and hydrogenated oil in snacks. Unaware or preoccupied parents fail to communicate to their children the value of productive accomplishment and discipline, so they sit unattended and passive in front of electronic entertainment, soothing themselves with sweet, fatty treats while life goes on around them but without them. And commercial interests continue to prey on these weaknesses. Like everything else we discuss in this book, not teaching your child proper diet and fitness habits increases the risk to your child's well-being—in this case, his physical as well as his emotional health.

I know that you are aware of this. Management of your child's eating presents all the same challenges as management of dating and sexuality, smoking, behaving responsibly with a car, and the like. It's another aspect of moral training: children need to learn the self-discipline necessary to eat the right foods and at the right times, and to respect their bodies so that they can later resist drugs, alcohol, and other physically toxic temptations. Like everything else I've discussed, risks and problems will be reduced by informing your child and role-modeling smart eating and exercise habits: serve plenty of fruits and vegetables, avoid sodas and snacks (don't even keep them in the house), and make time for physical activity every day, even if it is just an after-dinner walk.

THE LITERACY LETDOWN

As bad as these media messages are, there's another critical, often overlooked side effect: the damage that excessive media use is doing to our children's ability to learn. It has been widely reported that academic achievement is lower in children who watch more TV. Many researchers in neuroscience have long believed that the growing problem of children's brief attention span can be blamed on overexposure to the recurring cuts, edits, zooms, pans, and sudden noises the media provide—viewers are left craving more and constant stimulation.

According to Gloria DeGaetano, M.Ed., author of *Screen Smarts: A Family Guide to Media Literacy,* the earlier children acquire a passive TV habit, the more likely it is that their attention span will not develop normally. In her report "Visual Media and

Young Children's Attention Spans," published by the *Media Literacy Review,* the Media Literacy Online Project of the College of Education of the University of Oregon at Eugene, she writes: "Young children can be entrained to keep watching TV. The faster pace of the images they are watching, the more likely they will keep watching and the more likely the child's attention span will be jerked around."

A similar interference with development comes from the reset button on video games. When a child doesn't like the outcome of a game, he simply erases it and starts over. There is no need to attempt to rectify or improve a situation; the repetition leads to greater video game skill but gives him no real opportunity to study and learn, as a hobby like coin collecting or model airplane building does. If a child spends his allowance on a coin that proves worthless, he learns to do more research the next time around. You can't "disappear" a bad purchase.

Perhaps one of the most devastating effects of what education and media literacy professor Diane Levin, Ph.D., calls our "remote control childhood" is the declining state of literacy among children in this country. I don't mean they *can't* read—although that's certainly becoming a problem as well—but even those who manage to sound out words don't fully understand them. In psychologist Jane Healy's 1990 book *Endangered Minds: Why Children Don't Think and What We Can Do About It,* she surveyed teachers nationwide regarding their observations of their students' capabilities, and they unanimously responded that reading, writing, and oral skills were declining along with attention spans, even in the best and supposedly brightest neighborhoods. Classic classroom literature for middle and high school students such as *The Scarlet Letter, A Tale of Two Cities,* and *Evangeline* were proving beyond the reading skills of these students. One teacher reported that her high school seniors were graduating at lower reading levels than those of her junior high students in 1970. And this research was conducted in the late 1980s, mind you—before the advent of home computers, the Internet, and Game Boy. Imagine the state of literacy *now,* more than a decade later, with children receiving far more electronic information overload. According to the 1998 National Assessment of Educational Progress, 52 percent of twelfth-graders who watch an hour or less of TV a day read proficiently, whereas only 27 percent of those who watch four to five hours do. Only 14 percent who watch more than six hours read proficiently.

It seems obvious that if kids are watching TV, they're not spending the time reading, but let's also not forget that they're not *talking* either. "The brains of today's children are being structured in language patterns antagonistic to the values and goals of formal education. . . . The culprit is diminished and degraded exposure to the forms of good, meaningful language that enable us to converse with others, with the written word, and with our own minds," writes Healy in *Endangered Minds*. "The results are inevitable: declining literacy, falling test scores, faltering or circuitous oral expression, ineptitude with the written word that extends from elementary schools into the incoming ranks of professionals." While TV gets the lion's share of the blame, of course, Healy is quick to note that it's really but one symptom of the problem. Everything from stereo headphones to computer games to books on tape contributes, not to mention the sheer cacophony of our fast-paced frantic lives. "How can children bombarded from birth by the noise of the adult world learn to reflect, analyze, ponder?" she asks. "How can they use quiet inner conversations to build personal realities, sharpen and extend their visual reasoning? These qualities are embedded in brains by the experiences a society chooses for its children. What are we choosing for ours?"

Parents who choose to recognize the current state of media saturation and do something about it can clearly see the positive results in their children. Brenda, a mother of ten-year-old twin boys, gave me a heartening description of what her active media management has done for her children:

> My sons didn't start watching TV until they were three, and
> for the most part, the TV stays off during the week. They do

have a half day of school on Tuesdays, and if homework is done, they can watch an hour or two that day. I also monitor what they watch, which is pretty much limited to sports and Disney. I believe, and others have commented on the fact, that their reduced exposure to TV has contributed to both boys being self-entertainers, creative, excellent readers, and quite verbal. I have rarely heard either of them say, "I'm bored," and if they do it's usually because they've been playing too much electronics.

In recent years I've clearly explained to them why I limit their TV. I've told them that I notice more bad behavior when they watch more TV or play more Nintendo, and when that happens all electronics (which they understand to be computer, video games, and TV) are turned off indefinitely, even on the weekends. Conversely, if I feel that they've had a particularly tough day, or week, I will let them watch TV—I understand the need to "veg out" at times, and it doesn't always relate to a calendar.

Last summer I experimented during the first week of vacation. I didn't limit any TV, video, or computer games. It was a disaster: they played video games for hours, fought over the controls, ignored anything we said to them. My sweet boys completely disappeared. After that week I told them the electronics were being turned off indefinitely. And I stuck to it. Every so often I would reward them for good behavior with electronics, but rarely because they had asked me to. If they asked, the answer was always no, and so they stopped asking. Within a day they had rediscovered their building and construction toys, playing sports in the driveway, reading (one son read all four Harry Potter books in five weeks—2,200 pages!), drawing, and goofing around with our dogs.

CRITICAL MOMENT: Brenda recognized when the lack of limitation of media use was spiraling out of control, her sons' behavior was negatively affected. She quickly reinstated her rules and was rewarded with the return of creativity, responsibility, and respect in her sons.

MEDIA AS A SUBSTITUTE FOR FRIENDSHIP

Two other important developmental areas that tend to be negatively affected by media use are social and emotional growth. If children are focused exclusively on solitary, isolating experiences, they aren't interacting with their peers, sharing feelings, and practicing social skills and behavior control. Indeed, the Kaiser Family Foundation has found in its research that children ages eight to eighteen who are "heavy" media users—spending more than ten and a half hours a day involved in some form of media—score lower on a "contentedness" index. That is, they are less likely to report that they have a lot of friends, are happy at school, get along with their parents, or don't get into trouble a lot, and they are more likely to report being bored, sad, or unhappy. Conversely, I believe the child who had his full dose of motherese, who is used to regular dialogue and dinner conversation, who comes home from school bursting with news for his parents about what happened that day, will crave those sorts of productive interactions and not settle for isolated media activity.

Children can't possibly have time for meaningful relationships if they are in school six or seven hours a day, plugged into an electronic device another ten, and sleeping the rest of the time. And if they spend their early years in this manner, it's likely they will never learn how to form peer relationships in the first place. According to the research, one out of every six kids falls into this subset of heavy media users. That's about 16 percent of kids from third grade to high school who are well on the way to becoming isolated, alienated, distant, and unattached in their relationships to parents, teachers, and classmates—and by definition, to society.

The level of risk for these children is very high. When children are abstracted from life—psychologically structured so that reality is vague, more like a television image, and at a distance so that it is not fully real—the consequences of their actions are totally divorced from the action itself. Think of the shadow world of symbols portrayed in the movie *The Matrix*. To some children who have grown to live in such a state of abstraction, the shooting of people is merely a different form of video game. They act as though one could simply press a restart button and the mess and the consequences would disappear. In the game they can start over and over again, steadily gaining skill in indiscriminate, relentless, determined slaughter. But in real life they are left with blood and bodies on the ground.

When these kids are forced to go out into the world and interact, they may well do it in the way they have been taught by the media. Expressing themselves with verbal and physical aggression gives them in real life the same sort of payoff as watching *X-Men* or *Pokémon*. More than one thousand research studies over a thirty-year period have documented the fact that TV violence influences aggressive behavior in some children. That seems like an obvious outcome when you consider that the typical preschooler watching two hours of cartoons a day views ten thousand acts of violence annually, according to the National Television Violence Study (NTVS), the largest and most detailed analysis of TV content ever undertaken. This study also found that for preschoolers, who are not yet able to fully distinguish fantasy from reality, violence comes across as necessary, painless, and even desirable. Indeed, research has documented the fact that as children get older they become more detached in their opinions and analysis of the violent acts they hear about on the news, and why wouldn't they as it more and more becomes the norm in their lives?

The American Academy of Pediatrics, which has become increasingly vocal about the negative effects of media on children's lives, now counsels its members to question parents about media use when children have problems relating to weight gain, sleep, or behavior. Just as we can't know the exact dose level of alcohol it will take to damage a person physically, we don't know the exact amount of time it takes for a child to become injured by the media. But we do have evidence to say after a very specific amount of exposure—often as little as two or three hours—many children begin to react to it in negative ways. As parents, we need to catch these reactions and stem them as early as possible. Consider Penny's story:

> My three-year-old son, Eric, loves Power Rangers and has a couple of the plastic action figures I bought him. I bribed him to hold up his little sister for our Christmas picture, which he did happily upon learning he could get a Power Ranger toy. I know, not the best mothering skills, but sometimes you resort to that kind of stuff in desperation! Eric has seen the Power Ranger show, but it is very violent, and I found he was having a lot of night terrors. He is a very imaginative little guy, and watching these shows just sends him over the edge. He would sit in front of the TV for hours if I let him—even all day. He loves Cartoon Network and picks it over PBS any day. The straw that broke the camel's back was when he asked me for some cereal because it was "part of a good breakfast!"
>
> After that I disconnected the cable, got rid of the VCR so he couldn't view the Power Ranger tapes, and bought a DVD player. I explained to Eric that they do not have all those kid shows on DVD, so we can't rent them. I only allow him to see G-rated movies and PBS now. It took a couple of days of him pleading to put the TV on, but when he saw his old cable favorites wouldn't work anymore, he stopped asking for it so much. Now he is spending more time with his toys and tormenting his sister (usually when I am trying to cook dinner or talk on the phone). It is certainly harder when I am trying to get things done, but Eric is sleeping and eating better and is less fractious with the TV off.
>
> I find the house much quieter, actually calm. As a family, we are more connected and focused. The TV is a great baby-sitter, and I miss it, but we just went too far

over the edge. I am sure some families can control it better than we did. For us, turning the damn thing off has been the best solution. At the end of the day now we just listen to music and read and, you know, actually have a conversation—what a strange concept!

CRITICAL MOMENT: Penny recognized early on that Eric was proving to be unable to handle megadoses of media. In many homes aggressive behavior and sleep disturbances simply seem a part of everyday life. As I've noted in earlier chapters, parents who have abdicated control are used to complicated bedtime routines, nighttime wakenings, temper tantrums, hitting, bullying, and other antisocial behaviors in their children. Thus, these early deviant behaviors have grown "normal" in many homes, right along with excessive media exposure.

As with the violence-media connection, research is proving the correlation between sleep problems and excessive media use too. A team of pediatric sleep researchers headed by Judith A. Owens, M.D., of Brown University surveyed the parents of 495 children ages kindergarten through fourth grade and found that increased overall daily television viewing, and specifically viewing just before bedtime, was associated with bedtime resistance, sleep onset delay, anxiety around sleep, and short sleep duration. The shortest path to these sorts of sleep difficulties is to put a TV in the child's bedroom, Owens and her team found. In fact, one-quarter of the parents she surveyed reported that their child had a TV in his or her bedroom. Other surveys have reported that nearly one-third of kids ages two to seven, and half of the overall population of two- to eighteen-year-olds, have TVs in their rooms.

It's easy to imagine what TV does to the brain as children sit mesmerized in a trancelike state on the couch. It's also easy to see what violent video and computer games do: users work themselves into a frenzy, complete with red faces, sweaty brows, and bulging eyes. "I killed him! I killed him!" ten-year-olds report excitedly to their moms and dads, who respond, "Uh-huh," as they pass through the family room or glance up briefly from their laptops. With blood spurting and body parts flying, some of these video games are nothing but the pornography of aggressive impulses, designed to produce a path of distorted emotional discharge. But settling into a pattern of easily trig-gered violent actions is hardly consonant with a life that works well in our society. There are very few circumstances in the real world in which we don't have to modulate our emotions, and allowing children the freedom to act out violence instead of put-ting the brakes on aggression is the same as permitting an addic-tion to drugs or alcohol to form. A responsible parent surely wouldn't give a young child these games, just as they wouldn't permit the children to view pornography on TV or in a maga-zine. But as these children grow and adult supervision continues to decrease, access becomes increasingly easy and the addiction festers.

The violence of contemporary electronic media is not analo-gous to the violence of pre-electronic days. Batman's punches were laced with *zowies!* and *zams!* that at some level allowed us to identify with a good hero winning over evil, but without our participating in or identifying with sadistic violent impulses. Today's game controls, on the other hand, actually hook your motor system and emotional circuits in with the violent acts and become far more dangerous.

Of course, it's natural for us all to seek pleasure in our lives. Indeed, we're structured to react physically to things we enjoy, with our feel-good brain chemicals increasing in response to a pleasurable activity. But part of your job as a parent is to teach your child to discover the kinds of pleasures that are consistent with a productive and constructive lifestyle, pleasures that lead to continuing satisfaction rather than difficulties. You don't want your children to learn to trigger pleasurable and ecstatic responses from drugs, gorging, gambling, pornography, or promiscuity. Children need to be shown that they can derive their pleasure fix from a loving connection with another human being, from the accomplishments of work, from caring for a pet, and from doing good deeds. These are all pleasures that don't erode our personalities the way addictive habits and stimulations do. Parents need to train children so their neurological machinery picks out the loving, productive pleasures in life.

MEDIA IN MODERATION

You probably think I'm going to tell you to pull the plug on everything electronic in your home. I'm not going to do that. There's much that's good about the media: we learn of current events sooner and sometimes in more detail and have access to important information for everything from homework to vacation planning to finances. In fact, I would go so far as to say children need to know how to play video games with their peers—it's part of the socialization process now. The child who can't operate a joystick is at as big a disadvantage as the one who can't ride a bike. As a psychiatrist, I'm sure the day will come when I listen to a patient tell me he felt he was handicapped as a child because his parents never let him learn to play Nintendo.

Except for truly harmful behaviors, such as drug use or drunken driving, I'm reluctant to totally forbid anything. If children never get to watch TV or play video games, their curiosity becomes explosive—and dangerous in itself. But just as we wouldn't let a child who loves soccer play it seven hours a day, or we don't eat every meal at McDonald's, we must not let the media control our children's lives. Media in moderation can educate, inform, entertain, and satisfy a craving—as does the occasional dessert. Like vitamin A, the media can be extremely good and even necessary, but seriously toxic when given in too-high doses. Allowing a teenager free rein on the Internet is negligent.

How you manage your child's media exposure is a part of selecting the values you want to inculcate—and just as critical. If you abdicate this parenting task, your child's values may be determined by the media—and that's a scary thought. I want you to be well aware of the risk factors and consciously train your children in the values you will feel good about observing them display later on. I offer these guidelines to help you derive maximum benefit and minimum damage from the amount of time your family spends involved in the media:

Children Ages Five and Under

- **NO UNATTENDED TV WATCHING AT ALL.** If you're in the habit of turning on the TV for your kids then going about your life, stop now. Yes, you will have a period of discomfort as you try to find new ways to train your children to entertain themselves while you do what you need to do. But the good news is that they will quickly learn to do so. If you go on a trip with your children where there is no TV, such as camping or staying in a rustic cabin, as we did with our children when they were young, your kids will amaze you with the resourceful ways in which they learn to play in a totally unfamiliar environment.

   When you do watch TV with your very young child, talk about the program and its ethical issues. Explain the meaning and motivation behind commercials and programming; help her to understand fantasy and reality, the difference between a sales pitch and an honest evaluation.

Children Over Age Five

- **PERMIT *SOME*—BUT VERY LITTLE—UNATTENDED WATCHING OF QUALITY PROGRAMS OR MOVIES THAT YOU ARE FAMILIAR WITH, FOR NO MORE THAN TWO OR THREE HOURS A WEEK.** First, choose a program you have been watching with them, and try out an occasional brief absence while they are viewing it. Then, if that's working out, increase your absence. Also, limit the list to programs you would be willing to watch, not choices like the weekend morning cartoon shows. Their pace is too rapid, the sounds too jarring and repetitive, the commercials too abundant. Think of unattended Saturday and Sunday morning viewing as something like sending your children to the Sunday school of a place of worship that you don't belong to. Remember, the media are busy training your children to be consuming robots, to become passive absorbers of entertainingly camouflaged commercial pressures.

- **CONTINUE TO LIMIT TV VIEWING TO AN OCCASIONAL PLEASURE** as they get older, and try to keep watching most programs with your children.

- **DON'T CAVE IN WHEN THEY REACH ADOLESCENCE.** By now your children should be sharing—maybe reluctantly—your understanding of media and its effects and your values. If they are resisting your limits, you need to have a really good talk. It's far better to struggle with your adolescent about media than about drugs. It gives them the opportunity to rebel with less risk. For instance, it's far better for them to sneak some TV behind your back than to sneak some drugs. The fewer limits you offer here, the easier it will be for your child to stray into more dangerous consequences.

Children of All Ages

- **DON'T LET YOUR CHILDREN WATCH ANYTHING THAT YOU WOULDN'T BE WILLING TO WATCH WITH THEM.** If you can't bear to sit through an episode of *SpongeBob SquarePants*, it's not likely to be of any benefit to them either. Look at it this way: we all know that good children's books transcend generations. As a parent, I couldn't wait to read to my kids the same books I enjoyed as a child. Good children's TV should be the same—you should enjoy watching it as much as your children do.

When you do view programs together, notice how you feel as you watch. If the program feels jarring, or you see that your child either doesn't relate to the program or is upset by it, turn it off and discuss it. Be sensitive to the rhythmical yammering of the commercials. They are barraging your child in a way that will shorten his attention span. When this is going on, your child is literally being mugged right before your eyes.

- **SELECT SPECIAL PROGRAMS AND MAKE WATCHING THEM A FAMILY EVENT, JUST AS IF YOU WERE GOING OUT TO A MOVIE.** You can then have great discussions about the content, the story, the images, and the emotions and behaviors of the characters. You can use the program to share moral judgments and help form both your child's character and her ability to identify with your family and your community's culture. If you find yourself flinching or rejecting the notion of moral and ethical indoctrination, I suggest that you are feeling the pressure that this epidemic has placed on parents to succumb to the lowest common denominator of behavior. Remind yourself that you are administering a drug that might have value in very small doses but that increases its poisonous power as you increase your child's viewing time.

- **AVOID GETTING CAUGHT UP IN ONGOING TV SERIES.** Deciding on a series involves making a lot of decisions ahead of time that can interfere with more fruitful family time and interaction. On the other hand, if the series looks very promising and you know you will enjoy watching it with your child— as our family did with *Little House on the Prairie*—make it a regular date to share worthwhile entertainment together.

- **MODEL RESPONSIBLE MEDIA BEHAVIOR YOURSELF.** If you are flipping channels, if you leave the family all day to watch sports, ask yourself, "What are my values really?" If you find that you prefer the tube and the computer to more active pursuits, your kids will quickly pick up that value as well and come to believe that life is about being passively entertained.

- **SET COMMONSENSE RULES.** Media use should be permitted only after the day's work is done—chores and homework—and also not immediately before bedtime. Stop all media use an hour before bedtime, and use that time for reading, journal writing, talking, drawing, or playing a game together. As your child becomes involved in computer use and video games, make sure he stays within the guidelines you've already set. For example, the time allowed for media should include all forms of entertainment—including games and computers—not just TV watching. Don't then allow computer games after the TV time frame.

- **ALWAYS MONITOR YOUR CHILD'S COMPUTER USE.** Position the computer in a very public place within your home so that the screen is visible. If your children need to do research on the Internet, sit with them. With older children, your interested presence helps support their choices and use. Take advantage of parental controls and usage monitoring tools on services such as AOL to be sure that older children aren't gaining access to inappropriate information when you're not around. If you can afford to do so, invest in a laptop or notebook computer, but install only word processing and printing software on it. Keep the Internet service and e-mail confined to the desktop computer in the open space. This way, the older child who has to write a paper for school can take the laptop in her room and work privately, and you needn't fear she'll wander into trouble when you're not looking.

- **KNOW WHO YOUR CHILD'S FRIENDS ARE, AND TELL THEIR PARENTS ABOUT YOUR MEDIA RULES.** This may feel difficult at first, but treat it like a peanut allergy: you wouldn't hesitate to make sure your child wasn't given a peanut butter and jelly sandwich if you knew it would make him sick. Just explain, "My child is hard to manage after watching TV," or "He doesn't sleep well after TV," or "She gets carried away with the habit if we allow too much." If the other parents don't accept the limits you set, your child doesn't belong in that home. Remember, you have the right to make choices that affect your children. Media exposure is not a right—it is a powerful stimulus, and it is the job of parents to regulate the exposure of their child.

What do you do when other children come to your house and expect a fun-filled afternoon of media exposure? Be clear that "in this house we don't do that." Don't worry about other children's opinions. If a friendship is so shallow that it depends on constant media exposure, your child is better off without it.

Within the framework I have outlined here, there are many ways in which individual families can establish their own guidelines. To keep media exposure manageable, you may choose to ban TV and video games during the week but allow them for brief periods on the weekends. You may decide to take out your game system only occasionally, or to not buy one at all but rent one periodically for a treat. You may not introduce computers until your child needs it for schoolwork. Or you may choose to enjoy all these entertainments but impose hourly limits on their use.

Parents often ask me, "How can I stay in charge of my child's media use when they get older and I'm not always there?" This issue harks back to the moral training we discussed in chapter 6. If you began early to teach your child the value of moderation, he not only understands that TV or video games may be like a snack—we may crave them, but we can't constantly have them— but that understanding will have become part of his character, much like knowing not to steal. If you find your child has broken a media-related rule, sit down and ask him what's going on. Be loving but firm: he needs to know that you mean business, you feel strongly about the rule you set, and you feel disappointed when he doesn't live up to your expectation. If your child outright refuses to cooperate or breaks the rule again, put away all the media equipment until you know you can trust him again. You are in charge. Your rules will become part of his life, just like toothbrushing, showering, and schoolwork.

The following family profiles are full of good ideas and smart examples to follow. They illustrate learning experiences for both the adults and the children and provide a comfortable range of behaviors, including abstinence, moderation, and conscious enjoyment for the whole family. They ensure that your voice is the loudest in your children's lives.

THE GOLDMANS: LEARNING TO LIVE WITH LIMITS

"From the day we discovered we were pregnant with our first child, my husband and I made a quality-of-life decision that we would not let our children watch television or play video games," said Helen Goldman. "We believed that we needed to establish these things from day one, because it is all too easy to let them seep into daily life. Three years later we've found that it is really difficult to stick to it . . . more difficult than we imagined.

"There are two things that make sticking to the plan difficult for our son, Jeremy, and us. Jeremy does ask for TV, as he's been exposed to it at other people's houses. He knows about cartoons and gets excited about Elmo (what is it about that little red fuzzy guy?) just from seeing him on everything from bubble bath to clothes. On our end, we have a very energetic little boy who wants to be engaged all the time, so there are definitely times when I think fondly of setting him down in front of the TV just for some quiet time. It's taken a lot of resolve not to do it, and I typically pick up books instead.

"What keeps my husband and me going is how we feel when we go to a friend's house and see their kids staring at the tube, or when I hear a toddler demanding over and over again to watch something. I watched quite a bit of TV as a child and still find that it's my preferred method of relaxing when I don't have a good book going, and sometimes even when I do. I feel guilty about it when I've spent an evening watching television, because it's such a waste. But at the same time, I think the habit took hold from a young age, and I have yet to break it. That's a major reason that I don't want Jeremy or the second child I'm now expecting to fall into that behavior. My husband grew up in Florida on a river, where he spent his days on the water, fishing, running around in boats, real Huck Finn kind of stuff, and so I think that's where his strong feelings about Jeremy being active and not sitting in front of a TV come from.

"We did buy Jeremy a video for Christmas because it came so highly recommended by several people we know. It's called *The Snowman,* and it has a wonderful story and beautiful music. It's also only twenty-seven minutes long. Jeremy loves it so much, he'll often ask to watch it, and we often allow him. We'll probably get him another video produced by the same company because now I'm starting to feel as if he should have some variety if he's going to spend the time watching something. I'm so cautious because it would be easy to just slide down that slope and keep buying more stuff for him to watch, and then he'll be begging to sit down in front of the TV several times a day.

"As Jeremy gets older we'll try to make sitting down and watching special things a family event. For example, he's watched some of the Olympics. We talk about what the sport is about, what's happening, why they do certain things. I'd also eventually like to institute a family movie night on Fridays, when we all sit down and watch something together.

"I know not allowing computer and video games is also going to be really tough as Jeremy gets older. I have such an aversion to it because I have a fourteen-year-old nephew who plays video games constantly. He'll stay inside and play for hours on end, and he's the same way with the computer and Internet.

Not only is he overweight, but he's hard-pressed to put three sentences together when speaking with an adult, even though he's practically one now himself.

"What's interesting is how our friends comment on the no-TV thing. It's kind of like being a vegetarian. We're definitely meat eaters, and we roll our eyes and make comments about tofu this and soy that. Well, our friends do a bit of that to us with the whole TV thing—'Oh . . . that's right, you don't allow TV in your house,' and 'I forgot, Jeremy has never seen *Theodore Tugboat'*—and they look upon our poor, deprived child with a bit of pity. Still, I have to say that I'm proud that Jeremy doesn't watch TV, because he has great verbal skills, is very social, and loves being read to."

THE LAGANOS: STEERING CLEAR OF CABLE

I applaud the following family for their efforts. They are holding out more than most parents. But the slope they are on is becoming more slippery. By that I mean that TV use, albeit carefully controlled, has become a daily habit. As I mentioned earlier, any regular or extensive viewing is enough to addict and impair children, regardless of content.

"Our philosophy essentially is to limit but not ban," explains Donna Lagano. "Kids need to be part of the mainstream, and TV and movies are important in their world. The rule we developed for Caroline, five, and Brett, eight, is just one hour of TV or video watching a day. This was pretty easy for my husband and me because we hardly watched TV anyway, but we knew even the youngest kids are very attracted to it. They typically watch PBS shows from 5:00 to 6:00 P.M. or a video, but only after homework is done. We do allow for some flexibility, though—if the kids are sick, they can watch kid programming during the day. We take them to movies regularly and rent new videos for a treat when we occasionally go out for the evening and hire a baby-sitter.

"At this stage, Caroline is somewhat more interested in TV

than Brett, but I think that's because the programs they routinely are allowed to watch, such as *Dragon Tales*, are geared more toward her age level. Because we don't subscribe to cable, Brett doesn't know a lot about older—and usually more violent—shows targeted at his age and gender group. And so far none of his closest friends have PlayStations or Nintendo, which sounds odd in our typically middle- to upper-middle-class suburb of New York City, where most families have every consumer item—and then some! Brett does have a Game Boy, which he is allowed to play on car trips and for an hour or so each day on weekends.

"A real plus to limiting commercial stations has been that the kids' exposure to advertising is minimal. Brett does seem to understand the commercials he sees when watching sports with his dad. We've tried to explain that a lot of TV programming is just filling air space between opportunities to sell something, and that most shows for kids are aimed at getting them, and their parents, to spend money on related merchandise.

"I think that because we started limiting TV as soon as we started our family, it has been easier for us to stick to it and develop an environment in which the kids are encouraged to read, draw, paint, or play with friends. The rules with play dates are the same, of course, and we find that most kids are easily persuaded to do something other than TV, but it does require some parental involvement. Parents use the TV as a baby-sitter way too much. I suspect that changing parents' attitudes toward TV is a lot harder than keeping kids away from it!"

THE HOVORKAS: PRETEEN PITFALLS

The mother of a fourteen-year old told me about an upsetting episode with her then twelve-year-old daughter, which she was wise enough to turn into an important lesson for both of them.

"I have always thought that I monitored my three children's

TV, video game, and computer viewing. I kept the computer and TV out in the open in the family room, never behind a closed door," Karen Hovorka told me. "But as my oldest reached middle school, she began to demand more independence, and I really wanted to trust her. Kids are suddenly aware of so much around them (including their changing bodies) that their curiosity can get them into trouble. I didn't realize how much common sense she actually lacked, and quit looking over her shoulder as much. She was online with classmates constantly, and buddy lists were shared among friends of friends. Some of the chats were inappropriate.

"One time someone instant-messaged her because he read her profile, which said she was interested in track and music. As the chat went on she realized he was thirty years old, and she freaked out. Fortunately she told me about it and even saved the chat so I could read it. I could tell the scare alone taught her a lesson, but I still restricted her computer use (only homework, no socializing) for a few weeks after that to drive the point home. And I talked to her a lot about the dangers involved and about never giving out information about herself. We also talked about the media, and I tried to empower her to be able to critique media content by explaining that the images on TV, in movies, and on the Internet are being forced on her by money-hungry Hollywood businessmen. Their motive is simply to be so bizarre, violent, and inappropriate that they get your attention. It helped her to look at all this stuff with a more critical eye. Now she is more careful about whom she connects with.

"My second child has now reached middle school, and the battles I have with him are more about R-rated movies he wants to see. He is online with friends and on the Internet a fairly small amount of time. He is more interested in video games, playing basketball, and skateboarding. Since I pay for the video games he requests, screening for violence is easy. I just try to always be very open about discussing everything they see—sex, drugs, violence— and appeal to their intelligence and sense of responsibility."

HOW IS MY CHILD DOING?

If you follow the recommendations I outlined for media exposure, your child should be able to handle the level of TV, computers, and video games in his life. Still, it's important to be aware of the following warning signs, because children react to media stimulation differently. Be careful if your child:

- Often substitutes TV watching or video game playing for creative activities, and whines or cajoles when you try to take away or cut back his media use
- Has become more aggressive in play with other kids
- Has become more aggressive and disrespectful when talking back to adults
- Shows an unnatural level of excitement when playing computer or video games (bulging eyes, licking of lips, perspiration, doesn't react when spoken to)
- Frequently parrots expressions and behaviors of unappealing characters on TV programs
- Frequently begs for toys, snacks, and other amusements advertised on TV
- Eats unhealthy foods more often, particularly when accompanied by weight gain
- Prefers media use to outdoor activities, reading, or family outings
- Wants to watch TV even when playmates are visiting or you are in the middle of a get-together at someone's house and other kids and amusements are readily available

stepping-stone to financial security. That concept, which was once in the background of our aspirations, has now moved front and center. Parents have always worried about getting their children into the right college, but now each step in the educational process has become so critical to the next stage that the struggle has trickled down to preschool. In Berkeley, California, where I practice, parents tell me of long waiting lists and a need for influential references to ensure placement in certain preschools. Some parents even retain school placement experts who groom these very young children for their "interviews." The *New York Times* has reported the extent to which certain parents are willing to go to obtain a place in an esteemed nursery school, such as the highly desirable Ninety-second Street Y in Manhattan. Parents are afraid for their children's future, and the children learn at an early age that they will be limited as to what they can accomplish by the time they begin preschool.

The educational rat race is obliterating the shelter that was once the precious domain of early childhood. That shelter was characterized by what some parents would now consider idle pursuits: splashing in puddles, meandering through a park picking clover and playing peek-a-boo behind shrubs, scribbling chalk drawings on a driveway. Parents, too, once relaxed in this way: taking the family fishing on Saturday afternoon, sitting down to a Sunday pot roast, towing the kids in a red wagon on evening strolls around the neighborhood. But today's struggling, achievement-oriented parents see things quite differently. Even if it goes against their instincts, they feel forced to buy into dog-eat-dog competitiveness lest they hurt their child's chances for success. As a result, kids have become commodities to be sold to the next school or the next enriching activity. This quest is affecting family life dramatically by producing a pressure-cooker environment—for parents, who spend a lot of their free time rushing to games, competitions, and practices, as well as for the kids themselves, who feel the tight grip of the relentless pressure to succeed. Let's take a look at how it plays out on a daily basis:

Terry and Clark Broderick live in a distant suburb of San Diego, where they are able to afford a comfortable house and traditional neighborhood environment for their children. The trouble is that they are seldom home. They both work in the city and commute an hour each way. To avoid leaving their two children—Hannah, three, and Kelsey, eight—far away from them during the day, they have enrolled the girls in a day-care center and parochial school near their offices. Each day the family rises at 6:00 A.M. and is out the door by 7:00 so that they can drop Hannah at her day-care center at 8:00, drop Kelsey at school by 8:30, and arrive at their offices at 9:00. When Kelsey gets out of school at 2:30, she is bussed over to the day-care center, which has an afternoon program for older kids. At 5:00 P.M., the cycle reverses as the couple leave their offices, pick the girls up, and arrive home at about 7:00 P.M. Dinner is thrown together, Kelsey tackles homework, and Hannah falls asleep in front of the TV as her parents pay bills and try to catch up on housework. The day ends around 10:00 for the exhausted family. Weekends are hectic, too, because it's the only time the family has for shopping, yard work, and the kids' activities, which include dance lessons and soccer.

Michael Spence is in the fifth grade in a New Jersey public school. He loves hockey, baseball, basketball—those all-American team sports to which some parents tend to be too ferociously committed. Depending on the season, Michael has practice for one or two sports most days of the week after school and games virtually every weekend. He also averages two hours of homework a night. He gets off the bus at about 4:00 P.M. and grabs a snack, and his mom rushes him out the door to the playing field, gym, or rink. He gets home at 6:30 or 7:00, wolfs down his dinner, and does homework until 9:00 or 9:30. After that, it's an hour or so of TV or Nintendo to wind down before bed.

His dad is a sports nut, too, and they spend much of their weekend time together attending Michael's games, which involves a fair amount of car time since he's on competitive "traveling" teams. Or they catch a pro game at nearby Yankee Stadium or Madison Square Garden in New York. Michael's mom, Alicia, is glad that Michael gets to spend a lot of time with his dad and that they can bond over sports together. Still, she wishes her son had more downtime, because his life is so scheduled and competitive, and she'd certainly like to see his grades improve as well.

Sarah Smythe is a second-grader in the Georgetown section of Washington, D.C. An only child, she attends a private school that required testing for admission and has an accelerated academic curriculum. She's always been precocious, and her parents want to take advantage of every opportunity that may help Sarah reach her potential, so why shouldn't Sarah try everything? She takes piano, dance, and figure skating lessons. Her favorite activity, though, is an arts and crafts class on Saturday morning in which she can get nice and messy and just play around. Her mom, Jennifer, is not so thrilled with it, but she wants to be sure her daughter has some fun penciled into her demanding schedule. When questioned by her own mother about how busy Sarah is, Jennifer responds, "But all the other kids are doing this stuff, and I don't want her to miss out. And she says she enjoys all the activities. It's not like I'm dragging her to them in tears."

And so goes childhood in America in the twenty-first century. A longitudinal study conducted by the University of Michigan's Institute for Social Research showed that children's free time has decreased by one-third since 1981, and sadly, much of it is probably spent watching TV. Instead of having weekends devoted to leisurely fun, kids are tagging along with their parents as they do all the errands they can't get to during the workweek. This suggests that the adult time crunch has trickled down to the youngest members of the family.

The three scenarios just described illustrate the main factors that seem to be at work here: parental workloads are negatively affecting children, as in the Broderick family; too much emphasis has been placed on scheduled activities such as sports, as in the Spence family; and parents have become overly invested in their children's academic performance, as with Sarah. Their children's accomplishments become a major source of their own pride and feeling of success. As class distinctions fade, an individual's grades and social skills are the means for the later garnering of money and power.

The fact that so many children are growing up in high-pressure environments is very troubling. So far I have outlined some key "vitamins" a child needs to reach his potential: a strong bonding experience and continuing intimate and loving communication; routines and a disciplined environment; and moral training. But there's another ingredient that's equally critical for children's development: downtime. Just as a certain amount of fat is critical in young children's diets for brain development, quiet and reflective downtime is critical to their emotional diet. This is when they knit together the experiences of their day, develop individual interests, and build a personality. It allows a child to go inside himself and emerge ready to deal with the world. A dearth of downtime interferes with a child's centeredness, his ability to learn who he is and what he truly wants, and his self-expression and contentedness. No parent wants her child sitting around all the time with nothing to do and no one to interact with, but eliminate the opportunity altogether, and your child will never get a chance to develop her own identity. An identity will be projected onto her by adult-driven activities and ideals that have absolutely no place in this stage of life.

THE DANGERS OF PREMATURE STRUCTURE

In the discussion of the effects of child care in chapter 4, I noted the possibility that the reason children in group child-care centers sometimes show a higher level of cognitive and language development is that these skills accelerate when children have to cope with difficult environments. They must figure out how to get by and function in a large group on their own. Some child development professionals see this situation as positive, but I question it. These children are being forced to grow up and fend for themselves sooner than is best. That kind of coping is always going to be a risk of group child care, but the possibility also exists for children who are thrust out into the world prematurely by a demanding, overscheduled lifestyle.

The whole idea of having a calm, loving, sheltered, gentle childhood is that the child develops her personality naturally, at her own pace. If a child is forced to develop coping structures that are inappropriate to her stage of development, these structures will persist as she grows older. But because they are immature structures, she is not as capable of adapting to situations as a child who developed coping structures when truly ready to do so. Let's say she has to learn to interact with other children for many hours in a child-care center as a two-year-old, even though coping skills sufficient to such a task aren't normally developed until later. Exposure to this kind of stress has to be carefully adjusted to the age and developmental maturity of the child. Some might argue that children in big families would be in the same situation. But in large families with children of many ages, you have older siblings helping younger ones out with negotiations and tasks they can't handle on their own when Mom or Dad isn't available for the moment. This experience also happens in a safe place, not in a stressful, unfamiliar environment. In child-care situations, children are grouped by age, so your child is dealing with potentially half a dozen equally immature two- and three-year-olds. A toddler may learn to get her way by grabbing things and physically pushing others around rather than negotiating ("Can I use that toy after you?"), as a four-year-old would do. To a child who feels unsupported and alone, a seemingly small matter can feel totally frightening. The child learns to escape feeling vulnerable by grabbing control. She will be more likely to have persistent problems than kids who develop at a more normal pace. These are exactly the problem behaviors that are now showing up in the kindergarten-age children in the NICHD study we discussed in chapter 4. Again, researchers and parents are trying to rationalize them away, but the fact is that growing up in this environment has quite possibly skewed part of these children's development, and that's a risk that I urge you to minimize.

Downtime mixed with periods of effort leads to creativity. If parents create a complete, totally scheduled, and seamless world for their child to inhabit, one in which she never has to think about what to do or how to entertain herself, she's never given a chance to feel frustration or draw upon her own creativity. If instead she's gifted with regular free time—and certainly we're talking about time free of electronic media—she learns to exercise her imagination and come up with her own ideas for entertainment. Then a bit more of her internal structure develops. These moments become occasion for new expressions of creativity and development of the self.

The model for what I'm talking about is the delightful interplay between mother and child that I discussed in chapter 2. The mother carefully tailors the environment to meet her child's need for social contact and downtime. Early on in the baby's life the mother's being is loaned, so to speak, to the child so that he doesn't have to cope with emotions he can't yet handle. She seldom if ever allows him to feel frustrated—a sense of security is more important at this stage. But as the baby's bond with her grows, she can begin to pull away a little more, giving him the opportunity to feel frustration and develop coping mechanisms, forming his own personality in the process. The frustration is provoked by the mother in appropriate doses that the child can handle without having to improvise desperate coping strategies, such as a full-blown, throwing-himself-on-the-floor-writhing-and-screaming temper tantrum. Rather, the child is stretched within his ability, but not too far. It will be a very long time before he's totally ready to be independent. After all, we don't send our kids away to live on their own at six or ten or even sixteen. That's simply too much to expect. Nor are they ready to cope with day after day crammed full of activities that require them to practice and perform and function entirely on their own. Kids will always need to develop within a slowly unfolding cocoon of support, carefully meted out by the wise parent.

I've seen many adult patients in my practice who are survivors of the various wars and persecutions of the last fifty years. As children, they grew up in areas where bombs were falling around them and their safety was constantly threatened. Many of these patients became extremely successful as adults, and very wily in dealing with the world, but are often short on empathy. We have to consider that the same thing may well be happening to children who are put in other sorts of stressful coping situations too soon; their cognitive development may proceed, but at the expense of their emotional intelligence. I can't say it has been proven at this point, but the data strongly suggest that, as parents, we have the obligation to consider such risks.

PERFORMANCE PRESSURES

In previous generations parents made mistakes, such as expecting the oldest son to take over the family business even though he might have had other passions. The modern-day version is plotting out your child's path to an Ivy League doctorate before he's old enough to read, or training him for a career in the National Hockey League when he should be spending more time playing with peers or studying. Parents hate to admit that they are pressing a preconceived career path on their child. Yet they go from pumping Mozart into the womb to plopping infants in front of brain-exercising videos to taking toddlers to gymnastics classes and foreign language lessons. As these children progress through elementary school, they receive private tutoring in everything from soccer to reading to violin. In high school the roster of activities is carefully constructed to round out their résumés for college acceptance. Why? As parents say: "I just want her to try everything to see what she likes," "I want her to have everything I missed out on," and "Everyone's doing it, and I don't want her to fall behind her peers."

These parents think they are doing their best for their child, but in reality, the pressures of our toxic culture have clouded the issue. Parents have been made to feel that they are neglecting or depriving their children if they don't push them as far as they can go in every direction. Child psychiatrist Alvin Rosenfeld, M.D., explained the idea well in his 2000 book, *Hyper-Parenting: Are You Hurting Your Child by Trying Too Hard?* He writes:

> The entire American middle class now reads articles trumpeting the premise that all children can be smarter, more socially adept, and far superior if we parents take their development seriously and foster it actively. Child development research findings are presented as if our current state of knowledge were complete and ready for full implementation in every family. Reports pinpoint crucial periods of brain development almost down to the phase of the moon, telling us exactly what is needed (weekly piano lessons) and when (between a child's third and fourth birthday) for superior mathematical prowess to blossom. As for feeding infants, no question can remain; breastfeeding, we are told, boosts IQ by (precisely) eight points.

Psychiatrists see it, pediatricians see it, and teachers most certainly observe it day in and day out. Now administrators at Harvard—that heavenly prize for which parents strive—have spoken out. These administrators courageously describe how paradoxical and counterproductive the consequences have become in an article I received in a mailing from Harvard, "Time Out or Burn Out for the Next Generation?" by William Fitzsimmons, Marlyn McGrath, and Charles Ducey.

> The pressures placed on many children, while undoubtedly inculcating a constricting discipline in a child's life, probably have the unintended effect of delaying a child's finding herself and succeeding on her own terms. . . . Parents and students alike could profit from redefining success as fulfillment of the student's own aims, usually yet to be discovered. Burn-out is an inevitable result of trying to live up to alien goals.

These Harvard administrators are rightly appalled. They know what should be done, but the real question is going to be: Will parents heed the pleas for a more relaxed and self-instituted life for their children? The true heart of the epidemic is our failure to do so. All the information about how we are harming children is right there, yet society continues along the same detrimental path. And just think: these are the *good* kids caught in the epidemic. They're burnt out by other people's goals for them. These pressured children are alienated from themselves, whereas the Columbine shooters were alienated from society as well as themselves. They may not go on to shoot up their peers in anger, but they may well become Enron-style executives, clawing their way to the top, cheating and taking advantage of whoever gets in their way. They've been given the cognitive training to succeed but may be lacking a moral compass to guide them. Research has in fact demonstrated that even as early as middle school, putting too much demand on grades and performance may lead to cheating if children have not achieved a good degree of stabilization of character. Often students see cheating as a means of survival. Certainly they have somehow gotten the message that the reward is more important than actual achievement.

Other burnt-out overachievers struggle on, living outwardly successful, inwardly empty lives, as described by Fitzsimmons and his colleagues in their paper:

> Professionals in their thirties and forties—physicians, lawyers, academics, business people and others—sometimes give the impression that they are dazed survivors of some bewildering lifelong boot-camp. Some say they ended up in their profession because of someone else's expectations, or that they simply drifted into it without pausing to think whether they really loved their work. Often they say they missed their youth entirely, never living in the present, always pursuing some ill-defined future goal.

Then there is the group that "just can't take it anymore": they drop out, turn to substance abuse, even suffer emotional collapse. Consider the case of the MIT student Elizabeth Shin, who allegedly committed suicide by setting herself on fire. Her over-scheduled, stress-ridden, unsupportable life was described brilliantly in the April 28, 2002, issue of the *New York Times Magazine*. Reading the article, it's hard to imagine how Elizabeth's parents could not have noticed that she was self-destructing under all that pressure. Yet the parents are said to have filed a lawsuit against the university, supposedly because they feel they were kept in the dark about their daughter's emotionally distraught condition.

A CAREFUL BALANCING ACT

How do you put the brakes on today's fast-forward childhood? First by being aware and recognizing when things aren't working for your child. The in-tune parent doesn't need a prescription for the right amount or kind of activities. She can see when her child is happy, when his schedule is just right, and when he's overwhelmed. One mother I know thought she was doing her son a favor by signing him up for after-school golf lessons because he loved the sport. But he had to spend Tuesdays and Thursdays racing to the golf course and worrying about how he would get his homework done when it was all over. Evenings involved rushing through dinner and crying over spelling words and math problems that were normally no trouble for him. But this sensitive mother was quick to pick up on the problem, and they dropped the lessons after the eight-week session was over. He's much happier, she notes, having a "decompression period" after school when he can ride his bike or listen to music.

This mother recognizes that her child—like all kids—needs to go home and play after school, to integrate all the things he learned that day. Deep in our hearts we all know how that works. That's why we say things like, "I have to sleep on it." Ideas and decisions take time to gel, and it's no different for children, particularly when you consider how much new information they must process every single day.

Other kids seem to have different needs. I know an eight-year-old named Lilly who skips happily from horseback riding to dance classes. Depending on the season, she also squeezes in soccer, Brownie meetings, and ice skating, not to mention school and an hour of homework a night. Even in the summer, when her mother tries to keep the calendar wide open, Lilly begs to be on a swim team. Some kids are incredibly adventuresome, energetic, and seem to need less sleep than others. Trying to rein such a child in tends to feel unnecessary. Even so, even these high-energy kids need to have a reasonable amount of downtime. This is when you have to read your child's personality carefully and cautiously, and be honest with yourself about what happens when she's confronted with an opening in her schedule.

If she has trouble occupying herself, that issue constitutes a more critical problem that she needs to learn to deal with.

Of course, an active child also can be a burden for parents. If you are overstressed trying to get her everywhere, take care of your other kids, and put dinner on the table, your child needs to be told that. Otherwise you risk becoming a mother who, by doing everything for her kids, teaches them nothing about real life. There's nothing wrong with saying, "One or two activities a week—you can pick the ones you prefer." Then stick to it. You're not telling your child she can't try everything she wants—she just can't try them all at once.

Endlessly drifting from one activity to another is not a desirable situation either. Letting your child survey activities is one thing, but make it clear that some require more than a passing interest. Craft class may simply be a survey of what's available, for instance, but taking up piano requires a bigger commitment, and you will have to prepare your child to follow through. Explain to her, "If you want to try it, you have to agree to stick with the lessons for six months and practice two hours a week. We'll mark the time on the kitchen calendar." It's the same with a sport like hockey, which requires a certain degree of technical expertise, as well as a significant equipment expense on your part.

It sounds so simple to put it this way. But I am well aware that it is not. To reduce your child's activities enough to provide significant downtime, you have to go through some soul-searching and confront the fear that you're not doing enough. Ask yourself, "Is this what I really want for my child? What is a Palm Pilot full of appointments teaching him about morality, friendship, helping others?" "What's more important—my child's résumé or her heart and soul?"

Don't cram your child's schedule just because the activities seem valuable or sensible. Like spending money, there is always something that seems like a wise purchase or a practical investment, but the aggregate of too many things may prove toxic to your financial well-being. Look at your child's schedule item by item, decide what's dispensable, then schedule in that all-important downtime on a regular and consistent basis. Remember, no one is competing with franchises for karate and tutoring centers and music lessons trying to sell you lessons in downtime. You have to be your child's advocate in this area. You may feel guilty at first; you may be frightened that you're cutting your child off from something important, because our current culture has infected you. Parents are being taught to feel that life is difficult and dangerous and they must be on the defensive; they feel that no pressure means they're failing to do enough to help their child cope. Children in turn feel nervous, anxious, grasping, worried.

Though you've been told that it's the courses and lessons and competitions that best prepare children for the future, I believe—and hope you do as well—that it's really the family dinners, the weekend hikes, and the bedtime chats that make a child feel as if he matters, as if he can make a difference. After the World Trade Center terrorist attacks, many of us watched the documentary *9/11* by French brothers Jules and Gedeon Naudet, which followed a rookie firefighter as he experienced his first real "job" that day. In the early part of the documentary, the rookie, Tony, explains why he chose firefighting as a career. "I wanted my life to matter. I wanted to help people," he replies. My preference is to raise that kind of child—what's yours?

HOW IS MY CHILD DOING?

Watch for these warning signs that your child is experiencing unnecessary stress:

Behavior Symptoms

- Becomes unusually afraid or worried about something; suffers from nightmares
- Becomes clingier or regresses to babyish behavior
- Loses emotional control easily, flying off the handle when angry or dissolving into tears over seemingly minor issues
- Starts wetting the bed after nighttime dryness has ceased to be an issue
- Starts biting her nails or engaging in other anxious habits
- Begins to lie frequently
- Experiences a drop in grades

Physical Symptoms

- Experiences a decrease or increase in appetite
- Frequently complains of stomach pain, diarrhea, constipation, or headaches
- Suffers from panic attacks
- Develops insomnia

9

Out of Contact, Out of Control

The worst sin toward our fellow creatures is to be indifferent to them; that's the essence of humanity.

—George Bernard Shaw

BETH IS FIFTEEN YEARS OLD and beautiful in a childish way, but so sullen that it's painful to look at her. She calls her mother "stupid," "wimpy," and "embarrassing" right to her face. Beth outright refuses to do anything to help around the house, sulks frequently, and gets angry and snippy when inconvenienced. She won't always tell her mother, Marylu, where she is going or who she is hanging out with. Not having met them, Marylu is familiar with many of Beth's friends by name only and has no idea what kind of families they come from. Marylu is almost certain Beth is having sex; with whom she is not certain, but she is scared.

Marylu herself is very busy, involved in self-improvement workshops and a part-time nursing job. She wonders frequently what she could do to get better control of her daughter. In her despair, she's even thought of sending Beth to live in a nearby suburb with her father, from whom Marylu has been divorced since Beth was four. But she seldom follows through on any plan for improving communication or gaining control of the issues she has with her daughter.

Describe Beth to many of today's parents of teenagers, and they will solemnly nod their heads in recognition. For many parents, their child's adolescence has become a stage of not knowing, not understanding, not communicating. It's not a natural course of development, however, for communication to dwindle, relationships to break down, and parents and children to drift apart to this extent. Sure, children deserve more freedom as they get to middle and high school—it's absolutely necessary, in fact, to prepare them for eventual life beyond their families, in college dormitories, and on their own. But a child with a strong attachment, trained to consider moral and ethical issues within a healthy family structure, can accomplish all this without becoming alienated. Such a child may argue with you and certainly will press for privileges, but she won't become disaffected.

If your child isn't communicating with you, I guarantee that this problem has been building for a long time. There are two ways parents and children develop communication problems:

- They fail to bond from the outset and never really develop the kind of mutual dance we've talked about;
- They bond in infancy, but as the child starts to exert his independence, the parents fail to set appropriate limits on the testing and self-expressive actions of their child, thereby losing control of him.

Either way, the more difficult to manage the child becomes, the more frustrated and defensive the parents get. Communication between them ranges from confrontational and angry ("What the hell is wrong with you? I told you never to hang out with those kids!") to wimpy and weak ("You know I feel nervous when you go there. You won't do it any more, will you?"). As parent-child communication becomes negative, fearful, and shameful, it naturally begins to break down. Both parent and child want to avoid arguments and begin to avoid each other in the process.

There are three dominant characteristics of parents with an out-of-control child:

1. **Uncertainty:** If you are not sure of your own convictions, discussions of major issues such as dating, sex, and alcohol use will be vacuous and vague, thereby promoting contempt and rebellion in your child. When you know what you want for your child, and it comes from deeply held beliefs, your child will for the most part accept your limitations.

2. **Inauthenticity:** Your decisions have to be about what is good for your child and not about some vague, symbolic, politically correct notion. When it comes to your family and your values, don't allow yourself to be swayed by popular opinion. Look to see what you really do care about.

3. **Guilt:** If you are reluctant to confront and question your child, a good result is unlikely.

Any out-of-control child, whether three years old or seventeen, constitutes an emergency that must be handled. It is critical to restore communication rapidly. Children need room for disagreeing, room for anger, room for dissatisfaction, but all these emotions have to be borne in the context of parents holding the final responsibility and making the final decisions.

Often out-of-control children do an abrupt about-face and become unbelievably loving and cooperative when their parents finally take hold of the reins. There is no reason it has to take years or involve very serious crises. Good parental management will bounce most of them right back, and even the most seemingly lost children can have amazingly good outcomes in residential treatment programs. What cures them in these environments is good surrogate parenting, but you can provide this yourself if you are willing to do the work necessary to change your own practices.

The first step is to get back in communication with your child. Tell her, for example, "I hope you know that I love you, but we are on the wrong footing. We need to understand each other better." Then discuss firmly and clearly the issue at hand. Say your child has broken her curfew. Tell her, "I won't tolerate your coming in late. You and your friends just got your licenses, and I don't want you to be driving alone after dark." Or "10:00 P.M. is late enough to allow you to go to a 7:00 movie and get an ice cream afterward. You don't need to be roaming the mall longer than that." Then "Before I can let you go out again, I need to know you understand this rule. We'll talk about it more and see how each of us feels."

You see, if you can lovingly tell your child what will work and even bring your child into the process of coming to an agreement, the two of you can be brought closer together. If your child responds that everyone thinks she's uncool because she has to be home so early, ask her what would be more reasonable, in her opinion. Of course, if she comes back with 2:00 A.M., you're not going to say yes, but giving her an additional hour may be within your boundaries and could satisfy her need for acceptance, assuming her track record is good and you feel you can trust her during that hour. It won't always be possible to negotiate an issue in this manner, but take advantage of such opportunities when you can so that your child knows she has a voice and you are not simply imposing some arbitrary rule structure.

If every step of discipline is done with a smile, respect, and a clear voice saying, "You just can't do that," your child will grow into an overall centered and balanced adolescent who does not find it offensive when his parents ask about his life outside the home. Well-adjusted, bonded teens don't feel as if they're being spied upon; they continue to want to share and communicate and maintain their relationship with you. They may not tell you every little secret, but they don't shut you out entirely either. Don't believe anyone who tells you withdrawal is just typical teenage behavior. You're giving in to the pressure of a society that's telling you, as a parent, that you don't matter. It amounts to shirking your parental duties if you allow him to continue to walk around in such a noncommunicative state. I maintain that if even one committed person had insisted on connecting with Eric Harris and Dylan Klebold to help them work through what was going on in their clearly unhappy lives, the Columbine massacre would not have occurred. What makes us uniquely human is that we communicate. In the end, it is our most necessary way of connecting.

It is not good for teenagers to live in ambiguity. They're too involved in the struggle between the growing awareness of their physical impulses and the attempt to develop and define their character structure and personality so as to be able to function in a wider circle than the family. Like soft-shelled lobsters in their molting season, teenagers are tender. They don't know how to be in the world. They cast around for guidelines. If they don't find them at home, they can be easily pushed and seduced by peers. This combination of their own impulses and social seduction becomes irresistible if they do not have a moral grounding and an involved, supportive parental presence in their lives.

WATCHING THE DOOR CLOSE

When we think of communication issues, teenagers come first and foremost to our minds, but the truth is that the problem begins well before adolescence. In some families the door to loving communication was never fully open in the first place. These parents may have never really bonded with their children for a variety of reasons: they may not have understood the commitment that children require before they entered into parenthood; they may have adopted some of the many problematic approaches to parenting we have been discussing; or they may have had issues growing up in their own families that prevented them from learning how to really be in a healthy relationship.

Even in families that start off on the right track, the door between the lives of parents and their children may slowly begin to shut as they grow more and more influenced by today's warp-speed world. As the child moves full-time into school, parents tend to move further out of the family as well. Many stay-at-home mothers go back to work at this point, eager to build up the college fund and reestablish their own identities after a few years of being joined at the hip with little ones. As for the children themselves, their activities increase in proportion with their age, so that not only are they gone six or seven hours a day at school, but they scatter elsewhere when the bell rings. They carpool with other families, so travel-time chats get whittled down as well. When you think about it, even the safety laws that relegate children to the backseat have helped cut off the opportunity to talk. One mother who came for counseling for a variety of problems with her child actually remarked to me during a session recently that she loved her new minivan because the kids were seated so far in the back that she couldn't hear them! Of course, if you can't hear them, you don't have to deal with them. It's exactly that kind of attitude—do what you can to avoid the tough issues and conversations—that contributes to the breakdown.

Thus, it becomes quite possible to spend seriously little time with your children by the time they are ten or twelve. Even weekends are no longer sacred by this time: while we once accompanied preschool kids to play dates and birthday parties and got to observe the other parents in action, we now just drop them off and pick them up, paying very little attention to what's going on in other homes. You may be in the stands during your child's Little League or soccer game, but however attentive and caring it is to show up for your child's games—and the support is wonderful—it actually promotes far less communication than playing catch in the backyard. If your time really is in short supply, you're better off spending it just hanging out and talking.

That parents feel comfortable dropping out of sight so soon is yet another product of our hands-off child-rearing era. Society has been telling parents for so long now that they must not crush their kids that parents have developed the destructive habit of treating privacy and trust as inalienable rights. They are most definitely not. They are earned privileges, meted out to the gradually maturing child and maintained by behavior that conforms to family mores. Trust is built up over time but destroyed in a moment. Privacy is a privilege that is steadily earned as the child matures. It is downright dangerous to give a two-year-old privacy. If parents are to adequately protect their child from the dangers of the world, they need to know everything she plays with, whom she associates with, what she is doing or eating, and where she is at every waking moment. As the child grows and her parents learn that she can control her impulse to run into the street, they can begin to let go of her hand or let her walk at a greater distance from them. But if even once she bolts off into the street, her parents are right to watch her more closely until they are confident she has learned not to do that. The child might be impatient and want to let go of that parental hand, but her mother and father must not be guided by some notion of her "space" or "rights" and let go until they are certain she will walk safely.

We are living in a time of incredible commitment to ideology, and many parents now consult child-rearing books that preach philosophies of trust, privacy, and other "rights" of the child and "duties" of the parents. In my opinion, those books are spouting utter nonsense. Children learn to behave and move through the world with guidance from their parents, who must exercise common sense and loving consistency. That commitment does not end, nor should it diminish, when the child steps through the schoolyard gates.

Once again, research bears this out. In a 2002 study of 4,544 fifth- through eighth-graders by researchers at Dartmouth College, it was found that preteens whose parents placed no restrictions on their viewing R-rated movies appeared much more likely to use tobacco or alcohol. R-rated movies are supposed to be restricted for viewers under seventeen, but only 16 percent of the students—the vast majority of whom were under age fourteen—said their parents never allowed them to watch R-rated movies. About 33 percent of those who had no movie restrictions reported having tried smoking, but only 2 percent of those who were not allowed to watch R-rated movies said they had smoked. Forty-six percent of the group with no restrictions said they had tried alcohol, but only 4 percent in the restricted group had.

The kids who aren't permitted to see R-rated movies have parents with a strong sense of what they consider appropriate for their child and are willing to enforce it. They are willing to take charge and set the standards for the family. That position teaches the child that he is a child—that he is being raised by parents who have the ultimate authority and responsibility, just as a school principal or teacher or coach has. The child learns to accept the kinds of restrictions that are necessary for getting along well and being happy. In time, usually around age six, the child learns that there is a structure of what is good and what is not, and wants to be the kind of person who does the right thing.

If unthinking, trend-of-the-moment type parents arbitrarily imposed such restrictions, I doubt they would do any good. The child would see through the behavior and not take the restrictions seriously. But if parents are consistent in their words and behavior, they will build moral structure along the way and diminish the appeal of the temptations of the outside world, which all children will ultimately confront.

RECOGNIZING WHAT'S NORMAL AND WHAT'S NOT

Certainly teenagers don't need as much supervision as toddlers, and it's downright impossible (not to mention unhealthy) to know what they're doing every minute of the day. A teenager wouldn't be normal if he didn't demand some level of privacy, nor would he grow into a fully functioning adult if his parents didn't provide it. But there is a difference between giving a child some space and never communicating, between mischievous behavior and pathological behavior, between being able to feel some shame and remorse when caught and not being able to have those feelings. That critical difference is a moral foundation, the crux of family life, and the very basis of our society.

Of course, even generally well-behaved teenagers have their limits. In a family session just the other day, the parents reported that their son broke a school window, snuck into the building, and got caught. When the father confronted the son about why he would do such a thing, the boy's incredibly simple yet profound reply, with a look of chagrin, was, "I just couldn't be good anymore." He had no deviant intentions, no thought of truly harming anyone or vandalizing anything. He just fell off the good behavior wagon with his buddies. In this instance, his parents chose not to impose a punishment of their own because he clearly demonstrated that he knew he had misbehaved, and he was willing to face the consequences of the school's disciplinary action. Overall, he handled the situation responsibly and maturely, and his parents did not consider him to be out of control.

But sometimes pranks go too far. You will know by how you feel inside about your child's behavior. A number of years ago another family came to me on referral from their school guidance counselor because their son and some other kids had bought and released two thousand crickets in the lobby of his high school. It was clear as I got to know this child that he was actually doing fine in his development. This was heavy-duty mischief, but he was willing to take responsibility for it. He refused to turn in his accomplices but agreed to do some two hundred hours of service work at school.

I have a friend whose daughter brought home a marijuana plant, told her mother it was a carrot, and actually tricked the mother into watering it for a few weeks. Against the law, sure. Is she a hardened drug user or dealer now? Hardly. In all these examples, we are describing mischief, the excitement of being naughty, a thrilling escape from the confines of rules. It's very different from the behavior of a child who has hostile, destructive impulses.

How do you make this distinction between simple, expected rebellion and total abstraction and alienation from society? All kids do some naughty things; it wouldn't be normal if they didn't. All kids get moody at times, particularly during puberty and adolescence. The operative word here is "sometimes." There's a big difference between a child who cuts school so often that his grades are slipping and one who gets spring fever and skips out on a Friday afternoon. There's a big difference between a kid who goes out and parties on an odd Saturday night and one who is getting high every morning before class. There's a big difference between a kid who gets caught in an isolated shoplifting incident and one who steals your car after you've told him he can't have it that night. In fact, a kid who is stealing your car has a very serious problem: not only does he not understand property rights, privileges, or his place in the family, but he is driving around in anger with reckless abandon. You have totally lost control of this kid, and it's only going to get worse. Yet I hear parents telling of incidents this extreme as if they're about everyday behavior. They bypass the alarm signals, such as shoplifting or smoking pot, then come to family therapists like me when the kid finally gets pregnant or arrested and say, "We seem to be having some trouble controlling him." But by then it's much more difficult to turn the situation around. If you have had years of close association and frequent talks, you know your child so well that you can have confidence in how to assess whether his behavior is out of control or simply mischievous.

Here's another common example: cliques, especially among girls. There have always been cliques, of course, just as there have always been bullies and jocks and geeks. There have always been the hyper-indulged kids with every possible accoutrement and the ones who feel as if they never have the right jeans or backpacks or skateboards. But last year the *New York Times Magazine* ran a cover article by Margaret Talbot entitled "Girls Just Want to

Be Mean" that documented a trend toward an especially nasty type of behavior. Schools are instituting programs to help these girls see just how cruel and unjust they are acting and to teach them more empathic attitudes. Once again, all this training would have been better accomplished at home early in the child's life. Now schools are being forced to spend money to try to fix the neglected and distorted development of their students.

These mean girls, termed "Alpha Girls" and "Queen Bees" in the article, do things like dictate what their clique members have to wear on given days of the week, which parties they're permitted to attend, who is allowed to sit with them at the lunch table (in one clique, a member can invite an outsider to sit with them only after it has been approved by the whole group), and trick and betray each other in callous ways, like three-way phone calling, in which one girl calls up another and gets her to gossip about a third girl, who is listening silently on the other end. These kids raised with the epidemic practices described in this book will do anything to belong and seem eager to submit to anyone who will provide clear commands (the Alpha Girl). I wish they had had a wise "alpha" at home.

There is widespread knowledge of this behavior among parents and educators, and I find it extremely sad that they tolerate such abuse. These girls are guilty of self-esteem murder rather than physical murder, verbal violence rather than physical violence. Like the Columbine group that called itself the Trench Coat Mafia, to which Eric Harris and Dylan Klebold belonged, these girls are attaching in a symbolic way, not by bonds of love and friendship but by sworn affiliation to cliques, clubs, and gangs that are self-identified by clothing, colors, race, common activities. They are reflecting a need to feel important and loved because their self-esteem-regulating system was never properly developed at home. They turn for self-aggrandizement instead to the disciples and groupies at school who kowtow to their dictates. They view their peers (and indeed all people) merely as that which pleases or that which displeases. They don't have the bond of love to curb their aggressive instincts. Their attachments are narcissistic, their relationships manipulative, acquisitive, stereotyped.

No doubt many of these girls are expressing the same skewed values that characterize some of their parents: that what matters in life is what you wear and what you drive and how much money and power you have over others. Indeed, when we meet the mother of one of these Queen Bees in the *Times* article, she seems to brag about the fact that her daughter, an only child, has a bedroom suite bigger than some people's apartments, that she has traveled a lot and spent long hours away from her daughter because of her high-powered career, and that she doesn't mind the clique because it doesn't really hurt anyone and it will make her daughter a bigger person and more worldly in the long run!

Would you really want to be the parent of a girl whose life is about maintaining her self-esteem this way? Would you want your son to have her as a girlfriend? How would you feel about someone who has no empathy or concern for others, just a drive to satisfy her narcissism, being the mother of your grandchild?

Those of us who recognize and expect ethical, empathic, socially acceptable behavior from our children know in our gut when something is wrong, that when a child is behaving in such an extreme manner, it signifies more than a stage or trend or typical adolescent rebellion. You can see it in those empty pools of blue or brown or green no longer sparked with life, the sneering response—or total lack of acknowledgment—at your attempts at communication. You can hear the contemptuous tone when those children speak to their parents or other adults or less worthy peers.

These children are lacking a very important trait: the ability to see the consequences of their actions, the pain felt by their victims, and what people think of them. The kid who steals his parents' car doesn't consider what it would be like to pull into the driveway and find his father and a cop standing there waiting for him. The girl who dumps her friend never considers that she could someday be the one who goes home to cry alone in her bedroom. And Eric Harris probably couldn't imagine that we'd view his behavior as a manifestation of a serious collapse of his personality structure; rather, he imagined that he'd finally be the one in control. You and I can see how misguided these children are, but they have no idea because they also have no emotional or moral understanding of what life is supposed to be about, only a superficial view that is far from gratifying for them. Instead of spending time with their parents—the most critical issue throughout child-rearing—and receiving guidance through ongoing family discussions, they're left to haplessly figure things out on their own and with the help of their often equally uninformed peers.

It may not be politically correct to control your kids, but you have to accept that responsibility if you want your child to grow up emotionally healthy. The world will hold you responsible for everything from the unruly behavior of your toddler to preventing another horror like Columbine. There is a restaurant called The Dock, on Montauk, Long Island, with a sign on the front door that says, "If you can't control your kid, don't come in." You will always know when and if your child is manifesting the symptoms described in this book. You may feel uncertain how to handle it, or somewhat anxious or upset. It is painful to watch a distressed child acting out. Unfortunately, too often parents ignore these feelings and jump to rationalize what happened: he's in a bad mood, tired, under too much pressure, and so on. If this is your tendency, gauge your child's behavior against this checklist of warning signs from the American Academy of Child and Adolescent Psychiatry. Whether your child is depressed, angry, has low self-esteem, has developed violent tendencies or substance abuse problems, or is even suicidal, the constellation of symptoms is often the same.

- A drop in academic performance
- A change in eating habits, appetite, or body weight
- Sleep difficulties or oversleeping

- Withdrawal from friends and activities he once enjoyed
- Sudden mood changes and outbursts
- Defiant behavior (such as staying out past curfews, refusing to attend family functions, skipping school)
- Feelings of sadness, hopelessness, crying bouts, lethargy

Any child who exhibits such symptoms for more than a few weeks needs professional help. Needless to say, more extreme behaviors, such as violence toward others, vandalism, stealing, and known substance abuse require immediate treatment. No excuses (adolescent angst, sowing his oats) should ever be made for such behavior.

LEARNING TO RECONNECT

If you know you're not communicating with your child as well as you would like—and especially if you fear he's doing something improper or dangerous—the first step is to talk about it. You need to discuss what's happening, and not punitively: "We cannot and will not have this going on. Do you think it is an unfair rule? If so, what do you think would be acceptable? Things are going to have to change, but I am willing to work with you on exactly how we do it." Watch to see how your child reacts. If your child seems remorseful and willing to cooperate, it's probably safe to continue to remedy the situation on your own for a little longer. Set reasonable expectations for your child, explaining, for instance, that driving your car is a privilege, and if he wants permission to do so, he will need to maintain a certain standard of behavior—good grades, not smoking or skipping school, and so on. If his behavior is questionable, say, "I don't want you driving my car until you pull your grades up." Or "It is unacceptable to smoke pot. It is unhealthy, dangerous, and illegal." Above all, you want your child to know exactly what you expect, and what you won't permit.

Try as often as possible to turn such situations into lessons in ethics. For the child whose grades are slipping, explain that school is her main job, and life is at its best when you do your job well. Learning to study now will prepare her for a productive, successful, rewarding adulthood later. We all want our children to do well in school, but remember, grades are important only as a barometer of how things are in her world. If she's a first-grader and having trouble, naturally you're going to be concerned about some learning disability and look into an evaluation. By the same token, if your child is older and her grades are starting to plummet, you need to evaluate other aspects of her life that might be affecting school performance. By now you know it's nothing cognitive, or it would have shown up earlier. What is she feeling? What is disrupting her? You have to find out. Resolving this crisis is critical for her future well-being.

If necessary, employ a consequence when behavior is inappropriate, such as refusing to drive your child to the mall or to a movie when she's being uncooperative at home, or taking away computer or car privileges for a more serious infraction. But keep in mind that consequences for the most part should be related to the crime and short-term. For instance, if your child goes to a friend's house after school without telling you first, his consequence may be missing some other event or outing that evening or the next day. Keep in mind that one of the most important jobs of parents is to inspire their children to have a vision—help her to see that doing this now (and *not* doing that) will lead to an exciting and interesting life later. Don't punish or shame your child into behaving; convince her that it's the best thing she can ultimately do for herself.

TAKING BACK CONTROL

If you are dealing with an out-of-control preteen or adolescent, the task ahead is not easy, or even necessarily manageable. The biggest red flag is the child who refuses to communicate, who is unwilling to discuss events. Kids who pull further away and behave contemptuously are often feeling unloved and unimportant, as if they're not being nurtured. They're not reacting to what's happening at the moment, but rather to a deeper sense of loss they feel inside. The pain of those feelings jumps out of the heart and into the head, and instead of communicating, they solve their feelings by withdrawing and acting out.

As I said before, you are most likely dealing with lifelong patterns that have crippled your child's development. You can't settle for empty gestures like "grounding" or cutting off computer privileges for a week. Far more communication will be required to have any real impact. You may well need professional help for your child and yourself—to learn how to parent in a more productive manner. By the time a teenager is seriously out of control and is being rude or contemptuous, cutting school, breaking curfews, using drugs, being sexually promiscuous, running away, and threatening parents with violence to get his or her way, no intervention is going to work without extensive therapy and behavior control—not just for the child, but for the parents as well. A family that produces a child like this is so dysfunctional that I believe it is beyond the power of this book to be the sole source of help; such families must seek professional sources of help. It is a serious error to keep acting as if the problem is simply the young person's. Therefore, I do not intend to spell out steps to take with such an out-of-control child. The gap in communications, the lack of genuine affection, and the lack of bonding family practices are too severe for the family to go it alone. This is an emergency situation.

If that's what's happening in your home, I would suggest that you go directly to a family therapist who can sit down with your family and help you talk to each other, moving away from the nasty defensive behavior many parents and children fall into. Toughlove International (www.toughlove.org) is another option; this organization has helped many parents learn effective strategies for dealing with problem teens.

You must tell your child something like, "Honey, we can't seem to get this under control by ourselves. I've made an appointment next Wednesday to see a therapist. We're going to learn to talk to each other better so we don't keep getting into these same old fights." Make it clear that although you are willing to work with your child, his behavior is going to have to change. Be prepared to follow through with every available opportunity to get him the help he needs. If family counseling is not yielding results, you may end up needing a therapeutic boarding school for problem children, residential treatment center, wilderness therapy program, or a disciplinary boot camp. Your therapist will be familiar with specific programs and their effectiveness and can make suggestions about which would be the best option for your child. Another possibility is to have him live with another family for a while—a relative or foster family who may be able to handle him more objectively.

Whatever you choose, be sure it's a program or person that will go to the wall to get control of your kid. Some settings are locked, institution-style, because such troubled kids often have no qualms about trying to escape. But you will also have to do your homework to find a solution. Some camps and schools are well known and highly regarded; others are fly-by-night operations run by people trying to capitalize on family troubles. Again, most professionals recommend that parents make such decisions in consultation with their child's therapist, but you can also begin by consulting the National Association of Therapeutic Schools and Programs (www.natsap.org) which was established in 1999 to develop a set of guidelines and ethical standards for the industry. (There is no central licensing organization, however.) The Independent Educational Consultants Association (www.iecaonline.org) also provides a listing of programs it considers reputable, as well as a consultant referral service. These professionals will provide you with a psychological evaluation and match your child up with an appropriate program.

The costs for these programs can run into the thousands,

and plenty of parents balk at spending their children's college funds, but let me assure you: if your child is this far gone, he's not going to go to college anyway unless you take action. Plenty of parents who've had to resort to these programs realize that the only other alternatives are to watch their children go to jail or to the grave. The Kane family has been through such an ordeal with their son, Evan, whose learning difficulties were carefully managed for years in a private elementary school. But when he was deemed ready for a mainstream high school program, behavior issues that had been neglected at home, owing to his parents' sympathetic disciplinary style, resulted in a very out-of-control child. Listen to his mother, Laura:

> When Evan was between fourteen and fifteen, we began to experience significant behavioral challenges. He was flunking out of high school, smoking pot on a daily basis, stealing money from his older sister and us, and hanging around with some really creepy friends. We took him to a psychologist who helped us see that we had never disciplined Evan enough and taught us that keeping kids in line is not any one strategy but definitely must include a consistent pattern of limit-setting and enforcement.
>
> Still, when we began ratcheting up the discipline, Evan's behavior got even worse, if you can imagine that. He started sneaking off, not coming home at night, that kind of thing. I realized I had completely lost control of him at this point. His refusal to accept our limits and stop the drug use led us to put him in a religious boarding school where he has to adhere to a strict, structured code of behavior.
>
> He's still not out of the woods yet, but I have seen that when he comes home to visit, his behavior has improved dramatically. I think sending him to this school proved to him I was going to do really tough things. He says he's not going back when he's eighteen, but we told

him that if he didn't, he could no longer live at home—he would be on his own and have to support himself after that. He seems to believe me—the assistant principal at the school said Evan told him he wasn't allowed to live at home anymore. We also told him that if he gets kicked out of this school, we will have him declared an out-of-control child and he will become a ward of the state and be put into a boot camp, which is the next step for well-off parents but something we could never afford on our own.

It's a terrible thing when you get to a point where you don't want your child in your house anymore. The day I dropped Evan off at the school I cried all the way home. But I also was so relieved. Going to the psychologist was another very good thing. He was just as hard on us as he was on Evan. Our intentions were good, but Evan was a smart, aggressive kid who knew how to take advantage, and we just weren't on top of things. The fact that I can't even remember what I did to discipline him when he was younger tells me I wasn't doing enough. When he was little and people would tell me he had behavior problems, instead of getting it checked out with a professional, I just got defensive and angry toward the person who said so. I found out the hard way that children have to know there are consequences, and they have to be immediate.

The Kanes did exactly what they had to do. Now seventeen, Evan appears to be back on track and functioning, but clearly there has been a tremendous amount of damage to his development. Will he recover? Perhaps. Hopefully. What the parents finally did has certainly given him his best chance.

His mother also told me that Evan lacks motivation and may well have self-esteem issues. "A lot of kids overcome this kind of stuff successfully, but not Evan. He has no hopes, no aspirations, no mission in life," said Laura. "And he refuses to talk about his feelings—he just clams up. He was a happy little boy at home, but when he got to a much bigger high school and the outside world, that seems to be what put him over the edge."

Without structure, routines, limits, and a bonded relationship at home, kids don't have the moral foundation and emotional stability that would give them the power to resist the toxic temptations of the outside world. The Kanes are smart people and probably had the very best intentions, but they were lured into a sense that they were doing the right thing when they clearly weren't—and a child's life may have been wasted.

At the other end of this spectrum is the Roth family. They have two boys, ages twelve and fifteen, and have done really well within the parenting framework I have outlined in this book. As a result, their sons are smart, likable, and on the right track to a happy and productive adulthood. As a family, they clearly enjoy each other's company, and even as teenagers, that doesn't embarrass these boys! It seems fitting that I leave you with their story, as told by their mother, Ilene, and the hope that your home will ultimately be equally happy:

> Before we had kids, my husband, Paul, was a college basketball coach who was on the road the entire season. I was a TV news reporter who worked many, many hours as well. But we made some big changes when we decided to start a family. We moved to a robust Jewish community because we wanted religion to be an important part of our lives. Paul left his college coaching job and became an assistant principal at a high school. I quit my job and did freelance work from home for the next decade.
>
> I try to always be there for the boys. I made sure I was home during the most important years, and Paul is here, too, at the end of the school day. We eat dinner together most nights, and I have always stopped what I was doing and consciously listened to them when they

wanted to tell me about something. We talk about sex, their friends, the way they behave. Because my husband is an assistant principal, we openly discuss the problems he handles at school—the offense and the consequence—so that our children know if they do something wrong they will have those consequences as well.

Lately I have had a few problems with attitude. For instance, when I asked my older son to carry a folding chair for me at a sporting event, he replied, "I'm not your slave!" Paul and I decided that the best consequence for that remark was to make him be our slave for a day. We said, "Here are your jobs for the day," and had him weeding the garden and cleaning the toilet bowls. When it was over with, I just said, "Let's not talk about slaves around here anymore." [*Author's note:* While I wouldn't have handled this matter exactly the way the Roths did, it is clear to me that the commitment these parents had to handling the episode accomplished a tremendous amount of good. It is testimony to the fact that you don't have to be perfect every time to get good results.]

He's a great kid, though, the kind to whom I can just say, "I'm really disappointed," and it breaks his heart. We just have to reel him back, help restructure his teenage brain, and move on. I think it's because we've laid some solid groundwork, and the few times we've had issues they've been relatively easy to resolve because of our earlier efforts.

We've never let up on school being their number one priority, closely followed by religious requirements (Hebrew school, bar mitzvah training, services, and so on), and then come sports and friends. Both boys play competitive baseball and basketball and have been coached by their father for many years. We know our children's friends and their families, and we have a grasp on their lives.

What Every Parent Needs to Know

Train up a child in the way he should go and when he is old, he will not depart from it.

—Proverbs 22:6

IN THIS BOOK I have attempted to make a strong case for a return to a lovingly firm, less laissez-faire, less permissive form of parenting. I do not believe that discipline is by its very nature oppressive or dictatorial or arbitrary or unfeeling, as some of today's so-called child-rearing gurus would have you believe. Quite the contrary, limits lovingly presented free your child from the confusion and frustration of not knowing his or her role in the family and open the child's heart and mind to developing a loving, fulfilling, enriching relationship with the most important people in the world: Mom and Dad. From there, your child will enter the world at large with an understanding of what it takes to maintain healthy social relationships and the moral and emotional foundation necessary to cope and achieve and enjoy life.

The evidence of what works and what doesn't is all around us. And I know that you have always known it, too, in your heart. Now I very much hope that you have the support you need to carry out what's best for your child and your family. I've talked about why you *should* do it, and how you *can* do it. In a nutshell, here are the main points you must take away from this book and apply to your new lives.

PLAN FOR PARENTING

It is important to be aware that child-rearing is an unbelievably demanding undertaking, emotionally, psychologically, financially, and energetically. Your life will be totally altered. You do not have to take on this responsibility. There are many ways to be close with children and help them develop: being a devoted aunt or uncle or a foster parent, volunteering for programs such as scouting or Big Brothers–Big Sisters of America.

Should you decide to start a family of your own, you can avoid many of the problems of the epidemic by planning well. Long before you actually have a baby (or add more siblings to the family), start planning some of the things that will have to happen for you to be a "good enough" parent. For instance, many couples might be able to afford high-quality child care and continue to have both parents working with one child, but would find the cost prohibitive with two or three. Or they might find themselves physically or emotionally unable to devote the necessary time or attention to their children as the family grows. Know your personal limits, and accept that it may take extraordinary circumstances to raise your family given the way you live your life now. I am talking about making time to be with your children, making sure you have the necessary support and help, and making the major philosophical, ethical, and moral decisions that will influence how you manage them.

Prospective parents should work out their agreements and compromises in all these areas so that they are both supported in their parenting. When things are left so that one parent is protecting the child from the other, openings for mischief are created. Parents who can manage their child's sleep, early tests of willfulness, and toilet training teach their child exactly who is in charge through their commitment and determination. As a result, they produce a bonded and attached child who nestles in and fits into the household in a comfortable way. These parents have the time, the energy, and the concern necessary to be in charge of their child and are willing to do it.

NEVER FORGET WHAT CHILDREN REALLY NEED

If you *bond* with your infant, he will become attached, develop high self-esteem, and be motivated to please you. From this bonding he will then experience pleasure, reward, and deep satisfaction from feeling your love, which becomes a motivator of his future "good" behavior. He will not be the typical child who shows up in child psychiatry clinics.

If you *train* and *acculturate* your child by supplying a clear structure and expectations (the two "emotional vitamins" that are necessary for proper child development), she will tend to relate to the world with empathy and morality. If children do not have the successful early experience of bonding and attachment, they simply learn to accommodate rather than express themselves confidently. In other words, they learn to follow an external rules system when necessary, but left to their own devices, they do not have the internal code, the understanding of right versus wrong, to behave ethically and empathically on their own. These children need help and positive bonding and acculturating experiences to overcome their problems. It is often not too late to remedy the most difficult situation, even for those who need professional help.

In addition, if you *acknowledge, praise,* and *reward* real—and only real—accomplishment, your child will then be more likely to focus on and work toward goals with a sense of completion and accomplishment. Again, this step in rearing must be preceded properly by bonding and training experiences. If it is not, the child runs the risk of being either self-centered and grandiose or overly accomplishment-oriented and obsessive. These children ultimately show up in my office, whether their parents bring them for out-of-control behavior or they show up later as adults. Many have achieved material success but are stressed, burnt out, depressed, and unable to maintain healthy relationships because they really have little to give except their work.

RECOGNIZE WHEN DEVELOPMENT IS GOING AWRY

Parents have to understand that even the earliest symptoms I have mentioned—excessive tantruming, persistent bedtime issues, aggression toward playmates—are signs that development is going awry. The quicker the parent recognizes this and refuses to settle for the notion that a child is going through a stage, the easier it is to remedy the situation. If the problem behavior goes unchallenged, the character and worldview of the child will be steadily warped, and he will only become more difficult to manage. In the early stages of skewing it is easy for the parent just to take charge and the child will behave accommodatingly. But once a child has regularly been placated and given in to, it can be very difficult to extinguish this behavior. The next thing you know, the parents have decided that this child is simply a naturally defiant child whom no one could have managed. This eases the terrible guilt of the parents but doesn't help the child or the family as a whole.

The child who is not bonded, attached, or morally trained is at tremendous risk for settling for power and control as the main goal of his striving. Those are very poor substitutes for love and satisfaction. This is a catastrophic outcome for a child. The more cut off from warm and affectionate human connections he becomes, the more impaired are his self-esteem and overall development. But unfortunately, our society glorifies—in magazine and television advertising by high-profile fashion and lifestyle designers—the stupefied, absent, joyless look of children caught in this epidemic. Their faces have gradually become colder, more sullen, indifferent to others. Yet these pictures are held up as a statement of what looks desirable and cool to our children and their parents. The control and power these children glorify are the booby prize in life, not a real reward.

How do parents happen to raise such children? Our current child-rearing culture gives you this recipe for disaster.

FIFTEEN WAYS TO RUIN YOUR CHILD AND YOUR LIFE

1. **Don't plan ahead.** Don't admit to yourself that when you become the parent of a young child you will be vulnerable and in need of support. Don't think early on about arranging the possibilities for having a secure home in which to raise a child. Especially, don't pick a husband or wife with character traits that would make him or her a true partner and support throughout your child-rearing. Don't plan how to nurture your infant ahead of time; just assume it will all work out. Don't think about who is going to take care of your child if you work and who is going to provide financially if you stay home. Don't think through the details of how you will integrate work and child care.

2. **Leave your infant to be raised by an inadequate or unconnected caretaker for too many hours.** Choose one who has completely different ideas and experience with how a child should be raised. Especially, put your baby in circumstances where one person is dealing with several infants all day long. Even more effective are long periods in large child-care facilities, regardless of their quality.

3. **Keep yourself stressed and busy.** Be exhausted when you come home. It's especially effective to feel guilty about being away.

4. **Give in to your child's whims on everything, and demand nothing in return.** That will make up for your neglect.
5. **Facilitate your child's ascent into the world of consumerism.** Be understanding and accommodate his endless urges for the latest, coolest, most attractive, most superficial things.
6. **Let your child think he is the boss of the universe.** That way you can avoid frustrating or regulating her.
7. **Live without thoughts of the larger meaning of your life and your child's.** Live a life of scrambling, surviving, and grabbing a piece of the pie. Relate to all the "vices" in a way that you don't want your child to.
8. **Don't subscribe to a code of ethics or morality that can override your own impulses—and definitely don't expose your child to such a code.**
9. **Be sure your three- or four-year-old child sleeps in your bed, suckles, wears disposable underwear, and is pushed around in a stroller while you get your exercise.**
10. **Don't supervise your child's entire life.** Pay no attention to his friends, how he does in school, and what he does with his spare time.
11. **Let your child enjoy all the TV, videos, and video games he wants.**
12. **Act as though your child is on his own already.** There's no need to share news, activities, problems, and dilemmas. After all, he deserves his privacy.
13. **Don't take her out for genuine, loving times together with no interruptions, no chores.** Don't just hang out and have fun— it's also effective for children to have their days scheduled to the minute.
14. **Don't mess with your child's relationship to sex, drugs, tobacco, and alcohol.** He probably doesn't want to talk to you about those things anyway.
15. **Of course, don't ever give her chores or expect her to be a partner in running the house.**

Children raised in this manner often end up in clinics and guidance counselors' offices and, in worst-case situations, with the juvenile authorities or the police. They will go on in this direction until someone or something takes control of them. In years past it was common to recommend military service, and those too far gone ended up in military prisons or were discharged dishonorably. Now we have therapeutic boarding schools and boot camps as options, at least until these problem children reach adulthood and continue by themselves on their path of self-destruction.

How would you feel toward your child if she reached such a point? How happy do you think such a parent can be? Although many of the choices I discuss can be difficult and time consuming, they don't even compare to the consequences of not making them. And I can assure you from my clinical experience that almost any situation can be turned around. Raising children should be a deep, enduring pleasure. I know that it can be so for you.

Staying in Touch

AT THIS POINT you have the awareness and knowledge to fight this epidemic and save your child from it. I am concerned because the process of refining your child-rearing decisions can at times seem perplexing and difficult. To outline what has to be done is easy, and in fact simple, but the doing may be daunting.

I am committed to your success. I have written this book because I want to give your children the opportunity to be what they can be. To help you bring that about, you can stay in touch with me and get the support you need through my website, stoptheepidemic.com. It is devoted to providing information and a place to exchange ideas with other parents in the struggle and together to find more ways of insulating children from the more toxic aspects of our culture.

Stoptheepidemic.com contains:

- A monthly column by myself and/or special guests containing ideas that I believe will work for you
- A feedback page where you can report what works and what doesn't work for you
- A page on which the questions you ask are posted and answered
- A page on which parents can post messages and dialogue with each other
- A page on which you can search an archive of frequent problems and their solutions

- A question-and-answer of the month culled from your messages
- Capsule reviews of child-rearing literature and recommendations of books that foster non-epidemic-promoting parenting practices
- A "Treasury of Great Ideas from Parents" culled from the successful practices you report to me
- A guest column that is selected from thoughts we receive from you

I am open to suggestions for new features that would help parents, as well as any offers or help in maintaining the site.

For Further Reading

THE FOLLOWING BOOKS will give you additional insight into the many critical areas of development we have discussed in *The Epidemic*. They include excellent hands-on, time-honored, day-to-day strategies for many of the challenges parents face. They also differ enough that you can pick the one whose style speaks to you. If these additional resources don't help, rapidly get some professional guidance. If you get help as soon as trouble starts, it will be much easier for you and your child to get back on a good track.

EARLY DEVELOPMENT

Bruer, John T., Ph.D. *The Myth of the First Three Years*. New York: Free Press, 1999.

Coles, Robert. *The Moral Intelligence of Children*. New York: Random House, 1997.

Eliot, Lise, Ph.D. *What's Going on in There: How the Brain and Mind Develop in the First Five Years of Life*. New York: Bantam Books, 1999.

Gopnik, Allison, Ph.D., Patricia Kuhl, Ph.D., and Andrew Meltzoff, Ph.D. *The Scientist in the Crib*. New York: William Morrow, 1999.

BONDING AND CHILDCARE

Amini, Fari, M.D., Richard Lannon, M.D., and Thomas Lewis, M.D. *A General Theory of Love*. New York: Random House, 2000.

Greenspan, Stanley I., M.D., with Jacqueline Salmon. *The Four-Thirds Solution: Solving the Childcare Crisis in America Today*. New York: Perseus, 2001.

Karen, Robert, Ph.D. *Becoming Attached: Unfolding the Mystery of the Infant-Mother Bond and Its Impact on Later Life*. New York: Warner Books, 1994.

Schore, Allan N., Ph.D. *Affect Regulation and the Origin of the Self*. Mahwah, N.J.: Lawrence Erlbaum Associates, 1994.

—. *Affect Regulation and the Repair of the Self*. New York: W. W. Norton, 2003.

TRAINING AND TEACHING YOUR CHILD

Dinkmeyer, Don, Ph.D., and Gary McKay, Ph.D. *Raising a Responsible Child*. New York: Fireside, 1996.

Eagle, Carol, Ph.D. *All That She Can Be: Helping Your Daughter Maintain Her Self-Esteem*. New York: Fireside, 1994.

Gurian, Michael, *The Good Son*. New York: Tarcher, 1999.

Henner, Marilu, and Ruth Velikovsky Sharon, Ph.D. *I Refuse to Raise a Brat*. New York: ReganBooks, 1999.

Kindlon, Dan, Ph.D. *Too Much of a Good Thing: Raising Children of Character in an Indulgent Age*. New York: Hyperion, 2001.

Newberger, Eli H., M.D. *The Men They Will Become*. New York: Perseus, 1999.

Rosenfeld, Alvin, M.D., and Nicole Wise. *Hyper-Parenting: Are You Hurting Your Child by Trying Too Hard?* New York: St. Martin's, 2000.

HANDLING UPSETTING BEHAVIOR

Bodenhamer, Gregory. *Back in Control*. New York: Prentice Hall, 1983.

Condrell, Kenneth N., Ph.D., with Linda Lee Small. *Wimpy Parents: From Toddler to Teen*. New York: Warner Books, 1998.

Levy, Ray, Ph.D., and Bill O'Hanlon, M.S., L.M.F.T., with Tyler Norris Goode. *Try and Make Me! Simple Strategies That Turn Off the Tantrums and Create Cooperation*. Emmaus, PA: Rodale Press, 2002.

Ricker, Audrey, Ph.D., and Carolyn Crowder, Ph.D. *Backtalk: Four Steps to Ending Rude Behavior in Your Kids*. New York: Fireside, 1998.

Sells, Scott P., Ph.D. *Parenting Your Out-of-Control Teenager.* New York: St. Martin's, 2001.

Wolf, Anthony E., Ph.D. *Get Out of My Life, but First Could You Drive Me and Cheryl to the Mall?: A Parent's Guide to the New Teenager.* New York: Farrar, Straus and Giroux, 2002.

EDUCATING YOUR CHILD

Bennett, William J., Chester E. Finn Jr., and John T. E. Cribb Jr. *The Educated Child.* New York: Free Press, 1999.

Healy, Jane M., Ph.D. *Endangered Minds: Why Children Don't Think and What We Can Do About It.* New York: Touchstone, 1990.

THE DANGERS OF MEDIA

Healy, Jane M., Ph.D. *Failure to Connect: How Computers Affect Our Children's Minds—And What We Can Do About It.* New York: Touchstone, 1999.

Levin, Diane E., Ph.D. *Remote Control Childhood? Combatting the Hazards of Media Culture.* Washington, D.C.: National Association for the Education of Young Children, 1998.

Mander, Jerry. *Four Arguments for the Elimination of Television.* New York: William Morrow, 1977.

Winn, Marie. *The Plug-In Drug: Television, Children, and the Family.* New York: Viking Penguin, 1977.

References

1. STRICKEN CHILDREN, STRICKEN FAMILIES

Asimov, Nanette. "Exam Too Hard—Reprieve Likely." *San Francisco Chronicle,* May 2, 2003.

Breggin, Peter, M.D. *The Ritalin Fact Book.* New York: Perseus, 2002.

Benton, Sherry A., John M. Robertson, Wen-Chih Tseng, Fred B. Newton, and Stephen L. Benton. "Changes in Counseling Center Client Problems Across 13 Years." *Professional Psychology: Research and Practice,* February 2003.

Butterfield, Fox. "Teenagers Are Sentenced for Killing Two Professors." *New York Times,* April 5, 2002.

Carter, Chelsea J. "For Their Own Protection: Four Who Didn't Tell of Threat Suspended." Associated Press, March 9, 2001.

Coles, Robert. *The Secular Mind.* Princeton, N.J.: Princeton University Press, 2001.

"Columbine Killer Told of Violent Thoughts." Associated Press, October 6, 2002.

"Cops Seek Motive for School Shooting." cbsnews.com, May 9, 2003.

"An Evil Smile: Witnesses Say Suspect Looked Like He Was Getting Even." abcnews.com, March 6, 2001.

"From Suburbs to Taliban Ranks: One Man's Saga." Reuters, December 5, 2001.

Gibbs, Nancy, and Timothy Roche. "The Columbine Tapes." *Time,* December 20, 1999.

Goode, Erica. "Study Finds Jump in Children Taking Psychiatric Drugs." *New York Times,* January 14, 2003.

Green, Chuck. "Killers' Parents Selfishly Silent." *Denver Post*, December 9, 2001.

Hu, Winnie. "Now, High Schools' Sex Gossip Is Scrawled on Web Site Walls." *New York Times*, June 6, 2001.

Lewis, Michael. "Jonathan Lebed: Stock Manipulator, SEC Nemesis—and 15." *New York Times Magazine*, February 25, 2001.

"The Lost Sibling: Michael Williams Says He Didn't See Brother's Pain." abcnews.com, March 15, 2001.

Nicholson, Kieran. "Harris Wrote of Massacre Plan." *Denver Post*, December 5, 2001.

Powers, Ron. "The Apocalypse of Adolescence." *Atlantic Monthly* (March 2002).

"Principal: School Will Seek Expulsions for Hazing." cnn.com, May 13, 2003.

Roche, Timothy, Brian Bennett, Anne Berryman, Hilary Hylton, Siobhan Morrissey, and Amany Radwan. "The Making of John Walker Lindh." *Time*, October 7, 2002.

Seibert, Trent. "Normal Boys Hid Darker Side." *Denver Post*, May 17, 1999.

Silverman, Jay, Ph.D., Anita Raj, Ph.D., Lorelei A. Mucci, Ph.D., and Jeanne E. Hathaway, M.D., MPH. "Dating Violence Against Adolescent Girls and Associated Substance Use, Unhealthy Weight Control, Sexual Risk Behavior, Pregnancy, and Suicidality." *Journal of the American Medical Association* 286 (August 1, 2001): 572–79.

"Sticks and Stones: School Shooter Explains What Drove Her to the Edge." abcnews.com, April 13, 2001.

Stolberg, Sheryl Gay. "Preschool Meds." *New York Times Magazine*, November 17, 2002.

Taranto, James. "Zero Tolerance Makes Zero Sense." *Wall Street Journal*, May 18, 2001.

Zernicke, Kate. "Crackdown on Threats in School Fails a Test." *New York Times*, May 15, 2001.

Zito, Julie Magno, Ph.D., Daniel J. Safer, M.D., Susan dosReis, Ph.D., James F. Gardner, Sc.M., Lawrence Madger, Ph.D., Karen Stocken, Ph.D., Myde Boyles, Ph.D., Frances Lynch, Ph.D., and Mark A. Riddle, M.D. "Psychotropic Practice Patterns for Youth: A 10-Year Perspective." *Archives of Pediatric and Adolescent Medicine*, January 2003.

2. TEACHING YOUR CHILD TO LOVE

"Adapting to New Life Difficult for Romanian Orphans." Press release. Simon Fraser University, Burnaby, British Columbia, March 24, 1997.

Belkin, Lisa. "Life's Work: New Baby, Same Old Job." *New York Times,* June 7, 2001.

Eliot, Lise, Ph.D. *What's Going on in There?: How the Brain and Mind Develop in the First Five Years of Life.* New York: Bantam Books, 1999.

Goleman, Daniel. "Finding Happiness: Cajole Your Brain to Lean to the Left." *New York Times,* February 4, 2003.

"How Babies Acquire Building Blocks of Speech Affects Later Reading and Language Ability." Press release. University of Washington, Seattle, July 26, 2001.

Karen, Robert, Ph.D. *Becoming Attached: Unfolding the Mystery of the Infant-Mother Bond and Its Impact on Later Life.* New York: Warner Books, 1994.

"Mom's Warmth Influences Kid's Ability to Get Along with Others." Press release. Pennsylvania State University, University Park, April 22, 2001.

"Mother's Depression Impedes Baby's Development." Press release. Center for the Advancement of Health, Washington, D.C., May 21, 1999.

National Institute of Child Health and Human Development. "Maternal Depression Linked with Social and Language Development, School Readiness," September 3, 1999.

Schore, Allan N., Ph.D. *Affect Regulation and the Origin of the Self.* Mahwah, N.J.: Lawrence Erlbaum Associates, 1994.

———. *Affect Regulation and the Repair of the Self.* New York: W. W. Norton, 2003.

3. STARTING DOWN THE RIGHT PATH

American Academy of Pediatrics. "Breastfeeding and the Use of Human Milk," *Pediatrics* 100, no. 6 (December 1997).

Brody, Jane E. "An Enriching Change for Infant Formula." *New York Times,* July 17, 2001.

Corbett, Sara. "The Breast Offense." *New York Times Magazine,* May 6, 2001.

"Examining How Babies Sleep" [books on health]. *New York Times,* July 3, 2001.

Goode, Erica. "Clash Over When, and How, to Toilet Train." *New York Times,* January 12, 1999.

Ryan, Alan S., Zhou Wenjun, M.S., and Andrew Acosta, M.B.A. "Breast-feeding Continues to Increase into the New Millenium." *Pediatrics* (December 2002).

4. THE TRUTH AND CONSEQUENCES OF CHILD CARE

Greenhouse, Stephen. "Report Shows Americans Have More Labor Days." *New York Times,* September 1, 2001.

Greenspan, Stanley I., M.D., with Jacqueline Salmon. *The Four-Thirds Solution: Solving the Child-Care Crisis in America Today.* New York: Perseus, 2001.

Karen, Robert, Ph.D. *Becoming Attached: Unfolding the Mystery of the Infant-Mother Bond and Its Impact on Later Life.* New York: Warner Books, 1994.

Kornbluth, Karen. "The Parent Trap." *Atlantic Monthly* (January/February 2003).

Lewin, Tamar. "Study Finds Little Change in Working Mothers Debate." *New York Times,* September 10, 2001.

McLaughlin, Emma, and Nicola Kraus. *The Nanny Diaries.* New York: Griffin, 2003.

National Institutes of Health. NICHD Study of Early Child Care. April 1998.

Stolberg, Sheryl Gay. "Researchers Find a Link Between Behavioral Problems and Time in Child Care." *New York Times,* April 19, 2001.

———. "Public Lives: Another Academic Salvo in the Nation's 'Mommy Wars.'" *New York Times,* April 21, 2001.

———. "Science Studies and Motherhood." *New York Times,* April 22, 2001.

"Survey of Ohio's Working Families." Press release. University of Cincinnati, Kunz Center for the Study of Work and Family, August 1998.

5. WHOSE HOUSE IS THIS ANYWAY?

Ehrensaft, Diane, Ph.D. *Spoiling Childhood: How Well-Meaning Parents Are Giving Children Too Much—But Not What They Need*. New York: Guilford Press, 1997.

Gibbs, Nancy. "Do Kids Have Too Much Power?" *Time*, August 6, 2001.

Kindlon, Dan, Ph.D. *Too Much of a Good Thing: Raising Children of Character in an Indulgent Age*. New York: Hyperion, 2001.

Knoester, Chris, Ph.D. "Childhood Behavior Problems Predict Emotional Baggage for Young Adults." Press release. Center for the Advancement of Health, Washington, D.C., September 13, 2000.

Lavigne, John V., Ph.D. "Preschoolers Who Sleep Less Have More Behavior Problems." *Journal of Developmental and Behavioral Pediatrics* (June 1999).

Morris, Bob. "Correcting Manners of a Brat? Easy as 1--2--4." *New York Times*, December 23, 2001.

Owens, Judith A., M.D., M.P.H. "School-Aged Children Need Screening for Sleep Disturbances." *Journal of Developmental and Behavioral Pediatrics* (February 2000).

Owens-Stively, Judith, M.D. "Permissive Parenting May Be Hurting Kids' Sleep." *Journal of Developmental and Behavioral Pediatrics* (October 1997).

Padgett, Tim. "Monster Alert." *Time*, August 6, 2001.

6. RAISING MORAL CHILDREN IN A VALUELESS WORLD

Angier, Natalie. "The Urge to Punish Cheats: Not Just Human, but Selfless." *New York Times*, January 22, 2002.

"Bullying Is Not Limited to Unpopular Loners, Say Researchers; Many Children Bully Each Other, Especially in Middle School." Press release. Center for the Advancement of Health, Washington, D.C., August 20, 1999.

Coles, Robert, M.D. *The Moral Intelligence of Children*. New York: Random House, 1997.

Huffington, Arianna. *Pigs at the Trough: How Corporate Greed and Political Corruption Are Undermining America*. New York: Crown, 2003.

Goode, Erica. "School Bullying Is Common, Mostly By Boys, Study Finds." *New York Times*, April 25, 2001.

Hastings, Paul D., Ph.D., Carolyn Zahn-Waxler, Ph.D., JoAnn Robinson, Ph.D., Barbara Usher, Ph.D., and Dana Bridges. "The Development of Concern for Others in Children with Behavior Problems." *Developmental Psychology* 36, no. 5, September 2000.

Schwartz, John. "The Librarian's Web Dilemma." *New York Times,* June 20, 2002.

Slater, Lauren. "The Trouble with Self-Esteem." *New York Times Magazine,* February 3, 2002.

Stout, Maureen, Ph.D. *The Feel-Good Curriculum: The Dumbing Down of America's Kids in the Name of Self-Esteem.* New York: Perseus, 2000.

Schembari, James. "For Teenagers, an Introduction to Self-reliance." *New York Times,* May 26, 2002.

"The 2000 Report Card on the Ethics of American Youth." Survey report. Josephsen Institute of Ethics, Los Angeles, Calif.: April 2, 2001.

7. DON'T TOUCH THAT DIAL!

American Academy of Pediatrics. "Understanding the Impact of Media on Children and Teens." *Media Matters* (2002).

Cantor, Joanne, Ph.D. "Does Your Patient Have Sleep Problems? Ask About TV First." *AAP News* (September 2000).

"Field Guide to the Children's Televison Act." Center for Media Education, www.cme.org.

DeGaetano, Gloria, M.Ed. "Visual Media and Young Children's Attention Spans." *Media Literacy Review,* University of Oregon at Eugene, www.growsmartbrains.com.

——. *Screen Smarts: A Family Guide to Media Literacy.* Boston: Houghton Mifflin, 1996.

Edelson, Ed. "New Video Game Link to Violence Reported." HealthScout.com, July 19, 2001.

Guernsey, Lisa. "Looking for Clues in Junior's Keystrokes." *New York Times,* July 19, 2001.

Healy, Jane M., Ph.D. *Endangered Minds: Why Children Don't Think and What We Can Do About It.* New York: Touchstone, 1990.

——. "Understanding TV's Effects on the Developing Brain." *AAP News* (May 1998).

"Kids and Media @ the New Millenium." Survey report. Kaiser Family Foundation, Menlo Park, Calif., November 17, 1999.

Kubey, Robert, and Mihaly Csikszentmihalyi. "Television Addiction Is No Mere Metaphor." *Scientific American* (February 2002).

Levin, Diane E., Ph.D. *Remote Control Childhood?: Combating the Hazards of Media Culture.* Washington, D.C.: National Association for the Education of Young Children, 1998.

Mander, Jerry. *Four Arguments for the Elimination of Television.* New York: William Morrow, 1977.

Owens, Judith, M.D., Rolanda Maxim, Melissa McGuinn, Chantelle Nobile, Michael Msall, and Anthony Alario. "Television-Viewing Habits and Sleep Disturbances in School Children." *Pediatrics* (September 1999).

Robinson, Thomas N., M.D., M.P.H. "Kids Demand Fewer New Toys When They Cut Down on TV." *Journal for Developmental and Behavioral Pediatrics* (June 2001).

Rutenberg, Jim. "Survey Shows Few Parents Use TV V-Chip to Limit Children's Viewing." *New York Times,* July 25, 2001.

Schifrin, Donald, M.D., FAAP. "Three-Year Study Documents Nature of Television Violence." *AAP News* (August 1998).

Tedeschi, Bob. "Information Overload." *Parents* (November 2000).

Winn, Marie. *The Plug-In Drug: Television, Children, and the Family.* New York: Viking Penguin, 1977, 1985.

8. WHO STOLE MY CHILDHOOD?

Byrd, Robert A., Michael Weitzman, and Peggy Auinger. "Increased Behavior Problems Associated with Delayed School Entry and Delayed School Progress." *Pediatrics* (October 4, 1997).

Day, Sherri. "Learning Can Be Fun, at Least for the Makers of Electronic Toys." *New York Times,* November 27, 2002.

Fitzsimmons, William, Marlyn McGrath Lewis, and Charles Ducey. "Time Out or Burn Out for the Next Generation." Harvard University. www.college.harvard.edu/admissions/time_out.html.

Fuchs, Marek. "Tutoring Gives Pupils an Edge . . . for Preschool." *New York Times,* July 31, 2002.

Goldman, Victoria. "The Baby Ivies." *New York Times,* January 12, 2003.

Goode, Erica. "A Boy Genius?: Mother Admits Faking Tests." *New York Times,* March 2, 2002.

Hofferth, Sandra L., and Frank Stafford. "Major Changes in How American Children Spend Their Time." Survey report. University of Michigan, Institute for Social Research, November 9, 1998.

Rosenfeld, Alan, M.D., and Nicole Wise. *Hyper-Parenting: Are You Hurting Your Child by Trying Too Hard?* New York: St. Martin's Press, 2000.

Sontag, Deborah. "Who Was Responsible for Elizabeth Shin?" *New York Times Magazine,* April 28, 2002.

9. OUT OF CONTACT, OUT OF CONTROL

Brody, Jane E. "Adolescent Angst or Deeper Disorder? Tips for Spotting Serious Symptoms." *New York Times,* December 24, 2002.

Dalton, Madeline A., Ph.D., James D. Sargent, Leina A. Mott, Michael L. Beach, M. Bridget Aherns, Jennifer J. Tickle, and Todd F. Heatherton. "Revolution Between Parental Restrictions on Movies and Adolescent Use of Tobacco and Alcohol." *Effective Clinical Practice,* January/February 2002.

Jang, Sung Joon. "Study Finds Parental Influence Still Important During Adolescence." Press release. Center for the Advancement of Health, August 30, 1999.

Nagourney, Eric. "Behavior: When 'R' Stands for Risky Teenagers." *New York Times,* February 26, 2002.

Rimer, Sara. "Embattled Parents Seek Help, at Any Cost." *New York Times,* September 10, 2001.

Simons-Martin, Bruce, Ed.D., M.P.H. "Parents and Peers Influence Teen Smoking and Drinking." Press release. Center for the Advancement of Health, January 22, 2001.

Talbot, Margaret. "Girls Just Want to Be Mean." *New York Times Magazine,* February 24, 2002.

Acknowledgments

NO ONE CAN MATURE into a loving and content human being without having experienced a full measure of care and nurture. I am filled with gratitude for the people who made my life possible, and I share here a little of my life story to illustrate how dedicated people have provided me with some of the experiences anyone needs to grow properly. When we reflect back upon those who helped us in our own development, we can sense how much our own loving attention can mean to our own children and how critical our caring is for their souls.

I want you to know that in my own life, a hardworking mother loved me very much and was determined to ensure that there was someone available who would provide her child with a good bonding experience. My mother, Sadie Shaw, was a born entrepreneur. Raised on the Lower East Side of New York City, at age fifteen she was earning her living selling clothing from a pushcart. By the time I was born, she was married and running a nationally known, successful apparel business and had neither the time nor the inclination to learn or speak "motherese." Resolute and forthright, she did, however, teach me about determination and what it takes to be successful; she gave me the sense that I could do anything or connect with anyone.

Although my mother could not be there for me in certain ways, she did provide for me by hiring Bertha, a young German immigrant, who became my loving nanny and who lived with us for twelve years. Bertha taught me about being loved and cherished. She was the one I went to when hurt or in pain, the one I wanted to marry when I grew up. I felt like the center of her life (as I am certain you want your child to feel about you). On her day off, Bertha would take me out for lunch at the Automat and then to a movie, or a zoo, or a museum. She exemplified loving-ness combined with firmness when necessary.

I adored my father, Charles Lionel Shaw. We were extremely close, and by his wonderful example he taught me to think criti-cally, logically, and ethically and to know that things often aren't what they seem. He inspired in me a commitment to bring about change.

I was fortunate to train in child psychiatry at Mount Sinai Hospital in New York, and even more fortunate to have Abraham Blau as my chief. Abe was brilliant and charismatic—an inventive and original person who believed that we could affect and help any patient. He was relentless and taught me never to give up. He trusted me and gave me responsibilities beyond anything I could have dreamed possible. Abe was my empowering mentor for the six years we worked together, and after that always a resource.

My other significant mentor was Abe's assistant chief, Wil-fred Hulse. An urbane and worldly child psychiatrist and a refugee from Nazi Germany, he was charming, wise, and gra-cious, and now, years after his death, he is still a figure of awe to me. Our intimate lunches at his home were a significant part of my training. Surrounded by works of the leading artists of the nineteenth and twentieth centuries, we discussed my treatment of patients and therapy in general, and always with a dollop of art history. An extremely perceptive man, he shared his wisdom about the practical considerations of managing relationships with patients and their families as well as with fellow staff mem-bers. He taught me to make sure my interventions actually made the difference I wanted to make.

I could not have written this book except for the many indi-viduals and families who have come to me for therapy and allowed me into their lives. Their willingness to work and grow has made my professional life a joy.